International Financial Centres after the Global Financial Crisis and Brexit

International Financial Centres after the Global Financial Crisis and Brexit

Edited by
Youssef Cassis and Dariusz Wójcik

OXFORD
UNIVERSITY PRESS

OXFORD
UNIVERSITY PRESS

Great Clarendon Street, Oxford, OX2 6DP,
United Kingdom

Oxford University Press is a department of the University of Oxford.
It furthers the University's objective of excellence in research, scholarship,
and education by publishing worldwide. Oxford is a registered trade mark of
Oxford University Press in the UK and in certain other countries

First Edition published in 2018
Impression: 1

Published in the United States of America by Oxford University Press
198 Madison Avenue, New York, NY 10016, United States of America

British Library Cataloguing in Publication Data
Data available

Library of Congress Control Number: 2018932385

ISBN 978–0–19–881731–4

Printed and bound by
CPI Group (UK) Ltd, Croydon, CR0 4YY

This book is dedicated to the memory of one of its contributors, Richard Roberts, who died unexpectedly and prematurely in December 2017.

Preface

Ten years have passed since the collapse of Lehman Brothers on 15 September 2008 triggered worldwide financial panic on a scale unseen since 1929. The concerted efforts of governments and central banks prevented a depression, but a great recession ensued, which in turn led to a fiscal crisis in many countries, particularly in Europe. A wave of new financial regulation has swept the world, but not on a scale or at a speed as radical as many had initially expected or have called for, even if for others we have already witnessed a regulatory overkill. Growing inequality, aggravated by the crisis and more recent austerity policies, combined with the perceived inadequacy of financial-sector reforms, have added fuel to anti-establishment and anti-globalist political and social movements, culminating in the UK vote to leave the European Union and the election of President Donald Trump in the United States. And as if the times were not interesting enough for the financial sector, new financial technologies, referred to as 'fintech', promise to revolutionize finance, threatening to destroy millions of financial and related jobs in the process.

This book analyses the events of the last decade, by focusing on their impacts on international financial centres (IFCs). IFCs epitomize modern capitalism, acting as central nodes in international financial networks and command centres of the global economy. The crisis brewed in IFCs, with New York and London in the lead. In the aftermath of the crisis, many would expect financial activity and power to move gradually towards Asia. Many might also expect the position of European financial centres, particularly Frankfurt and Paris, to be weakened by the ongoing Eurozone crisis. On the other hand, economic history teaches us that the map of financial centres changes very slowly, and it takes major political upheavals to redraw it. The book tests these predictions of change versus inertia, showing how the global map of international financial centres has changed since 2008 and why. In addition, it outlines the likely implications of the UK's EU referendum and the new US presidency on the financial map of the world. Finally, given the emergence of potentially transformative new financial technology, the book asks whether in the future we will need international financial centres as we know them.

These questions are addressed by a diverse team of contributors with financial historians and geographers in the lead. One of the lessons of the crisis is the need for more interdisciplinary and heterodox thinking about money and finance in space and time. Specialization in research and science is necessary, but without dialogue across disciplines, it can degenerate into silo thinking, with disciplines turning into echo chambers reinforcing their internal biases and limitations, and fine-tuning existing models and canons, rather than questioning them and allowing disruptive innovation. In this context, our project is a major engagement between financial history and geography. This interdisciplinary approach helps us recognize a broad range of factors affecting the development of IFCs including, but not limited to: changes in the size and structure of demand for financial services, macroeconomic policies, domestic and international financial regulation, political instability, pressures from civil society, reputational issues, changes in the culture of financial institutions, and technological developments.

The core chapters focus on the case studies of New York, London, Paris, Frankfurt am Main, Zurich and Geneva, Beijing, Hong Kong, and Shanghai, Singapore, and Tokyo. These are complemented with two chapters providing a global overview from a historical and a geographical perspective. Our focus on eleven leading financial centres in eight countries was influenced by our knowledge of the top end of the IFC hierarchy, as well as the need to keep the volume compact. This does not mean, however, that developments in other countries and cities are ignored. To complement the case studies, the introductory and concluding chapter present a global perspective on the evolution of IFCs, with additional data and analysis. In these chapters, and throughout the book, we consider the results of the Global Financial Centres Index, published biannually by Z/Yen Group in London since 2007, but we do so critically. In contrast to the GFCI, our book will focus on the actual activity of IFCs as measured, for example, with stocks and flows of transactions and employment, and on specific changes in strategies and policies affecting IFC development. Our goal is not to create a competing index, but to better understand what has actually happened in the leading IFCs, why it has happened, and with what implications for their future, and for the future of the world economy.

The book is illustrated with data, tables, and figures, documenting an eventful decade in the history of IFCs. The interdisciplinary and accessible style of the book, and the evidence presented herein, will hopefully make it attractive to scholars in economics, management and business studies, geography, history, sociology, political science, and area studies.

The idea for the book was born during a meeting in Florence between the two editors on 22 June 2016. We discussed the financial history and geography since the crisis, and decided that the tenth anniversary of Lehman Brothers' collapse was the right moment to reflect on the changes brought about by one of modern history's most violent financial shocks, particularly if we could assemble an interdisciplinary team of scholars who are experts on leading IFCs. The title for the book appeared obvious: International Financial Centres after the Global Financial Crisis. Only forty hours later we found out that the Leave campaign won the UK's EU referendum by a small margin. The result sent the British pound into decline, and an industry of forecasts and speculations about the impacts of Brexit took off. While this outcome took us by surprise and made the project more challenging, it probably reinforced our resolve to pursue our plan, though with an extended title considering the potential impacts of Brexit on IFCs.

The project unfolded as an interdisciplinary conversation, with a dialogue between financial historians and financial geographers at its heart. To foster these interactions, we organized a workshop in Oxford in June 2017, where our contributors presented draft chapters. While geographers among us were eager to detect changes and transformations around every corner of global finance, the accounts of historians had a cooling effect, reminding us of the slow, long-term nature of the processes underpinning the evolution of IFCs. The workshop was a genuine tour around the world of financial centres accomplished in two days. We have learnt a lot from each other, and hope that this project will lead to more interdisciplinary collaborations on finance.

As editors, we would like to thank first of all our contributors for engaging with our idea and for following a tight and demanding timetable. Adam Swallow from Oxford University Press led us smoothly through the stages of the publication process, with the assistance of Katie Bishop and Catherine Owen. Dariusz Wójcik has received funding for the project from the European Research Council (ERC) under the European Union's Horizon 2020 research and innovation programme (grant agreement number 681337). His contribution to the book reflects only his views and the ERC is not responsible for any use that may be made of the information it contains. The Oxford workshop was made possible with funding from the School of Geography and the Environment and from St. Peters College Oxford. Theodor Cojoianu at Oxford provided exemplary assistance with the project, organizing the workshop logistics (only a month before his own wedding), and contributing to the final stages of collating and editing chapters, in addition to co-authoring the final chapter. His enthusiastic approach has been most appreciated, as well as the creative input of his wife Alet Meiring to the design of the book cover. Both Dariusz and Theodor drew inspiration and motivation for the book from the Global Network on Financial Geography (www.fingeo.net), a worldwide network of scholars and practitioners interested in the evolution of finance in space and time and its impacts on economy, society, culture, and the environment.

Youssef Cassis and Dariusz Wójcik

Florence and Oxford, November 2017

Contents

List of Figures

List of Tables

List of Contributors

Youssef Cassis is Professor of Economic History at the European University Institute, in Florence. His work mainly focuses on banking and financial history, as well as business history more generally. His most recent publications include *Capitals of Capital. A History of International Financial Centres, 1780–2005 (Cambridge University Press, 2006, 2nd revised edition, 2009), Crises and Opportunities. The Shaping of Modern Finance (Oxford University Press, 2011),* and, with Philip Cottrell, *Private Banking in Europe: Rise, Retreat and Resurgence (Oxford University Press, 2015).* He has also recently co-edited, with Richard Grossman and Catherine Schenk, *The Oxford Handbook of Banking and Financial History, (Oxford University Press, 2016).* Youssef Cassis was the cofounder, in 1994, of *Financial History Review (Cambridge University Press).* He was a long serving member of the Academic Advisory Council of the European Association for Banking and Financial History (EBHA) and past President (2005–2007) of the European Business History Association.

Theodor Cojoianu is a Marie Skłodowska-Curie Research Fellow at the Michael Smurfit Graduate Business School, University College Dublin and a Smith School Doctoral Scholar at the Smith School of Enterprise and the Environment, University of Oxford. Theodor's research focuses on the innovation, finance and geography of sustainability transitions. Theodor has previously held appointments in the sustainable finance space in both academic and finance industry organisations. He worked in academia within the Centre for Responsible Banking and Finance at the University of St. Andrews, the ICMA Centre at the University of Reading and the University of Edinburgh Business School. He was previously an analyst with MSCI ESG Research in London and affiliated with Sociovestix Labs and Sustainable Investment Partners.

Karen P.Y. Lai is Assistant Professor of Geography at the National University of Singapore. Her research interests include geographies of money and finance, markets, service sectors, global city networks and international financial centres. Her recent projects examine how aspirations of households and financial centre development are intertwined through financialisation processes, and the global financial networks of investment banks in mergers and acquisitions, and initial public offerings. She is on the Standing Committee of the Global Production Networks Centre at NUS, executive committee of the Global Network on Financial Geography (FinGeo), and editorial board of *Geography Compass* (Economic section).

David R. Meyer is Senior Lecturer in Management at Olin Business School, Washington University in St. Louis. Previously he was Professor of Sociology & Urban Studies at

Brown University. His publications include five books and monographs and over sixty articles and book chapters. He published *Hong Kong as a Global Metropolis (2000, CUP)*, *The Roots of American Industrialization (2003, Johns Hopkins UP)*, and *Networked Machinists (2006, Johns Hopkins UP)*. His recent publications focus on the development of Asian finance, including network governance at the State Banks of China, banking networks of Asian financial centers, private wealth management in Asia, high frequency trading on exchanges, Hong Kong and Singapore as network hubs of global capital, Shenzhen in China's financial center networks, Hong Kong's enduring global business relations, Bank of China International in Hong Kong, and Hong Kong and Singapore exchanges confront high frequency trading.

Laure Quennouëlle-Corre is director of research at the CNRS in Paris. She received her Ph.D. from the Ecole des Hautes études en sciences sociales (EHESS) in 2000 and published her first book *La direction du Trésor. L'Etat-banquier et la croissance 1947–1967* in the same year. Her works focuses on economic and financial history, especially international capital flows, financial institutions and regulation. Her last book deals with the role of Paris as International Financial Centre: *La place financière de Paris au XXe siècle. Des ambitions contrariées (2015, Comité pour l'histoire economique et financière de la France)* where she explores the role of different financial institutions throughout the century.

Richard Roberts † was Professor of Contemporary Financial History at King's College London. His books include: *When Britain Went Bust: The 1976 IMF Crisis (2016); The Lion Wakes: A Modern History of HSBC (with David Kynaston, 2015); The Media and Financial Crises (coeditor, 2014); Saving the City: The Great Financial Crisis of 1914 (2013); Did Anyone Learn Anything from Equitable Life? Lessons and Learning from Financial Crises (2012); The City (2008); Wall Street (2002); City State: A Contemporary History of the City of London and How Money Triumphed (with David Kynaston, 2001); Take Your Partners: Orion, the Consortium Banks and the Transformation of the Euromarkets (2001); and Schroders: Merchants and Bankers (1992)*. He was on advisory boards of OMFIF (Official Monetary and Financial Institutions Forum) and the Gulbenkian Foundation, Lisbon, a trustee of the Barings Archive Trust, and wrote a monthly column for GlobalCapital.

Eike W. Schamp is professor emeritus in economic geography at Goethe University, Frankfurt/Main, Germany. He holds a doctorate in economics from the Faculty of Economics and Social Sciences at Cologne University where he also habilitated in economic geography. His research focuses on the reorganization of industrial production systems, the geography of knowledge and higher education, and financial geography. He has published widely in these fields, mainly referring to Europe and Francophone Central Africa. His recent books include *Innovation, Finance and Space (with A. Thierstein, 2003, Frankfurter Wirtschafts- und Sozialgeographische Schriften), Knowledge, Learning, and Regional Development (with V. Lo, 2003, Münster Lit.), Linking Industries Across the World. Processes of Global Networking (with C. Alvstam, 2005, Aldershot: Ashgate)* and *Finanzcluster Frankfurt. Eine Clusteranalyse am Finanzzentrum Frankfurt/Rhein-Main (with W. König, 2007, Frankfurt Business-Net)*.

Sayuri Shirai is a professor of Keio University and a visiting scholar at the Asian Development Bank Institute. She was a Member of the Policy Board of the Bank of Japan (BOJ) from April 2011 to March 2016. Prior to that she worked as Professor of Economics at Keio University. She also taught at Science-Po in France in 2007–08. She was an Economist at the International Monetary Fund (1993–98). She graduated from Keio University and holds a Ph.D. in Economics from Columbia University. She is the author of numerous articles in professional journals and published eleven books on China's exchange rate system, Japan's macroeconomic policy, IMF policy, European debt crisis, etc. The most recent book published in August 2016 was about the monetary policies of BOJ, ECB, and FRB. She is currently writing an e-book in English about BOJ's monetary policy and to be published from Asian Development Bank Institute at end-January or early February *2017 (Reflating the Japanese Economy—An Incomplete Mission to Achieve the 2 Percent Inflation Target with the Super-Easy Monetary Policy)*. She frequently comments on economic developments for Reuters, CNBC, Bloomberg, BBC, as well as Japanese TV programs and newspapers.

Tobias Straumann is a professor of economic history at the universities of Basel and Zurich, Switzerland. He has published books and articles on European financial and monetary history and Swiss business history, including *The Value of Risk: Swiss Re and the History of Reinsurance (2013, OUP, with Peter Borscheid, David Gugerli and Harold James)* and *Fixed Ideas of Money: Small States and Exchange Rate Regimes in Twentieth-Century Europe, Studies in Macroeconomic History (2010, CUP)*. He held visiting positions in Lausanne, Berkeley and Hong Kong. His latest publication is *"How the German crisis of 1931 swept across Europe: a comparative view from Stockholm" Economic History Review 1/2017 (with Peter Kugler and Florian Weber)*.

Richard Sylla is Professor Emeritus of Economics at New York University, where from 1990 to 2015 he was Henry Kaufman Professor of the History of Financial Institutions and Markets. He is also a Research Associate of the National Bureau of Economic Research, and chairman of the board of the Museum of American Finance. His latest books include: *Alexander Hamilton on Finance, Credit, and Debt*, published in March 2018; and *Alexander Hamilton: The Illustrated Biography*, a life of the founding father who launched a modern US financial system in the early 1790s, which came out in November 2016. His previous books include *The American Capital Market* and *A History of Interest Rates*. His writing has appeared in numerous publications, including the *Journal of Economic History, Explorations in Economic History, Small Business and American Life: A History and Business and Economic History*. He has served on the editorial board of many journals that include *Enterprise and Society, Economic and Financial History Abstracts*. He served as President of the Economic History Association and the Business History Conference.

Dariusz Wójcik is a Professor of Economic Geography at the School of Geography and the Environment, Oxford University, and Fellow of St Peters College Oxford. His research focuses on finance, globalisation, and urban and regional development. He has published several books and over 50 articles, and serves on the editorial board of *Economic Geography*, the *Journal of Economic Geography, Environment and Planning A*, and

GeoJournal. His recent books include *The Geography of Finance: Corporate Governance in a Global Marketplace (2007, OUP)* and *The Global Stock Market: Issuers, Investors and Intermediaries in an Uneven World (2011, OUP).* He is the co-editor of the *New Oxford Handbook of Economic Geography (2017, OUP).* He has held visiting positions at the London School of Economics and Political Science, Hong Kong University, National University of Singapore, Beijing Normal University, and the University of Sydney, and convened the Global Conference on Economic Geography 2015. He is the chair of the Global Network on Financial Geography (www.fingeo.net).

1

Introduction

A Global Overview from a Historical Perspective

Youssef Cassis

On the eve of the Global Financial Crisis, the world's eight leading financial centres were New York, London, Tokyo, Frankfurt, Paris, Hong Kong, Singapore, and Zurich (with Geneva). Ten years later, the top group was made up of the same capital cities, though in a different ranking order (Hong Kong and Singapore had definitely overtaken Frankfurt and Paris and possibly also Tokyo), plus one newcomer: Shanghai (with Beijing). On the face of it, the most severe financial crisis in modern history has hardly disturbed the world of global finance. In the same way, the established order does not seem to have been affected by another momentous, though much more recent, event: the Brexit vote of June 2016. But are these changes really minor? What hides behind the slow shifts in the hierarchy of international financial centres? While the ensuing chapters of this book will investigate the challenges faced by each of these centres, the object of this introductory chapter is to provide a global overview of the development of international financial centres in the last ten years and to put these recent events in a longer-term historical perspective.

Three sets of questions have to be addressed. The first concerns international financial centres: what are they, how are they ranked, and what should we make of existing rankings? The second is related to the effects that global financial crises have had on financial centres: have they led to the emergence of new centres, the rise of existing ones, and the decline of established ones? But financial crises also directly impinge on the activities of international centres: how far have they declined and how speedily have they recovered? How much have they been reshaped by new regulation? And the third question, which also has some relevance to the Brexit issue, has to do with the ability of financial centres to reinvent themselves in the face of new adverse conditions or, on the contrary, their inability to resist decline.

These are not entirely straightforward questions. The ranking of financial centres—like all rankings, whether of the largest companies or the richest countries—can be contentious, because of the criteria on which these rankings are based and because of the conclusions, at once illuminating and meaningless, that can be drawn from these rankings. Historical parallels can also be treacherous, yet without taking them into account there would be no learning from the past. Even if the general course of financial crises can be convincingly modelled, each crisis breaks out and unfolds within a unique context. There is thus as much to learn from the differences between each of them, especially between past and present, as from their apparent similarities. The rest of this chapter will consider in turn each of these three sets of questions before introducing the other chapters of the book.

1.1 The Hierarchy of International Financial Centres

Financial centres can be defined as the grouping together, in a given urban space, of a certain number of financial services; in a more functional way, they can be defined as the places where intermediaries coordinate financial transactions and arrange for payments to be settled. This concentration can chiefly be explained by external economies—in other words, the cost reductions that firms can achieve as a result of the competition, proximity, and size of the sector or the place in which they are operating. For a financial centre, what primarily matters is the liquidity and efficiency of markets; the diversity and complementarity of financial activities; the availability of professional services, technological expertise, and a skilled workforce; and access to high-quality information. The concentration of financial services can be found at several levels: national, regional (in the sense of one part of the world), and international—depending on the extent of the geographical area served by a centre; while the volume and range of financial services offered by a centre is correlated with the breadth of its geographical influence. In other words, there exists not only a variety of financial centres, in terms, for example, of specialization in certain services, leading to complementarity and cooperation, but also a hierarchy, and competition between them. Only a handful of financial centres perform a truly global role—hence their importance, as the nerve centres of international financial activities, and the significance of the changes that might affect the way they fulfil their role.

The financial capital(s) of the eight countries selected for this analysis can be considered as the world's leading international financial centres—but on what basis? Even though an implicit order of importance has always been recognized by practitioners and commentators alike, the systematic ranking of international financial centres is a fairly recent endeavour. Until the 1980s, the respective position of the leading centres was assessed on the basis of a number of quantitative and qualitative indicators of their financial activity (Cassis 2006).

As far as I am aware, the first wide-range ranking was attempted in 1981 by the American economist Howard C. Reed, who proposed an initial ranking of international financial centres, at intervals of ten to fifteen years from 1900 onwards, based on a set of quantitative criteria, such as the number of foreign and multinational banks based in a centre, and the amount of foreign assets and foreign liabilities held in the centre (Reed 1981). While establishing a ranking for the top ten or so, the study mainly provided a taxonomy of international financial centres. For 1980, the eighty centres under consideration were divided into five ascending categories: forty were classified as host international financial centres; twenty-nine as international financial centres; eight (including Frankfurt, Hong Kong, Paris, and Zurich) as supranational financial centres of the second order; two (New York and Tokyo) as supranational centres of the first order, and just one, London, as the supranational centre par excellence. Subsequent analyses have put forward a number of variations on this theme (Jones 1992; Roberts 1996). In addition, by the closing decade of the twentieth century, precise rankings became increasingly available for each of the various activities performed by an international financial centre (such as international banking, foreign exchange, capital markets, assets management, number of foreign banks, and others), with the order of precedence of the leading centres being determined on this basis—usually London, New York and Tokyo, Frankfurt and Paris, Hong Kong and Singapore (Roberts 1998).

Precise rankings of international financial centres have become available since the beginning of the twenty-first century with the attribution of overall scores aggregating multiple indicators. The Global Financial Centres Index, in particular, published twice a year since 2007 by the Z/Yen Group, first on behalf of the City of London, then of the Qatar Financial Authority, and most recently co-produced by the China Development Institute (GFCI 22, September 2017), has quickly established itself as *the* reference on the matter. However, the ranking of the Global Financial Centres Index is based on *competitiveness*, and only partly on size, volume of business, or international influence.[1] The two can, but do not necessarily, go together. While few would dispute the position of the top four (London, New York, Hong Kong, and

---

[1] Factors of competitiveness include: people, business environment, market access, infrastructure, and general competitiveness.

Singapore), many would be surprised by the position of Paris, which dropped from eleventh in March 2007 to thirty-seventh in March 2015 (behind Tel Aviv, Munich, Vienna, and Stockholm), before rising to twenty-ninth in March 2017; or that of Frankfurt, which dropped from sixth in 2007 and 2008 to nineteenth in 2015 and twenty-third in March 2017 (behind Osaka, Vancouver, and Geneva), though it climbed back to eleventh position in September 2017. Moreover, a ranking based on competitiveness tends to be extremely volatile (Shanghai, for example, jumped from thirty-fifth in 2009 to fifth in 2011 and back to twenty-fourth in 2013) in sharp contrast with the historical evidence of great stability in the position of international financial centres. Whatever its merits, in particular the dynamic perception of international financial centres that it conveys, the Global Financial Centres Index cannot be taken as an entirely reliable guide to identify the international financial centres that really matter in today's world. Competitiveness is essential, of course, and it will be discussed in the following chapters in connection with the effects of the Global Financial Crisis, but it must be distinguished from power and influence. Another, less influential ranking, the Xinhua·Dow Jones International Financial Centers Development Index, appeared between 2010 and 2014,[2] and has apparently ceased publication. However, its results were more realistic, with New York (consistently ranked number one), London, Tokyo, Hong Kong, Singapore, Shanghai, Frankfurt, and Paris featuring amongst the top ten in all five years.

An interesting conclusion of this brief survey is that, with the exception of the Global Financial Centres Index, all rankings, whether implicit or explicit, whether based on quantitative or qualitative data, or a mixture of both, point towards the same direction, the same group of financial centres and the countries that host them. Our choice of leading international financial centres to be discussed in this volume thus appears comprehensive and realistic—even if it does not include American financial centres such as Boston, Chicago, and San Francisco, which are clearly overshadowed by New York, and far from insignificant centres such as Sydney or Toronto, which nevertheless fall somewhat behind the selected ones in terms of global reach. There have been some questions about the top spot: New York or London? The answer has to be New York: London might have the edge in direct international financial activities, but overall Wall Street has retained its pre-eminence since the end of the Second World War. Moreover, it has been New York that has set the tone in international finance, if only because of the might of the American banks, mostly based in New York, and on which a great deal of London's international influence has depended.

---

[2] The ranking is based on the following criteria: financial market, growth and development, industrial support, service level, and general environment.

Another interesting point is the longevity of international financial centres. In 1913, the four leading centres were, in order, London, Paris, Berlin, and New York—the financial capitals of the four leading economies; Brussels, Amsterdam, and Zurich followed somewhat behind. One hundred years later, the same four centres were still amongst the leaders (though Frankfurt had replaced Berlin), Zurich was still following somewhat behind, and Amsterdam even further, no longer in the top ten. The newcomers were Tokyo, and Hong Kong and Shanghai, the financial capitals of the third and second largest economies respectively (taking into account the peculiarity of the relationships between the two Chinese cities), as well as Singapore (which, along with Switzerland—as two small centres that have been able to take advantage of favourable circumstances—could be viewed as the exception that confirms the rule). This long-term stability raises the question of the effects of systemic financial crises, as well as other upheavals, on the development of international financial centres.

1.2 Financial Crises and Financial Centres

There have been very few global financial crises since the late nineteenth century—and hardly any beforehand. In advanced economies, only eight events have reached this magnitude: the Baring crisis of 1890; the American Panic of 1907; the financial crisis of July–August 1914; the banking crises of the Great Depression, 1931–3; the financial instability of the early 1970s and the ensuing banking failures; the international debt crisis of 1982; the Japanese banking crisis of 1997–8; and the financial debacle of 2008 (Cassis 2011). None of them led to any real change in the hierarchy of international financial centres. Nevertheless, some centres suffered more than others in certain circumstances. New York was clearly weakened by the Great Depression, falling behind London in the issue of foreign loans (the only major financial activity where it ranked first in the 1920s), but still retaining its overall position as number two, ahead of Paris. Tokyo suffered major erosion in the wake of the Japanese banking crisis of 1997–8, and the bursting of the stock market and property bubbles earlier in the decade (with the yen dropping in terms of share of world currency turnover and a decrease in the presence of foreign banks), and was eventually caught up by Hong Kong and Singapore.

The major changes in the hierarchy of international financial centres have all been brought about by wars. The French wars led to Amsterdam's final demise and its replacement by London as the world's leading financial centre at the turn of the nineteenth century. Following the Franco-Prussian War of 1870–1, Paris was no longer able to compete with London for world leadership. The First World War enabled New York to rise to international

5

prominence, above Paris and Berlin—but not yet to overtake a weakened London. This took place after the Second World War, which further weakened Paris's position and completely eradicated Berlin as a financial centre. At the same time, wars mainly accelerate long-term processes already under way: London had already overtaken Amsterdam as a trading centre in the late eighteenth century; Paris's challenge to London in the second third of the nineteenth century was ultimately doomed, if only because of the economic balance of power between Britain and France; and with the United States' GDP already twice as large as that of Britain by 1905, it was only a matter of *when* New York was going to supplant London.

The main effect of global financial crises on international financial centres has been a slowdown in their activities. This is particularly visible in foreign issues and international capital flows, the primary function of international financial centres. They fell sharply in the wake of the Baring crisis of 1890: capital exports from Britain fell from £123 million in 1889 to £32 million in 1893, before gradually increasing from 1894 but not reaching their pre-crisis level before 1900 (Stone 1999); French capital exports also fell, from 913 million francs to 127 million francs between 1890 and 1891, though they picked up earlier than in Britain (Lévy-Leboyer 1977). They fell even more dramatically during the Great Depression: foreign loans offered in New York, the main provider of international funds, dropped from an average of nearly $1000 million between 1924 and 1929 to less than $100 million in 1932 and 1933. In London, foreign loans outside the British Empire ceased almost completely after 1931, though imperial issues continued throughout the decade, reaching £187 million between 1932 and 1938 (Balogh 1947). The impressive and regular growth of the Eurodollar market came to an abrupt end in the wake of the banking failures of the mid-1970s, especially that of the Herstatt Bank on 26 June 1974. Foreign loans, in the form of syndicated floating-rate Eurocredits, resumed a few years later, and then expanded dangerously, only thanks to the massive inflow of 'petrodollars' in the American and European banks following the oil shock of 1973 and 1978; and they did not freeze after the outbreak of the Latin American debt crisis, in August 1982, because of restructuring programmes arranged by the International Monetary Fund and the guarantees offered by the American monetary authorities (James 1996). Japanese banks retreated from foreign markets following the bursting of the asset price bubble in 1992 and the banking crisis of 1997–8.

Financial crises affected, in varying degrees, all activities of international financial centres and had broader economic consequences. This is not the place to discuss them in detail.[3] However, in connection with a discussion of

---

[3] Discussions of financial crises and their consequences can be found in Kindleberger (1978), Reinhart and Rogoff (2009), and Cassis (2011).

international financial centres ten years after the Global Financial Crisis, it is worth pondering a moment on the decade that followed previous global crises, in particular as far as recovery and regulation are concerned.

There is no systematic historical analysis on the speed at which, and the extent to which international financial centres bounced back from a global financial crisis in terms of employment and various indicators of business activity, though a number of studies have looked at economic recovery after a financial shock and an economic downturn (Goodhart and Delargy 1998; Bordo et al. 2001; Reinhart and Rogoff 2009)—and the two are somewhat linked. A broad pattern of prompt recovery—less than five years—can nevertheless be perceived. This was the case after four of the seven global crises that broke out before the financial debacle of 2008: the Baring crisis of 1890, the American Panic of 1907, the financial instability of the early 1970s and the ensuing banking failures, and the international debt crisis of 1982. The proportion is even higher (four out of six) if we leave aside the financial crisis of July–August 1914, which was entirely linked to the outbreak of the First World War. The major exception is the Great Depression, which consisted of four interrelated shock waves: the Wall Street Crash of October 1929, a series of banking crises occurring over a period of five years, the collapse of the world's monetary order, and an economic slump of dramatic proportions. The minor exception is the Japanese banking crisis of 1997–8, which was part of Japan's lost decade (or even two decades). As an international financial centre, Tokyo bounced back but never entirely recovered its former position.

Financial crises have tended to increase the level of financial regulation, with the aim of preventing the outbreak of a new crisis. The American Panic of 1907 led to one of the most important pieces of legislation in US banking, the creation of the Federal Reserve System. But financial regulation really started, in many countries, as a response to the banking crises of the Great Depression, widely seen as having aggravated the slump, but also a result of the *Zeitgeist* of the time, which strongly favoured state intervention. The most radical reforms took place in the United States within the framework of the New Deal with, in particular, the Glass–Steagall Act of 1933, which separated commercial banking from investment banking.[4] Similar measures were adopted in Belgium, Italy, and France, while universal banking was preserved but stronger supervision introduced in Germany and Switzerland. Only Britain did not introduce any banking legislation. The Standing Committee on Banking Regulation and Supervisory Practices, later known as the Basel Committee, was created in 1974, in the wake of the series of bank failures

---

[4] Other significant measures included the Securities Exchange Act of 1934 (which created the Securities and Exchange Commission), and the Banking Act of 1935 (which reformed the Federal Reserve System).

that erupted in the early to mid 1970s. It took another financial crisis, the international debt crisis of 1982, to finally reach, in 1988, an agreement on capital adequacy, known as Basel I.[5] These agreements took place within a new political and ideological climate, marked by the growing influence of a neo-liberal view of the world economy. From the late 1970s, financial crises did not prevent the process of financial deregulation from sweeping aside any resistance—a movement that culminated with the abolition of the Glass–Steagall Act in 1999 and included, among others, the 'Big Bang' in the City of London in 1986.[6]

It is often assumed that financial centres need to be regulated in order to prevent the outbreak of financial crises, but that they only thrive in an unregulated environment. And yet there is no historical evidence to indicate that increased financial regulation leads to a slowdown in financial activities. The reverse is true in the short term, as new regulation tends to restore confidence in financial institutions and markets. This was especially the case in the 1930s. The point is more debatable in the medium-to-long term, as the socio-economic context within which specific regulatory measures were introduced begins to change. There has been much debate about the benefits and costs of financial regulation in the third quarter of the twentieth century, and financial deregulation in the last quarter. What is clear is that decisions to regulate and deregulate were motivated by political considerations as much as (if not more than) economic necessities.

1.3 Brexit in a Historical Perspective

It is not obvious how to put Brexit in a historical perspective. The event, of course, has not yet happened. But even so, never before had the world's largest (or second largest) economic area been decoupled from its financial capital. One can find some remote parallels. One is Vienna after the First World War, which ceased to be the financial capital of the Austro-Hungarian Empire, a declining but not insignificant economic area. But this was caused by military defeat and the dismantlement of the Habsburg Empire, not Austria leaving it. Another is Montreal, which was replaced by Toronto as Canada's financial

---

[5] The Basel agreement was adopted in 1988 and implemented four years later, in 1992. It rested on three pillars: one measuring capital, a second weighting risk, and a third, with which Basel I is readily associated, setting a capital ratio of 8 per cent of risk-weighted assets. Despite weaknesses, it was a first step towards the establishment of a system of international regulation.

[6] The 'Big Bang' was a reform of the London Stock Exchange—the result of an agreement in 1983 between the government and the exchange to abolish by the end of 1986 fixed commissions, as well as the age-old separation between the functions of brokers and jobbers (or market makers). It was also decided to open up the stock exchange to the outside world by permitting banks to buy member firms.

capital as a result of Quebec separatism. In any case, it is hard to see what lessons can be drawn from these two cases, whether one considers the prospects for the City of London or those for the other major European centres after the United Kingdom has left the European Union.

Historical 'lessons' have to be looked for elsewhere, primarily in the conditions leading to the rise and decline of international financial centres. Contemporary economic and financial literature has identified a number of them—stability of political institutions, the strength of the currency, powerful financial institutions, liquid markets, firm but not intrusive state supervision, a light tax burden, a skilled workforce, efficient means of communication. While these conditions undoubtedly apply to all successful centres, they do not explain why only a handful of them have risen to become the world's leading international financial centres—those discussed in this volume that I have elsewhere called the 'capitals of capital'. Long-term historical analysis reveals that the rise of a major international financial centre is closely linked to the economic power of the country that hosts it (Cassis 2006): London and Paris in the late eighteenth and early nineteenth century, Berlin and New York in the late nineteenth century, Tokyo in the mid to late twentieth century, Hong Kong in the late twentieth century, Shanghai in the early twenty-first century. Each of the three cities successively ranked top in world finance—Amsterdam in the eighteenth century, London in the nineteenth and early nineteenth, and New York ever since—has at the same time been the financial capital of the dominant economic power of the day. There are a couple of exceptions that confirm the rule: Switzerland in the second half of the twentieth century, or Singapore since the 1980s, but they are both the result of exceptional circumstances.[7]

What can these 'lessons' tell us about the possible effects of Brexit on international financial centres? Let us first consider the prospects for London. London has always been an international rather than a domestic financial centre, far more than New York, Frankfurt, or Tokyo, and by the turn of the twenty-first century it had become a truly global financial centre. But London has also become a European financial centre and in many respects, especially wholesale financial services, the financial capital of Europe. Significantly, Europe's other financial capitals, especially Paris and Frankfurt, have gradually lost some of their importance and influence, a position not entirely dissimilar to that of Boston, Chicago, or San Francisco in the United States. After Brexit, London would no longer be the financial capital of a major economic power

---

[7] Switzerland benefited from its neutrality during World War II, capital inflows, and the role of refuge currency played by the Swiss franc, as well as to the relatively weak activity of other financial centres in continental Europe, especially Paris and Frankfurt, prior to the early 1980s. Singapore was able to take advantage of the emerging Asian dollar market from the late 1960s and of the absence of a major financial centre in South-East Asia.

and thus no longer meet the conditions required to be one of the world's top financial centres. This does not mean that the City of London would be eradicated from the map of major international financial centres in the short to medium term, or even the long term. The rebirth of the City of London in the 1960s when Britain had become a medium-sized power was also an exception that confirmed the rule. The exception is likely to be repeated after Brexit, if only because of London's unparalleled position in several fields of international financial business and its capacity to innovate and reinvent itself. But its international influence would be diminished and become more akin to that of Singapore than that of New York.

London would also benefit from the absence of real competition from continental Europe. But that would only be in the short term. In the medium to long term, as a leading economic power (even without the United Kingdom), the European Union would have to host one of the world's leading financial centres—a centre capable of competing with New York, Hong Kong, Shanghai, Tokyo, and Singapore in the same way as London, but not Frankfurt or Paris, does today. Such a centre would be more 'domestic', i.e. European, than international, with London retaining much of this role in Europe. It is not clear which city would emerge as the new financial centre of the European Union, though Paris and Frankfurt appear to be the most likely candidates, or how long this process would take.

1.4 International Financial Centres after the Global Financial Crisis and Brexit

The following eight chapters of this book draw a first balance sheet of the development of the world's leading financial centres in the decade that followed the Global Financial Crisis: New York, London, Paris, Frankfurt, Zurich/Geneva, Hong Kong/Shanghai/Beijing, Singapore, and Tokyo—the sequence of the chapters follows a geographical rather than a hierarchical order. The chapters also reflect on the possible consequences of Brexit a year and a half after the result of the referendum, but still before Britain actually leaves the European Union. They necessarily devote more attention to the former than the latter issue, which is admittedly far more elusive. The chapters deliberately take a short-term historical perspective—broadly speaking, they focus on the the twenty-first century, as the object of this book is not to write a new history of international financial centres, but to contribute to a better understanding of the changes brought about by two recent epochal events. While all addressing the same issues, each author has written his or her chapter in a personal manner, partly reflecting his or her academic discipline, which adds to the richness of the analysis. General conclusions regarding international financial centres after the Global Financial Crisis and Brexit will be drawn in the last chapter of the book. Beforehand, three main points will be addressed here, in connection with the three questions raised at the beginning of this introduction.

The first point concerns the hierarchy of international financial centres. The chapters do not deal directly with this issue, in other words they do no attempt to rank their respective centre in some kind of pecking order. Rather, most of them use the Global Financial Centres Index as an indicator of relative success or failure in the last ten years. The analyses conducted in the book confirm that global financial crises do not cause an upheaval in the hierarchy of international financial centres, yet they reveal strong internal dynamics within the group of leading centres. The respective positions of New York on the one hand, and the three Chinese centres (Hong Kong, Shanghai, and Beijing) on the other are particularly striking.

Richard Sylla confirms, implicitly rather than explicitly, New York's position as the world's top financial centre—because of the size of the market for US Treasury securities; the persisting role of the dollar as the world's main reserve currency; the Fed's actions as the world's central bank during the Global Financial Crisis; the size and restored strength of American leading banks, all located or with a strong presence in New York; and the size of its securities market, with the NYSE and NASDAQ being the world's two largest exchanges. There are of course other measures of the influence of international financial centres, but these make a very strong case for New York.

David Meyer underlines the complementarity between Hong Kong (the global financial centre), Beijing (the political, regulatory centre), and Shanghai (the commercial centre), as well as the density of their networks in the rise of China as a global financial power. None of the three Chinese centres is about to supplant New York as the world's number one—the conditions, in terms of rule of law, currency convertibility, or per capita income, are not yet met. But despite challenges, including the status of Hong Kong and the risks of financial instability, China's financial centres have gained strong momentum.

The second point relates to the effects of global financial crises. The Global Financial Crisis, despite its severity, appears to fit into the general pattern of being followed by comparatively prompt recovery, though with some variations between regions—South-East Asia, North America, and Western Europe. The Global Financial Crisis hardly registered in the East Asian financial centres (Hong Kong, Shanghai, Beijing, Singapore, and Tokyo), though it had some early impact on the economies of the region. The Asian financial crisis of 1997 mattered more, even if Hong Kong, Singapore, and to a lesser extent Tokyo (which went through its own banking crisis) were not the worst hit by the shock. In North America, New York recovered rather well from a crisis of which it was the epicentre.

The effects of the Global Financial Crisis were more strongly felt, in different ways, in the financial centres of Western Europe, where they were compounded by the Euro-crisis, which lingered until 2015, as well as some specific domestic problems. London maintained its leading position alongside New York throughout the period. Interestingly, Richard Roberts points out that, measured by employment figures in wholesale financial services, two earlier downturns (in the mid-1970s, and the early 1990s) were actually worse than that caused by the Global Financial Crisis—with respective falls of 19 per cent, 22 per cent, and 12 per cent from peak to trough. And even though the crisis was over by September 2009, business confidence, which had returned with the end of the crisis, continued to fluctuate, dipping again in 2011–12 and 2015–16. In Paris, employment barely declined after 2007 and increased steadily after a slight slowdown between 2007 and 2013. Laure Quennouëlle-Corre also points out that the solidity of French banks during the crisis reinforced Paris's competitive position as an international financial centre. However, the vitality of the Paris stock market was weakened by the failure of the Euronext NYSE merger. Conversely, Frankfurt suffered from the lasting troubles of the big universal banks (especially Deutsche Bank), the pillars of the German model of capitalism, though Deutsche Börse is described by Eike Schamp as one the winners of the crisis. Finally, the Swiss centres seem to have fared particularly badly, with its largest bank, UBS, one of the worst hit by the crisis, and banking secrecy ending de facto in 2009, putting an end, according to Tobias Straumann, to Switzerland's exceptional role in European capital markets.

The Global Financial Crisis also led to the introduction of tighter financial regulation—with Basel III at the international level, the Dodd–Frank Act in the United States, the Vickers Report in Britain, and the various steps towards the banking union in the Eurozone and several other countries of the EU. How have these new regulations affected international financial centres? The chapters convey a contrasting yet revealing picture. As the issue of post-Global Financial Crisis regulation is hardly discussed in five of the eight core chapters (those on Paris, Frankfurt, the Chinese centres, Singapore, and Tokyo), one can surmise that this has not been a prime concern for these centres.

Only three chapters, those on New York, London, and the Swiss centres, directly address the question of new regulation. In the three countries involved, the main issue at stake is whether regulation has gone too far in its burdensome and sometimes apparently unnecessary complexity and become a case of regulatory overkill—people in the profession talk of 'regulatory tsunami'. This is undoubtedly the view held by the banking community. In the City, throughout the post-crisis years ('one of the most intensive periods of regulatory change in modern history' according to the British Banking Association), regulation has been seen as a major problem and a serious threat to London's position. Swiss bankers have tried to push back the regulatory wave but their voice has remained unheard. Only in the United States has the backlash against the Dodd–Frank Act led to new legislative proposals in Congress. In contrast to the legacy of the Great Depression, which lasted nearly half a century, the measures taken as a response to the Global Financial Crisis are being questioned after less than a decade—a reflection of the differences between the two crises, but also of the economic context (the weight of finance in advanced economies), ideological climate (the persistence of neoliberal views), and international balance of power (the rise of East Asia) prevailing in the early twenty-first century.

Finally, the third point concerns the capacity of international financial centres to reinvent themselves, and seize new opportunities in order to resist decline. Here, the main post-crisis challenge does not seem to be Brexit, but fintech. Fintech is more than simply the application to financial services of innovations brought about by digital technology. It also refers to the possibly major disruptions that these innovations could bring to the financial sector, whether one considers the way of providing financial services or the firms providing these services.

All the chapters in the book discuss how the leading international financial centres have been dealing with the fintech challenge, in particular their respective competitive positions in the field. From this perspective, none of the leading centres appears to have missed the boat, even if the fintech industry is not as active in Tokyo, and Japan more generally, as in other advanced economies. New York can rely on its 'Silicon Alley' and looks unlikely to be disrupted by fintech. London, with its own 'Silicon Roundabout', can claim to be the fintech capital of the world. Frankfurt, together with Berlin and Munich, is part of a more decentralized development of fintech in Germany, which ranks third in the world behind the United States and Britain. Paris does not appear to be far behind, with the success of its 'finance innovation cluster', set up in 2007, and the launch in 2016 of a new 'French Tech Hub' in London. A 'guarded optimism' is prevailing in Switzerland, with the existence of a 'Crypto Valley' in Zug, near Zurich, and the government's encouraging stance. The Chinese centres, with Beijing in the lead, are riding high, accounting for 90 per cent of Asia-Pacific's investments in fintech; while Singapore has embraced the movement, not least with the formation in 2015 of a 'FinTech and Innovation Group' by the Monetary Authority of Singapore, and is positioning itself as a link with emerging centres in Indonesia, Malaysia, Thailand, and Vietnam.

Against this general optimism, the possible disruptions that may be caused by new technologies appear fairly remote. Nevertheless, Laure Quennouëlle-Corre underlines the threat that the development of private platforms has posed to official stock exchanges, and the possibility of blockchain technology reducing the volume of international financial centres' activities; while Richard Roberts points out that consumer banking, payments, and fund transfers face the highest risk of disruption. Significantly, most British financial firms believe that part of their revenues is at risk, and envisage responding through strategic partnerships with, or takeovers of, fintech firms.

Unlike fintech, Brexit increasingly appears as a regional rather than a global shock, seriously involving only three of the eight leading international financial centres: London, Paris, and Frankfurt. The East Asian centres are hardly going to be affected by it. New York is likely to gain some business, Zurich and Geneva much less so. The intricacies of Brexit, in particular the passporting rights and location of clearing houses, are discussed in some details, from the perspective of London, Paris, and Frankfurt, in the three chapters devoted to these centres. The authors remain cautious in their conclusions and even more so in their assessments of possible scenarios. For Eike Schamp, Frankfurt, usually considered as best placed to benefit from Brexit, 'will remain a small financial centre compared to post-Brexit London'. There has been an unprecedented mobilization of the various stakeholders in the fight for Paris's European leadership, but the outcome remains unpredictable. Much uncertainty surrounds London's possible or likely losses, but some leading players see the City as being eventually reshaped by fintech rather than Brexit, and remaining one of the most important and attractive international financial centres.

From the perspective of international financial centres, there has been more continuity than change in the decade following the Global Financial Crisis. The international financial hierarchy has hardly been modified, with only marginal changes resulting from the development of the world economy. As in the wake of previous crises, financial regulation has been tightened, but this has not coincided with a significant shift in ideological outlook. Financial innovation, an intrinsic part of the financial world for the last forty years, has moved one step further with fintech, which has the potential to transform the conduct of financial transactions though not necessarily the map of international financial centres. Brexit does not fit into this long-term historical development pattern. Yet its disruptive effects, especially on a global scale, should not be overestimated. Richard Roberts's closing words about the London financial elite's perception of the years to come could be extended to the other centres: no looking back to the financial crisis, the world has moved on, and a new array of challenges and opportunities—a vision at once worrying and promising.

References

Balogh, Thomas. 1947. Studies in Financial Organisation. Cambridge: Cambridge University Press.

Bordo, Michael et al. 2001. 'Is the Crisis Problem Growing More Severe?'. *Economic Policy* 16 (32): 52–82.

Cassis, Youssef. 2006. Capitals of Capital. The History of International Financial Centres, 1780–2005. Cambridge: Cambridge University Press.

Cassis, Youssef. 2011. Crises and Opportunities. The Shaping of Modern Finance. Oxford: Oxford University Press.

Goodhart, Charles and P. J. R. Delargy. 1998. 'Financial Crises: Plus ça Change, plus c'est la Même Chose'. *International Finance* 1 (2): 261–87.

James, Harold. 1996. International Monetary Cooperation since Bretton Woods. Washington, DC: International Monetary Fund and New York: Oxford University Press.

Jones, Geoffrey. 1992. 'International Financial Centres in Asia, the Middle East and Australia: A Historical Perspective'. In Finance and Financiers in European History 1880–1960, edited by Youssef Cassis. Cambridge: Cambridge University Press, pp. 405–28.

Kindleberger, Charles P. 1978. Manias, Panics and Crashes. A History of Financial Crises. London: Macmillan.

Lévy-Leboyer, Maurice. 1977. 'La balance des paiements et l'exportation des capitaux français'. In La position internationale de la France. Aspects économiques et financiers XIXe–XXe siècles, edited by M. Lévy-Leboyer. Paris: éditions de l'Ecole des hautes études en sciences sociales, pp. 75–142.

Reed, Howard C. 1981. The Preeminence of International Financial Centres. New York: Praeger.

Reinhart, Carmen M. and Kenneth S. Rogoff. 2009. This Time is Different. Eight Centuries of Financial Folly. Princeton: Princeton University Press.

Roberts, Richard. 1996. 'The Economics of Cities of Finance'. In Cities of Finance, edited by H.A. Diedericks and D. Reeder. Amsterdam: Royal Netherlands Academy of Arts and Science, pp. 7–19.

Roberts, Richard. 1998. Inside International Finance. London: Orion.

Stone, Irving. 1999. The Global Export of Capital from Great Britain, 1865–1914: A Statistical Survey. New York: St Martin's Press.

2

New York

Remains a, if not the, Pre-eminent International Financial Centre

Richard Sylla

2.1 Introduction

New York City became a—some would argue *the*—leading international financial centre a century ago, after World War I. In just a few years it transformed the United States from being the world's largest 'debtor' nation to the largest 'creditor' nation (Sylla 2011a). A century before that, New York emerged as the leading US financial centre, certainly after populist president Andrew Jackson in 1832 vetoed Congress's bill to re-charter the central bank, and possibly earlier.

Supporters of New York as *the* leading centre can point to the size of the US money and capital markets, which dwarf those of other countries. The US banking system until recently was also the world's largest, but since the Global Financial Crisis of 2007–9, it has been surpassed by China's, which rather remarkably has more than tripled in size since 2008. The Eurozone as a whole also has a substantially larger banking system than the United States, but that system is still not a banking union, and it has moreover contracted quite a bit since the financial crisis a decade ago. In 2017, it too was passed by China.

The case is stronger for regarding New York as *a*, not *the*, leading international financial centre. Its international business is large, but in comparison with other centres, notably London, a much greater proportion of its business is domestic rather than international. It serves mainly a US economy that until recently was the world's largest, and one that still accounts for about a quarter of gross world product.

On some measures, China by 2017 may have surpassed the United States in GDP. As a matter of arithmetic China, which has about four times the population of the United States, would have equalled it in GDP when its per capita GDP reached a quarter of the US level, and it seems China reached that level by 2017. Like the United States, China's financial system serves mainly its domestic economy. But the sheer size of China's economy suggests that Chinese financial centres could become increasingly important as world financial centres. That after all was the pattern followed by the US economy and the New York financial centre during the nineteenth and twentieth centuries.

There is another sense, however, in which New York can be said to be a very international financial centre. Its leading financial institutions—universal banks such as JPMorgan Chase and Citigroup, investment banks such as Goldman Sachs and Morgan Stanley, custodial banks such as Bank of New York Mellon, asset managers such as BlackRock, and private equity firms such as KKR and Blackstone—have strong presences in many of the world's other leading financial centres. If Brexit were to force London to have to contract some of its financial operations, as some expect, it would be a fairly simple matter for the American banks to transfer staff and operations to their existing operations in the Eurozone, in Asia, and even back to New York.

But the New York-based institutions just mentioned are not the only American financial companies with strong presences in other international financial centres. Bank of America, headquartered in Charlotte, North Carolina, is another, as is Wells Fargo, headquartered in San Francisco, California. Both of these major world banks also have substantial operations in New York, as do many of the world's leading banks headquartered outside the United States. New York is, therefore, a very international financial centre even if a relatively greater proportion of its business serves the US domestic economy than is the case with other international financial centres (such as London) located in countries with smaller domestic economies.

The New York financial centre is also home to five of the world's thirty largest insurance companies ranked in 2017 by assets: Metlife, Prudential Financial, AIG, New York Life, and TIAA, as well as leading hedge funds such as Bridgewater and Renaissance Technologies.

In this chapter, I first discuss the major developments affecting New York as a financial centre since the crisis of 2007–9. Next, I survey the regulatory responses to the crisis; regulation is very much an ongoing topic because the US Congress is currently considering altering, even undoing, the initial regulatory response embodied in the 2010 Dodd–Frank Act. Then I consider the potential impacts of fintech innovations on financial systems and financial centres. I conclude with some observations on the likely role of New York and other international financial centres in the years and decades ahead.

2.2 Impacts of the 2007–9 Financial Crisis

The New York financial centre in most respects has recovered rather well from the Global Financial Crisis a decade ago, at least in comparison to Europe's leading centres. There is some irony in the recovery because New York was the epicentre of the crisis, the most dramatic event of which was the failure of Lehman Brothers, a leading US and international investment bank, on 15 September 2008. The Lehman failure shocked the financial world because it was unexpected—in March 2008 the US government had arranged a bailout of Bear Stearns, an important investment bank but one smaller than Lehman, and its absorption by JP Morgan Chase, creating an expectation that Lehman would surely receive a similar bailout if it proved necessary. Then when this did prove necessary, it wasn't done. Panic broke out, and there were runs on even the most solid and reputable institutions, both in the United States and around the world.

What went wrong? And why was New York the epicentre of the crisis? A lot of ink has been devoted to answering these questions. Here a summary may be in order.

The crisis was often described as a 'subprime crisis' because its origins lay in the origination of home mortgage loans to borrowers with less than stellar credit in the United States in the years leading up to the crisis. Traditional underwriting standards for home loans would not have allowed many of these loans to be made. But in the US housing boom of the early years of the twenty-first century, up to 2007, underwriting standards collapsed. Mortgage brokers and underwriting specialists introduced compensation models that made their incomes depend on the fees they received for making new loans. So, the more mortgage loans they originated, the more income they received. They made a lot of loans they would never have made under traditional underwriting standards. Their justification was the argument that house prices never went down, so even if a borrower who had put no money down defaulted, the home collateral would be of sufficient value to avoid any loss to the lender. It was a convenient but flawed justification. While it might be said that home values had never declined nationwide in the United States since 1945, which was how far back the models used by the credit rating agencies extended, during the 1930s and some earlier episodes house prices had, in fact, declined nationwide.

A more telling justification for the origination of dicey subprime mortgage loans, but one more whispered than shouted, was that the underwriters' business model was 'originate to distribute'. This is where New York and Wall Street came into the picture. Instead of holding onto the mortgage loans, the underwriting firms sold them to New York banks that packaged them into mortgage-backed securities (MBSs), and even securities based on

MBSs called collateralized debt obligations (CDOs), and sold both types of securities worldwide to investors—usually institutional investors—hungry for yield in the low-interest-rate environment of those years.

It was a highly profitable business for the banks . . . while it lasted. Although the individual loans to subprime borrowers were risky, the credit rating agencies (New York-based S&P, Moody's, and Fitch were the big three that did most of this work) pronounced the MBSs and CDOs to be of low risk, hence highly rated, because each security was diversified in being backed by mortgage loans from different parts of the United States. So even if house prices fell in one part of the country, which was not unusual, and led to losses on a mortgage or two, a diversified MBS or CDO based on many mortgages was unlikely to go bad, and it still offered a higher yield than an investor could obtain on traditional fixed-income investments such as government and corporate bonds.

Some of the investors who bought MBSs and CDOs were so-called shadow banks, entities set up in order, they thought, to profit handsomely by holding the high-yielding long-term securities and financing the purchases with cheap, short-term money-market funding such as commercial paper and repo. New York banks set up such off-balance-sheet shadow entities because, being off balance sheet, they did not require that much, if any, bank capital to be held in the shadow bank, which enhanced the profit possibilities. But to get lenders to lend, the banks often agreed to take the off-balance-sheet entities back onto the balance sheet if anything went wrong.

It all worked fine until late 2006 and early 2007 when house prices topped out and unexpected numbers of individual mortgages went into default, often just a few months after the mortgage loans had been made. Moreover, when those involved in the business began belatedly to investigate the underlying collateral, which they had assumed to be owner-occupied houses, they discovered that many of the houses were standing empty and uncared for. Speculators had taken out mortgage loans to build houses they intended not to live in, but to flip at higher prices as long as the housing boom continued.

The protracted crisis began in early 2007 when several of the mortgage originators, for example, Indy Mac and Countrywide, failed, mostly because their own financing had dried up; some were taken over by larger banks—e.g. Countrywide, absorbed by Bank of America—usually to the later regret of the latter. By the summer two shadow-banking entities sponsored by Bear Stearns failed, and the crisis spread to Europe where banks discovered that some of their MBS and CDO investments were hard to value because no one wanted to buy them.

All of this happened more than a year before Lehman failed, but the signs were ominous. US equity market indexes topped out by October 2007, and then began a decline that would lead them to lose about half their value by the time the bottom came in March 2009. The US economy at the end of 2007 slipped into a recession—later dubbed the 'Great Recession'—that would last for eighteen months before it ended in May 2009. Unemployment rates approached 10 per cent in 2009.

Lehman's failure in mid-September was the defining moment of the crisis, but it was hardly the only major negative event. Before it happened, the US Treasury put the government-sponsored enterprises Fannie Mae and Freddie Mac, which guarantee home mortgages, purchase them from private mortgage lenders, and participate in mortgage securitization, into 'conservatorship', which effectively meant taking them over and channelling their earnings into the US Treasury. Shortly after Lehman failed, AIG, a large insurance company, was on the verge of insolvency because of its dealings in credit default swaps, and received an $80 billion bailout from the government. The money passed through one door of AIG and out of the other, onto the balance sheets of other banks with claims on AIG. Then Merrill Lynch, a large investment bank, avoided failure by selling itself to Bank of America; WAMU, a large mortgage originator failed and was absorbed into JP Morgan Chase; and Wachovia, a large commercial bank, failed and was ultimately absorbed by Wells Fargo after a weakened Citigroup made a failed bid for it.

It was a classical crisis with runs on the banks. The runs differed from earlier crises in one respect, but otherwise were similar. In earlier crises, depositors pulled their funds out of banks all at once, or tried to, and when the banks could not convert their liabilities into base money, they had to shut their doors. In 2008, the difference was that short-term lenders—the buyers of commercial paper and repos issued by bank holding companies and shadow banks—not depositors, asked for their money back and stopped lending because they feared the borrowing banks (and Fannie, Freddie, and AIG) might fail.

The solution was also classical. The US Treasury under Secretary Henry ('Hank') Paulson, formerly the CEO of Goldman Sachs, injected funds into the faltering institutions—first into Fannie and Freddie, and then via the Troubled Assets Relief Program (TARP) by means of injections of capital into all the leading banks, whether they wanted it, needed it, or not. And the Federal Reserve began a massive expansion of its balance sheet by lending to faltering institutions, including financial institutions and non-financial businesses in both the United States and Europe, and purchasing large amounts of US Treasury debt and MBSs to add liquidity to markets to keep them from breaking down.

The Fed made amendments to Walter Bagehot's classic rules for the lender of last resort in a crisis. Whereas Bagehot had said the central bank should lend freely on good collateral—or what in ordinary times is considered good collateral, e.g. government debt—at a high rate of interest, the Fed under the leadership of Ben Bernanke, formerly of Princeton University's economics department and a leading expert on what went wrong during the Great

Depression of the early 1930s, lent fairly freely on what could be considered dodgy collateral at low rates of interest.

While these central-banking solutions were implemented in 2008, the Federal Deposit Insurance Corporation increased its insurance on deposits to $250,000, to make sure the runs on commercial paper and repo did not spook bank depositors into making old-fashioned runs on their banks as happened in earlier crises. And the newly assembled Obama administration proposed, and Congress enacted, a $700 billion fiscal stimulus programme that helped, although it was poorly designed and implemented, and was less than it might have been given the magnitude of the crisis.

These measures stemmed the crisis in late 2008 and 2009. As mentioned earlier, US equity markets bottomed out in March 2009, and the Great Recession ended two months later. But the economic recovery from the crisis turned out to be painfully slow. Earlier recoveries from crises, associated economic downturns, and recessions unrelated to crises, featured short periods of expansion above the average long-term US growth rate of 3–4 per cent per year. The long expansion that began in June 2009, and is still in effect in late 2017, averaged annual growth of only 2 per cent, despite several years of continuing stimulus in the form of so-called quantitative easing by the Fed, which ultimately led the Fed balance sheet to more than quintuple to $4.5 trillion after 2007. Unemployment in 2017 has fallen to a 4–5 per cent range, virtually full employment, but real wages stagnated in what some pessimists term 'the new normal'.

Thanks to rising asset prices—houses and securities—the net worth of US households reached an all-time record $94.6 trillion dollars in 2017. This means that the average US household is three-quarters of the way to millionaire status, although the median household worth would be far lower, around $100,000. It is evident that most of the gains have been concentrated at the top of the wealth distribution; the rich own the biggest houses and the lion's share of stocks and bonds. So it appears that record household wealth is cold comfort to most American households. The election of populist Donald Trump to the presidency in 2016 was a strong indication that despite full employment and record household net worth, the new normal is not very attractive to wide swathes of the US citizenry. And the fractious national and state politics of the years since the crisis ended in 2009 shows no sign of going away early into the Trump administration.

Given the rather gloomy condition of the 'new normal' in the United States, and the lack of indications that it is going to go away anytime soon, one might think that New York's status as a leading international financial centre could be threatened. But that seems far from the case. The United States and the New York financial centre continue to have many advantages. In what follows I shall review these advantages, along with some associated disadvantages, within a framework that I developed in earlier work to study the historical development of modern financial systems regarding their key components (Sylla 2002; 2004; 2009; 2011b).

In that framework, there are six key components:

- Public finance and debt management
- Money
- The central bank
- The banking system
- Securities markets
- Corporations

Let's see how these apply.

2.2.1 *Public Finance and Debt Management*

Here the great advantage is the US national debt as embodied in the market for US Treasury securities—bills, notes, and bonds. This is the largest market in history for the obligations of a single issuer. In 2017, its size is $20 trillion, slightly more than US GDP. But $6–7 trillion of the total consists of securities the US government has issued to itself, as when collections of Social Security taxes exceed payments to retirees in the national pension system, as they have since the inception of the system in the 1930s. The Treasury borrows the surpluses to finance current spending, issuing an IOU—non-marketable Treasury debt—to the Social Security Trust Fund. The marketable debt in the hands of the public, including the Federal Reserve System, which owns a good chunk of it, is in the range of $13–14 trillion. The market for this debt is highly liquid; single transactions of billions of dollars can occur with little impact on market prices.

The US government has not defaulted or missed a payment on its debt since Alexander Hamilton, the first Secretary of the Treasury, set up the system to restructure Revolutionary War debts and to establish public credit and the Treasury bond market during his tenure in office from 1789 to 1795. The bond investors of the world know this history and consider US Treasury debt to be the safest of financial assets, as well as the best collateral one can offer when seeking a loan. Whenever there is turmoil, financial or other, in the world, worried investors sell riskier assets and park the money in US Treasury obligations. Asset prices fall in many other markets and yields rise, while the opposite happens in the Treasury debt market as prices rise and yields fall. The Treasury debt market has been international since its inception when European investors began to purchase US debt securities. By the first years of the 1800s, a majority of the debt was held abroad (Sylla, Wilson, and Wright 2006). This long tradition continues down to the present when trillions of dollars of US debt are owned overseas and often are major international reserves for foreign governments.

That foreign investors, both official and private, are willing to hold so much Treasury debt is an obvious advantage to the United States. It is also a great advantage to the New York financial centre because that is where much of the issuing and trading of Treasury debt occurs. The Federal Reserve System, America's decentralized central bank, manages its System Open Market Account at the Federal Reserve Bank of New York. It buys and sells Treasury debt securities as a method of implementing monetary policy and on behalf of the Treasury, which is in the market on a weekly basis, rolling over old debt for new, and frequently selling new debt. On the other side of the market are a number of primary dealers, largely American and a few large foreign financial institutions with headquarters or major offices in New York. Lesser institutions and individual investors buy and sell Treasury debt by dealing with the primary dealers.

As long as the Treasury debt market continues to play the role in US and international finance that it has for the past century, New York's status as a leading international financial centre seems assured.

The downside of a huge public debt market is the strain its management can place on public finance. Since 2008, the worst year of the Global Financial Crisis, the gross public debt of the United States has doubled, from $10 to $20 trillion. The extremely low interest rates that followed from the crisis to the present made the debt not too costly to manage. But as interest rates normalize, a process that has already begun, the interest cost of a $20 trillion debt will increase and put pressure on the federal budget.

The fractious US politics of the years since the crisis make it difficult to enact tax increases, so if more of the budget has to go to paying interest, there will be less left for other purposes. On top of that, the US Congress pretends to be fiscally responsible by enacting ceilings on the national debt. That creates a problem bordering on a crisis whenever the spending authorized by Congress bumps up against its previously imposed debt ceiling.

This periodical and silly debt-ceiling political charade is good neither for the United States nor for the New York financial centre. New York, the country, and the world would benefit from a greater sense of fiscal responsibility in Washington, DC. A lack of such responsibility could constitute a threat to US leadership in the world and to New York's position as a leading financial centre.

2.2.2 Money

The US dollar continues to be the main reserve currency of the world, as it has been for nearly a century. It accounts for about 60–65 per cent of foreign exchange reserves around the world, down from around 70 per cent before the advent of the euro, which is now the runner-up, accounting for about 20 per cent of reserves. The UK pound and Japanese yen make up most of the remaining reserves, with recent shares of 4–5 per cent each.

These percentages may be declining because the Chinese have been pushing the yuan (or renminbi) as a reserve currency, apparently with some success. This would seem to be a natural outcome of China's fast-growing weight in the world economy and international trade. But history shows a lot of persistence in leading reserve currencies. There have not been many of them since the advent of international money markets. One surmises that China faces a long and uphill struggle to have the yuan replace the dollar as the leading reserve currency.

The dollar's pre-eminent reserve-currency role confers on the United States an 'exorbitant privilege', in the words of 1960s French finance minister Valéry Giscard d'Estaing. The privilege consists in the ability of the US Treasury's Bureau of Engraving and Printing to print, say, a hundred dollar bill (the largest current denomination of US currency) at a cost of just a few cents, and then have the bill finance, directly or indirectly, $100 of imports of goods and services merely because foreign countries want to obtain those dollars and hold them as foreign exchange reserves.

The gain to the United States is obvious, and the financial crisis, perhaps because of associated problems of the euro, did little if anything to diminish it. A lot of foreign exchange trading is done in New York, but London for various reasons has done much more of it. One wonders if Brexit will diminish London's role. If so, it could be to the advantage of New York and other world financial centres.

2.2.3 *The Central Bank*

During the Global Financial Crisis, the Fed effectively acted as the world's central bank. The extent to which it did so was not known at the time, but came out later when Congress demanded a full accounting of its lender-of-last-resort operations during the crisis. The Fed accommodated other central banks and lent to financial and non-financial corporations within the United States and also in other countries. It did this in cooperation with other central banks.

The Fed's actions during the crisis are reminiscent of the late nineteenth and early twentieth centuries when London was the premier international financial centre and the Bank of England acted as the world's central bank. Then, as in the recent crisis, the Bank of England acted with the cooperation of other central banks, notably the Bank of France, and with major private financial institutions both in the UK and in other countries such as the United States, which then did not have a central bank.

Most students of financial history would deem it to the advantage of the London financial centre a century and more ago that it was also the home of the de facto world central bank. Now that the Fed has acted as a world central bank, it is probably to the advantage of the United States and the New York financial centre. There is a structural difference, however. Whereas the Bank of England had (and has) its headquarters in London, New York is home only to the most important of the twelve regional reserve banks in the Fed system, which has its headquarters in Washington, DC. Although there are instances in Fed history of disagreements and a lack of cooperation between the Fed board in Washington and the Federal Reserve Bank of New York, they are far in the past. In recent decades there has been close cooperation between the board in Washington and the New York Fed. So the difference between London in the old days and New York now is minor.

A more important difference between London then and New York now is the political climate. Whereas the Bank of England then enjoyed the support of the British government and the populace, the Fed now is not nearly as popular in the United States. When Congress discovered the extent of the Fed's world central banking operations in the crisis, it trimmed the Fed's powers in the 2010 Dodd–Frank regulatory reform act, discussed further in Section 2.3. The Fed's quantitative easing and low-interest policies in the period after the crisis have also proved controversial. For years the Fed's critics in and out of Congress have said that those policies would unleash inflation, and the fact that it has not happened yet does not appear to temper the criticisms.

The Fed's political problems appear to be the latest manifestation of a long tradition in the United States that worries about 'excessive' concentrations of financial power. Such worries early in US history prevented the first two central banks, the Banks of the United States, from receiving charter renewals. That never happened in the long history of the Bank of England.

The Fed and some of its backers now think that the political climate in the United States could threaten the cherished independence of the central bank. Donald Trump voiced misgivings about the Fed and its leadership during the 2016 presidential campaign. He has an opportunity early in his administration to remake the composition of the Fed board, which had vacancies due to resignations, and in 2017 he nominated board member Jerome Powell to replace Janet Yellen as chairman on the expiration of her four-year term in 2018.

The Fed's ability to function as the world central bank is therefore more tenuous than that of the Bank of England in the days of the classical gold standard. Hence, the New York financial centre may not be in quite as strong a position as London once was. Nonetheless, New York would still seem to be in an advantageous position by being in the country that is the home of the world's pre-eminent central bank.

2.2.4 *The Banking System*

US banks were wounded by the crisis, but the wounds have mostly healed. As *The Economist* pointed out in a recent special report on international banking, since the crisis

> America's banks are significantly stronger. In investment banking, they are beating European rivals hollow. They are no longer having to fork out billions in legal bills for the sins of the past, and they are making a better return for their shareholders. (Economist 2017a)

The structure of the US banking system has also improved since the crisis, although perhaps not because of the crisis, since the trend began earlier. For most of its history, the United States had a banking system unlike that of most countries. There were thousands, even tens of thousands of independent banks, and most of them because of laws and regulations were limited to having one office, so-called unit banking. Regulation was by states, and when the federal government created a system of nationally chartered banks in the 1860s, federal regulatory authorities deferred to state regulation. Many other countries had fewer, larger banks and usually extensive, nationwide branching systems. For too much of this period (although libertarians might disagree), there was no central bank—1811–16 and 1836–1914. Unit banking was a problem; small, undiversified banks were prone to failure. The lack of a central bank compounded the problem. Americans probably had more access to credit than citizens of other nations for the past two centuries. A century ago, before World War I, the US system had more deposits than Britain, France, and Germany combined. But the US banking system was less stable, and crises more frequent, than elsewhere.

At the peak in the early 1920s, there were some 30,000 banks. The crises of the Great Depression knocked that down to around 14,000 in the 1930s, a level that persisted into the 1980s. Various financial crises during the 1980s and a decline in the banking system's share of total finance combined to stimulate regulatory change. During the 1990s Congress made possible nationwide branch banking, and it ended the 1930s Glass–Steagall Act's separation of commercial and investment banking. In 2017 there were fewer than 6,000 banks, mostly as a result of mergers and acquisitions, and that process is ongoing. Currently, there are a hundred or so large banks with more than $50 billion in assets along with some 5,000 so-called community banks with assets of $1 billion or less. US banking at long last looks more and more like banking in other countries.

During the 1990s and early 2000s, mergers and acquisitions along with regulatory relaxations created several gigantic money-centre banks or bank holding companies. Leading examples are JPMorgan Chase, Citigroup, Bank of New York Mellon, Goldman Sachs, and Morgan Stanley, all headquartered in New York, and Bank of America and Wells Fargo headquartered elsewhere but with large presences in New York. There were worries that these behemoths were 'too big to fail', and would have to be bailed out with taxpayers' money if they encountered difficulties. During the financial crisis several of these banks absorbed weaker rivals, becoming even more 'too big to fail'. And the two remaining large investment banks, Goldman Sachs and Morgan Stanley, took out bank holding company charters granting them access to Fed lending. That banks deemed too big became even bigger is one of the paradoxes of the recent crisis, and it has led to an ongoing debate about how to protect the taxpayers from too-big-to-fail bailouts.

Bank profits, hit hard during the crisis and then sapped by heavy fines for various misbehaviours in the lead-up to it, have rebounded. The five largest New York-headquartered banks—JPMorgan Chase, Citigroup, Bank of New York Mellon, Goldman Sachs, and Morgan Stanley—had combined net profits of $31.9 billion in 2007 and $56.5 billion in 2016 (data from Value Line 600, 2017). In between, profits were much lower and sometimes negative, most prominently Citigroup's negative profit (or loss) of $32.1 billion in 2008.

A decade after the crisis, the New York financial centre is either home or a second home to a number of the world's largest and strongest banks. That has to bode well for its future. Their presence in other world financial centres is most probably good for those centres as well, and it enhances the benefits of a well-integrated world financial system.

2.2.5 Securities Markets

New York is in an enviable position when it comes to securities markets. It is the home of the world's two largest stock exchanges, NYSE and NASDAQ. World equity market cap is estimated in the range of $60–70 trillion, of which the US markets' share is some 40 to 50 per cent. A similar ranking holds for the world's bond markets, which have an even larger cap of some $100 trillion; the US share, managed largely by New York institutions, is about $40 trillion, or 40 per cent. The largest components of the US bond market are US government debt, roughly $14 trillion in the hands of the public; mortgage-backed securities, $9 trillion; corporate debt, also about $9 trillion; municipal (US state and local) debt, $4 trillion; and federal agency issues, $2 trillion.

The New York securities markets serve the world, not just the United States. Asset managers—mutual and exchange-traded funds, pension funds, and insurance companies—in most developed nations are active participants in the large and liquid New York-based markets. Some of the largest, of course, are based either in New York (e.g. BlackRock and TIAA) or the northeastern

United States (e.g. Vanguard, Fidelity, and T. Rowe Price). The city and the metropolitan area also are home to some of the world's leading private equity firms (e.g. KKR and Blackstone), as well as the largest hedge funds (e.g. Bridgewater and Renaissance Technologies).

Given modern IT technologies, there is less reason than in the past for such financial organizations to be based in any financial centre. Asset managers, private equity firms, and hedge funds can and do operate in many other US and world cities. But as long as the largest and most liquid stock and bond markets are in New York, the rest of the world will continue to keep their eyes on it on a daily basis.

Although New York dominates securities markets, it has some problems. Companies listed on its exchanges are down to fewer than four thousand, half of the listings two decades ago. Mostly, that is a result of mergers and acquisitions (Economist 2017b). But it also results from private equity firms taking listed companies private, and from many companies choosing to remain private instead of listing their shares. Private companies avoid both the reporting requirements of public companies and the alleged incentives Wall Street gives public companies to focus on short-term financial results at the expense of long-term business planning. IPOs are also down from past levels. These problematic trends were in place before the financial crisis, but were exacerbated by the slow-growth economy that followed in its wake.

2.2.6 Corporations

The United States is home to many of the world's largest, most innovative and technologically advanced corporations. Since the financial crisis, a significant component of the rise in equity values has occurred in a relatively small number of companies with internationally recognized names, e.g. Alphabet (Google), Amazon, Apple, Facebook, Microsoft, Netflix, and Tesla. Most of them operate in many countries and earn significant portions of their revenues outside the United States. Because those portions would be taxed at relatively high corporate tax rates if they were brought home, the companies tend to hold huge cash balances overseas. There is much talk of changing the way the United States taxes corporate profits in order to induce those balances to come home. If that happens, it could boost anaemic US investment and growth, and it might make the companies less disruptive overseas.

The New York financial centre participates in the success of these world-class companies by virtue of having their listings on the NYSE and NASDAQ exchanges. Their shares trade worldwide, but share valuations are determined mainly in New York markets. That constitutes another advantage for New York among international financial centres.

2.3 Regulation

In response to the crisis of 2007–9, Congress enacted the Dodd–Frank Wall Street Reform and Consumer Financial Protection Act of 2010. It was the most comprehensive overhaul of US financial regulation since the New Deal reforms of the 1930s. Major features of Dodd–Frank include: (1) higher capital and liquidity requirements for banks; (2) creation of a Financial Stability Oversight Council made up of the heads of nine(!) other federal financial regulators and charged with monitoring systemic risks posed by entities termed 'systemically important financial institutions' or SIFIs, to be subjected to enhanced capital requirements, annual stress tests, living wills, and, if necessary, orderly liquidation; (3) creation of a Consumer Financial Protection Bureau to shield consumers of financial products from abuses, deceptions, and frauds; (4) a so-called Volcker Rule to prevent bank holding companies from engaging in proprietary trading or sponsoring hedge funds and private equity funds; and (5) a reduction of the Fed's authority to act as a lender of last resort in a crisis because Congress thought the Fed's use of that authority in the 2007–9 crisis increased moral hazard by bailing out entities deemed too big to fail.

As the various Dodd–Frank measures were gradually implemented after 2010, two things became apparent. One is that the act did reduce systemic risk in the US financial system compared to both pre-crisis levels and post-crisis levels in other countries, and it contributed to the more rapid recovery of US banks compared with banks in other countries. The other is that Dodd–Frank became an example of regulatory overkill with its many new regulations seemingly far exceeding what was necessary to contain systemic risks and perhaps contributing to the weak recovery from the 'Great Recession' that began in the crisis. Regulatory overkill led to a backlash.

So far, the backlash against Dodd–Frank has led to two major legislative proposals in Congress, namely the financial 'CHOICE' (Creating Hope and Opportunity for Investors, Consumers, and Entrepreneurs) Act, passed by the House of Representatives in June 2017, but with its prospects for Senate concurrence appearing dim. The other proposal is a 'twenty-first-century Glass–Steagall' act introduced by a bipartisan group of four senators early in 2017.

The CHOICE Act would dismantle much of Dodd–Frank, mainly in the form of an 'off-ramp' provision allowing any bank having a 10 per cent capital ratio (according to US accounting standards, which would allow banks to hold less capital than would international accounting standards) to be exempt from much of Dodd–Frank regulation. CHOICE would also eliminate the power of the Financial Stability Oversight Council to designate and regulate SIFIs; replace Dodd–Frank's 'orderly liquidation authority' with existing bankruptcy procedures with no access, even temporarily, to public funds; repeal the Volcker Rule; reform the Consumer Financial Protection Bureau to increase its accountability and restrict its power to ban financial products and services; and make the Fed have to defend any deviation from a simple monetary policy rule.

Critics of CHOICE view its main drawback as the pretence that there are no SIFIs that need stricter regulatory attention and enhanced capital requirements. Implementing CHOICE would make the financial system less safe. They also question CHOICE's attack on Fed independence. Otherwise, they go along with the repeal of the Volcker Rule because it has proved difficult to implement and, in any case, would not have prevented the 2007–9 crisis. They like the off-ramp provision for non-SIFI banks, the great majority of banks in the United States, which face excessive regulatory burdens under Dodd–Frank, but they think the 10 per cent capital requirement might be too low. And they see a need to make the Consumer Financial Protection Bureau more accountable but would retain its authority to protect consumers (Richardson et al. 2017).

The goal of the proposed 'twenty-first-century Glass–Steagall' act is to protect deposits of banks insured by the Federal Deposit Insurance Corporation by limiting what are deemed risky activities. It would prohibit commercial banks from engaging in, or being affiliated with institutions engaged in, investment banking, broker dealing, swaps dealing, futures dealing, and hedge-fund investing. The act is as much a backlash against the way the Volcker Rule was watered down into incoherence by negotiations after Dodd–Frank as to the Dodd–Frank Act itself.

The new version of Glass–Steagall has a number of problems. Had it been in effect before the crisis, it seems unlikely that it would have prevented the crisis, which began in investment banks such as Bear Stearns, Lehman, and Merrill Lynch. If deposit-taking bank holding companies divested themselves of the activities specified by the act, it is questionable whether the resulting less diversified income streams would enhance their safety. Lastly, the act would probably not make 'too big to fail' banks less common. Instead, as banks such as JPMorgan Chase and Citigroup got rid of their 'risky' assets and activities, Goldman Sachs and Morgan Stanley would divest their deposit banking operations and absorb the risky assets. So some big banks would become a bit smaller, and other big banks would become bigger.

In the regulatory outlook, the best bet would seem to be that neither the CHOICE Act nor the twenty-first-century Glass–Steagall Act will become law. Instead, the more onerous and less justified excesses of Dodd–Frank will gradually be eliminated. But the Dodd–Frank provisions regarding SIFIs, which cover the major New York banks, will be retained because they do appear to have reduced systemic risks.

2.4 Fintech

Thomas Philippon of NYU's Stern School of Business describes fintech as follows:

> Fintech covers digital innovations and technology-enabled business model innovations in the financial sector. Such innovations can disrupt existing industry structures and blur industry boundaries, facilitate strategic disintermediation, revolutionize how existing firms create and deliver products and services, provide new gateways for entrepreneurship, democratize access to financial services, but also create significant privacy, regulatory and law-enforcement challenges. Examples of innovation that are central to fintech today include cryptocurrencies and the blockchain, new digital advisory and trading systems, artificial intelligence and machine learning, peer-to-peer lending, equity crowdfunding and mobile payment systems. (Philippon 2016, p. 2)

Fintech represents an entrepreneurial opportunity as well as a threat to incumbents in finance, mainly because the financial system is not as efficient as it might be. Philippon (2015) and others have shown this in several path-breaking articles (Philippon and Reshef 2013; Greenwood and Scharfstein 2013). For more than a century in the United States, the financial sector has charged about $2 for every $100 of assets it intermediates. All the innovations that have revolutionized financial services, lowered trading costs in some areas, and dramatically increased trading volumes have not lowered the overall cost of finance. Where trading and other costs have fallen, the financial system has responded by increasing the proportion of total intermediated assets in higher-cost areas such as the professionally managed portfolios of mutual funds and hedge funds. So despite lower-cost finance in some areas, the overall cost of finance has stayed at around 2 per cent of assets for decades.

The high costs of current finance create the fintech opportunity. Peer-to-peer lending can grab market share from traditional bank lending. Crowd-funding can reduce the costs of IPOs and erode the profits of traditional investment banking. Blockchain technology can move money cheaply over long distances and across borders, undercutting the fees banks charge. In these and other ways, fintech should make finance more efficient and less costly.

Currently, it is far from clear that any fintech start-ups will become the next Apples, Microsofts, Amazons, Googles, and Facebooks, all of which were disrupters of old technologies, business models, and incumbent firms. Some knowledgeable observers think it more likely that competition will lead to fintech's incorporation into existing financial institutions, particularly the larger, well-heeled ones that already invest huge sums in technology.

The result is likely to be that finance will become more efficient as the cost of intermediation falls below the long-established norm of about 2 per cent.

That will be good for the consumers of financial products and services. But it also probably means that the higher levels of earnings employees and shareholders in the financial sector have enjoyed in comparison with other economic sectors will be eroded.

New York is unlikely to be disrupted by fintech. Its Silicon Alley, the New York version of the more famous Silicon Valley, is a centre of digital innovations that are, or will be, applicable to finance, and its existing financial institutions are well aware of the opportunities and threats of fintech. In 2017 Cornell University opened a high-tech research and graduate education facility, Cornell Tech, on Roosevelt Island in the East River between the New York boroughs of Manhattan and Queens. This is a project that was pushed by former mayor Michael Bloomberg, whose own fortune was built on innovative financial technology. It is expected that Cornell Tech will have a relationship with Silicon Alley similar to that of Stanford University with Silicon Valley. Only time will tell, but for now, New York seems to be more a central part of the fintech revolution in the United States than an old financial centre threatened by it.

2.5 Conclusion: The Outlook for New York

The New York financial centre has recovered from the crisis a decade ago. The recovery is most evident in the profits and equity-market valuations of the city's leading financial institutions. Employment as of 2016 had not quite returned to the peak levels of 2006 before the crisis (see Table 2.1). But that seems less a result of the crisis than a continuation of a long-term trend for employment in the US financial sector to shift away from New York City, New York State, and the Tri-State area to other areas of the United States. Table 2.1 shows that employment in finance shrinks cyclically in Wall Street downturns—the S&L crisis and recession of the early 1990s, the dot-com crash of the early 2000s, and the 2007–9 crisis—and then recovers, but usually to successively lower peaks in the three New York areas, while it generally increases in the rest of the United States. Total financial employment in the United States as of 2016 had not quite recovered to 2006 levels, but with the ongoing economic expansion there is no reason to consider 2016 a peak. And US financial employment levels in both 2016 and 2006 were well above previous peak levels in 2000 and 1990.

Modern information and trading technologies make these reallocations of financial employment possible, and economics—cities such as New York can be expensive places in which to live and work compared to other locations— makes such labour reallocations prudent for the bottom lines of the income statements of financial and other companies.

Table 2.1. US and New York financial industry employment, 1990–2016 (thousands)

Year	Financial Activities				Finance & Insurance				Securities, Commodities & Other Financial Investments			
	US	Tri-State	NY State	NY City	US	Tri-State	NY State	NY City	US	Tri-State	NY State	NY City
1990	6,596	1,149	771	515	4,967	915	605	407	485	190	161	151
1992	6,611	1,088	723	471	4,970	863	564	368	519	193	157	146
2000	7,830	1,164	754	495	5,807	903	567	373	884	290	217	200
2003	8,074	1,121	703	436	6,011	859	520	319	803	248	179	164
2006	8,393	1,159	735	467	6,222	890	548	345	885	282	205	184
2009	7,757	1,056	668	428	5,798	805	491	335	854	259	185	165
2016	8,370	1,099	708	460	6,209	829	517	332	934	261	193	172

Notes: The supersector Financial Activities is made up of Finance & Insurance (North American Industry Classification System 52) plus Real Estate and Rental and Leasing (NAICS 53). Finance & Insurance includes Federal Reserve banks, credit intermediation, and related activities; securities, commodity contracts, and investments; insurance carriers and related activities; funds, trusts, and other financial vehicles. The subsector Securities, Commodities, & Other Financial Investments (NAICS 523), included in Finance & Insurance, consists of investment banks; securities and commodity contracts brokers; securities and commodity contracts exchanges; portfolio managers; and investment advisors.

The Tri-State area is New York, New Jersey, and Connecticut.

Source: Author based on data from SIFMA (Securities Industry and Financial Markets Association), US Securities Industry Employment (www.sifma.org/research/us-industry-employment, accessed 9 Feb 2018), based on US Bureau of Labor Statistics data.

Despite modest declines in finance-related employment in the New York area, average salaries and bonuses remain quite high and well above the averages for non-finance jobs. This suggests that even as overall employment in finance gets reallocated to areas not part of the New York financial centre complex, the key decision makers and top talent will remain there.

The 2007–9 crisis led to political attacks on finance and the opprobrium of many Americans towards financiers. Financial leaders were chastened for a time, but that seems pretty much over. The culture of 'the Street' is little changed. The incentives to take risks with other people's money in the hope of making a lot of one's own money are still there. Regulatory reforms have not changed incentives.

One astute observer of the Street suggests that the only way to change incentives in ways that would promote greater financial safety and soundness is to take a cue from the Wall Street of some decades ago when most of the leading firms were partnerships rather than corporations (Cohan 2017). He calls for unlimited liability for the top managements of financial firms, so they could lose not only their jobs and bonuses, but also their financial wealth, houses, vacation homes, and yachts when their decisions lead their firms to crash à la Lehman. With more skin in the game, top management presumably would take more prudent risks and monitor their employees and operations more effectively. It's a good suggestion, but does not seem to have gained any traction.

If Brexit affects New York as a financial centre at all, it is likely to be to New York's advantage. The city's leading banks operate and often have strong presences in other leading financial centres of the world, so they are well positioned to expand in ones that grow and pare operations in ones that contract.

Other New York advantages derive from its being the financial centre of the United States, a wealthy country that continually generates pools of savings that become the raw material processed by a financial centre. The steady accumulation of wealth in the large American economy creates a more stable flow of raw material into the New York financial centre than perhaps is typical of centres that rely more than New York on international capital flows, which can be fickle for a particular financial centre.

More specific advantages discussed here include the US Treasury debt market, the dollar as the still pre-eminent reserve currency, a strong central bank in the Fed, a banking system that has shed many of problems of its earlier history, the world's largest securities markets and stock exchanges, and a large and dynamic corporate sector. None of these advantages of New York seem likely to go away soon.

If there is a current negative for New York, it might be the contentious politics and policy uncertainties emanating out of Washington, DC. Both reflect deep divisions among the US electorate. But such divisions are not a new thing in American history, and they are likely to diminish and perhaps even go away at some point.

Even these clouds may have a silver lining: New York is perhaps fortunate that the political capital of the United States is located in another city. It can go about its financial and other businesses without being as distracted as much as it would be if the political dysfunctions and sometimes clownish behaviours of the capital were taking place in its midst instead of far away in Washington, DC.

It was Alexander Hamilton, a New Yorker and lately even the star of a Broadway musical, who made the deal that moved the political capital out of New York in 1790, another of a great many things he did for which New York and the United States owe him more than a little gratitude.

References

Cohan, William D. 2017. Why Wall Street Matters. New York: Random House.

Economist. 2017a. 'Ten Years On: Banking after the Crisis'. Special Report, May 6th–12th issue.

Economist. 2017b. 'Schumpeter: Life in the Public Eye'. April 22nd–28th issue.

Greenwood, Robin and David Scharfstein. 2013. 'The Growth of Finance'. Journal of Economic Perspectives 27 (2), Spring: 3–28.

Philippon, Thomas. 2015. 'Has the US Financial Industry Become Less Efficient? On the Theory and Measurement of Financial Intermediation'. American Economic Review 105 (4): 1408–38.

Philippon, Thomas. 2016. 'The FinTech Opportunity', Working Paper. New York: New York University Stern School of Business. July.

Philippon, Thomas and Ariel Reshef. 2013. 'An International Look at the Growth of Modern Finance'. Journal of Economic Perspectives 27 (2), Spring: 73–96.

Richardson, Matthew P., Kermit L. Schoenholtz, Bruce Tuckman, and Lawrence J. White (eds). 2017. Regulating Wall Street: CHOICE Act vs. Dodd-Frank. New York: Center for Global Economy and Business of New York University Stern School of Business.

Sylla, Richard. 2002. 'Financial Systems and Economic Modernization'. Journal of Economic History 62 (2): 279–92.

Sylla, Richard. 2004. 'Hamilton and the Federalist Financial Revolution, 1789–1795'. New York Journal of American History 65 (3), Spring: 32–9.

Sylla, Richard. 2009. 'Comparing the UK and US Financial Systems, 1790–1830'. In The Origins and Development of Financial Markets and Institutions, edited by Jeremy Atack and Larry Neal. Cambridge: Cambridge University Press, pp. 209–40.

Sylla, Richard. 2011a. 'Wall Street Transitions, 1880–1920: From National to World Financial Centre'. In Financial Centres and International Capital Flows in the Nineteenth and Twentieth Centuries, edited by Laure Quennouëlle-Corre and Youssef Cassis. Oxford: Oxford University Press, pp. 161–78.

Sylla, Richard. 2011b. 'Financial Foundations: Public Credit, the National Bank, and Securities Markets'. In Founding Choices: American Economic Policy in the 1790s, edited by Douglas Irwin and Richard Sylla. Chicago: University of Chicago Press, pp. 59–88.

Sylla, Richard, Jack W. Wilson, and Robert E. Wright. 2006. 'Integration of Trans-Atlantic Capital Markets, 1790–1845'. *Review of Finance* 10: 613–44.

Value Line 600. 2017. Ratings and Reports, issues of August and September.

3

London

Downturn, Recovery and New Challenges—But Still Pre-eminent

Richard Roberts

3.1 Prologue: From Trade Finance to the Global Financial Crisis

London emerged as the world's foremost financial centre during the French wars that began at the end of the eighteenth century, taking over from Amsterdam at the apex of the hierarchy of international financial centres. Its pre-eminence was grounded in its leading role in the organization and financing of international trade, complemented by its development of the world's foremost bond market. In the nineteenth century, London became the epicentre of the sterling-based international gold standard, the leading centre for international banking with the world's key money market, and developed commodities and equity markets—an unrivalled constellation of financial activities (Roberts 2008).

London's international financial business was largely suspended during the First World War but revived in the 1920s. That conflict and its aftermath saw the emergence of New York as both a competing and complementary leading international financial centre during the inter-war decades (Cassis 2006). After the Second World War international finance was dominated by New York and the dollar. But London staged a remarkable comeback from the early 1960s as the focal point for Eurodollars and Eurobonds (Roberts 2008). Since the 1960s, London and New York have jointly occupied the pinnacle of the hierarchy of international financial centres, a position they occupied at the onset of the so-called Global Financial Crisis—more accurately a financial crisis among high-income countries—in 2007 (Wolf 2015).

During the nineteenth century, a succession of financial crises affected Britain around every ten years, notably in 1825, 1837, 1847, 1857, 1866, 1878, and 1890, associated with peaks of the business cycle. The gravest were the crises of 1825 and 1866, the latter featuring the failure of Overend Gurney, a major and systemically important financial institution—the Lehman Brothers shock of nineteenth-century Britain (Turner 2014; Mahate 1994). The threat of war in 1914 led to a breakdown of international financial markets, but the crisis was effectively managed by the state and damage to London as a financial centre was limited (Roberts 2014). The twentieth century saw a succession of sterling currency crises with major devaluations in 1931, 1949, and 1967. Subsequently, London's financial services sector was buffeted by the 'secondary banking crisis' of 1973, the UK's 1976 IMF crisis, the 1987 international stock market crash, and the 1992–3 ERM crisis. But thereafter the UK experienced 'the longest period of sustained economic growth in 200 years', with London thriving as an international financial centre and Gordon Brown, chancellor of the exchequer, famously declaring the end of the 'boom-bust economy' (Brown 2004).

The freezing of the international interbank credit market from mid-August 2007 was a massive shock. Northern Rock, a UK bank that funded itself in the wholesale short-term credit market, had to turn to the Bank of England for emergency liquidity assistance, the first substantial casualty of what proved to be a gathering financial crisis. When news of the support facility broke on 13 September there was a deposit run on Northern Rock with long queues outside branches, the first British retail bank run since 1866; in February 2008 Northern Rock was nationalized (Shin 2009). Spring 2008 saw moves by British banks to boost their equity capital and initiatives by the authorities to enhance support (Pym 2014). Nevertheless, Northern Rock appeared to be a one-off casualty of its particular high-risk business strategy, not a canary in the coal mine.

But financial stress was mounting in the United States and continental Europe with the US government-supported rescue of 'bulge bracket' investment bank Bear Stearns by JPMorgan Chase in March signalling the intensification of the strains. In July the US Treasury announced a rescue plan for America's two largest lenders, Fannie Mae and Freddie Mac, owners or guarantors of $5 trillion of US home loans. Mid-September saw the climax of the crisis in the United States with the failure of Lehman Brothers, a government bailout of insurance giant AIG, and the rescue of Merrill Lynch by Bank of America. The crisis climaxed in the UK in mid-October with the recapitalization by the state of RBS, Lloyds TSB, and HBOS. But the pressures in the financial system rumbled on accompanied by a deepening economic downturn that prompted a succession of interest rate cuts culminating in a reduction to 0.5 per cent, and the recession led to the initiation of a large quantitative easing programme in March 2009.

The spread of the banking crisis to continental Europe became clear with the state bailouts of banking giants Fortis and UBS in the wake of the Lehman shock. These moves were followed by the nationalization of Iceland's banks and state support measures for Ireland's lenders in early 2009. In April 2009 the G20 agreed a $5 trillion global stimulus package to combat the international recession, and this engendered hope that the worst of the financial crisis was over. But in the Eurozone the financial crisis morphed from a banking crisis into a sovereign debt crisis. The latter began in May 2010 with a massive bailout of Greece, followed by bailouts of Ireland in November 2010, Portugal in May 2011, Greece for a second time in July 2011, and Spain in June 2012 (Godby 2014). With the Eurozone in recession and potentially breaking up, in July 2012, Mario Draghi, president of the European Central Bank, declared that 'the ECB is ready to do whatever it takes to preserve the euro. And believe me, it will be enough' (Draghi 2012). Draghi's pronouncement marked a turning point, and the Eurozone crisis eased in the following years. But for London, Britain's 23 June 2016 referendum decision to leave the EU raised a host of new uncertainties.

3.2 London Wholesale Financial Services Sector Growth and Reversals

The most appropriate quantitative yardstick for the growth of London's wholesale financial services sector would be an annual economic output measurement, but such data do not exist. The quantitative indicator that is available is an input measurement—'City-type jobs', meaning employment in wholesale financial services and related professional services. Estimates of 'City-type jobs' are available from 1971, having been commissioned and published by the City of London Corporation from a succession of City-based economic consultancies, initially Lombard Street Research and more recently CEBR (Centre for Economic and Business Research). 'City-type jobs' include those in firms located in the City, London's traditional financial services hub, but also Canary Wharf and the West End. They focus on serving wholesale clients—corporations, governments, and financial institutions—and the measure excludes retail financial services jobs. The calculation of 'City-type jobs' estimates was discontinued after 2012.

Since 2007 annual estimates for financial services jobs in London have been published by TheCityUK, the 'representative body for the UK-based financial and related services industry'. The data, based on its London Employment Survey, provide annual estimates of financial and related professional services employment, with wholesale and retail jobs combined. The data is presented for three geographical areas: the whole of Greater London; the City of London;

and Canary Wharf. The aggregated number 'City & Canary Wharf jobs' can be regarded as similar to the 'City-type jobs' number, though including a minor retail element. However, the statistic does not include the cluster of jobs in London's West End, working mostly in hedge funds, asset management, private equity, and private banking, which numbers perhaps 5,000 to 15,000.

Over the four and a half decades from 1971 to 2015, the number of people working in wholesale financial services in London, as measured by these yardsticks, increased from 201,000 to 328,000, as shown in Figure 3.1. The long-term secular growth of London's wholesale financial services sector since the early 1970s reflects the expansion of international trade, capital, and other financial flows over these decades and increasing globalization from the 1990s. But growth was by no means continuous, with four significant reversals over the period resulting from adverse developments largely in the international financial and economic environment.

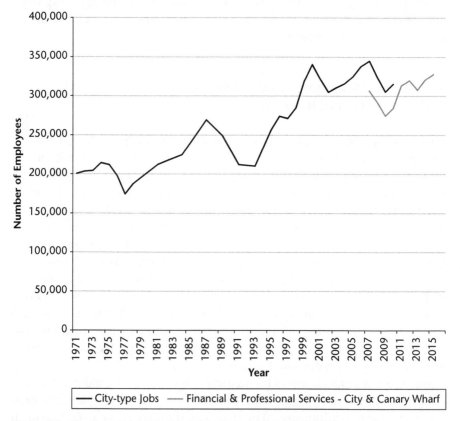

Figure 3.1. London wholesale financial services jobs, 1971–2015

Source: Author, based on data from: Corporation of London, Growth Prospects of City Industries (2003); The City's Importance to the EU Economy (2004); International Financial Markets in UK (May 2007) p.1; CEBR News Release Nov 2012, 2008–2017; CityUK, London Employment Survey, Oct 2015.

The first reversal occurred in the mid-1970s with 'City-type jobs' falling from 214,000 in 1974 to 175,000 in 1977, a three-year decline of 19 per cent from peak to trough. The downturn reflected the oil-price shock of 1973 and the consequent international recession, with Britain's 1976 IMF crisis adding a domestic downer (Roberts 2016). Growth resumed from 1978 and continued through the second oil shock of 1979 into the 1980s, with 'City-type jobs' reaching 270,000 by 1987. A second reversal followed the international stock market crash of October 1987, with the attrition continuing for six years through the recession of the early 1990s and the British and continental ERM crises of 1992–3 (Keegan et al. 2017); by 1993 the number of 'City-type jobs' had fallen to 210,000, a 22 per cent decline from peak to trough.

The 1990s saw strong advances in the number of London's 'City-type jobs', which reached 340,000 in 2000, reflecting the dynamic globalization of finance with London one of the key hubs in the process (Wolf 2010). But the early 2000s saw a sharp but short third reversal associated with the bursting of the dot-com bubble; 'City-type jobs' fell to 306,000 in 2002, a 10 per cent fall from peak to trough. Expansion resumed in 2003, and by 2007 'City-type jobs' reached a peak of 354,000. Confirmatory evidence on the growth of jobs in London's financial services sector before the crisis is provided by data from City recruitment consultant Morgan McKinley on the creation of new jobs from 2005 (Morgan McKinley 2015a). Morgan McKinley's statistics indicate a rise in 'London financial services jobs new to the market' from 78,000 in 2005 to a peak of 113,000 in 2007.

And then came the onset of the Global Financial Crisis in summer 2007, the fourth reversal; by 2009 the number of 'City-type jobs' had fallen to 305,000, a 14 per cent downturn from peak to trough. As measured by TheCityUK's 'City & Canary Wharf' employment metric, finance and related professional services jobs numbered 307,000 in 2007. By 2009 the number was down to 275,000, a 10 per cent reduction. Thus there was an average decline of 12 per cent in the aftermath of the Global Financial Crisis. Morgan McKinley's metric of new financial services jobs also fell during 2008 and 2009 to just 46,000 in the latter year. The 46 per cent drop was consistent in direction with the 'City-type jobs' and 'City & Canary Wharf' metrics, though much more severe in magnitude.

Comparison of the four reversals between 1971 and 2009 shows that, as regards the jobs headcount for London's wholesale financial services, two downturns were significantly deeper and longer lasting than the one associated with the Global Financial Crisis. This is perhaps surprising given the unprecedented impact of the 2007–8 financial crisis on high-income countries' banks, public finances, and the depth of subsequent recessions. In the UK, the recession was most acute in the manufacturing industry and in the industrial regions of the west Midlands and the north of England, and milder in the south and in financial services. As regards financial services, the crisis took a harsher toll of jobs in the regions than in London, resulting in increased concentration of the industry in the capital (Wojcik and MacDonald-Korth 2015). It has been speculated in a report by the London School of Economics for the City of London Corporation that possibly 'the massive "bail-out" of the banks, though intended to underwrite their balance sheets rather than to subsidise trading . . . may turn out to have provided some effective protection during the recession, not only for the "wholesale" financial service sector itself, but for the wider economy, particularly in London' (City of London 2009).

Each of the three London financial services jobs yardsticks recorded upturns in 2010: 'City-type jobs' increased from 305,000 in 2009 to 315,000 in 2010; 'City & Canary Wharf' jobs advanced from 275,000 to 284,000, and Morgan McKinley's new jobs series rebounded from 46,000 to 66,000. This suggested a resumption of the long-term secular expansion of London's wholesale financial services sector as had occurred after previous downturns.

However, 2011 saw a divergence in the estimates. The 'City & Canary Wharf' measure recorded a steady continuation of the recovery of London's financial and professional services sector, with jobs rising from 284,000 in 2010 to 328,000 in 2015, though with a fleeting dip in 2013. But the 'City-type jobs' yardstick recorded a contrary movement—a decline from 315,000 in 2010 to 250,000 in 2012, its final year of publication, representing a 21 per cent fall (CEBR 2012b). Douglas McWilliams, president of CEBR, commented that 'the combination of weak demand, aggressive regulation, high taxation and the rising competitiveness of financial centres in the Far East mean that London's position is weaker than before. London remains the top-ranked financial centre but its lead has narrowed' (CEBR 2012a). The Morgan McKinley series of new jobs declined from 2011 to 2013, which saw the creation of just 34,000 new positions. Commentary suggested that the strains in the Eurozone adversely affected financial activity in London in these years. But 2014 witnessed an upturn with a rise to 42,000 new financial sector jobs, a dynamic that continued through 2015 and into 2016.

3.3 London Financial Services Activities since the Crisis

Jobs numbers for six financial and related professional services activities are available for the years 2007 to 2015: banking; asset management; insurance; market infrastructure; legal services; and accounting and management consultancy. The data, published by TheCityUK, is for combined wholesale and retail jobs. The Global Financial Crisis was first and foremost a banking crisis. Five of the eight major British banks received injections of public funds to support and recapitalize them, suggesting a probably significant effect on London's banking jobs. Indeed, during 2008 and 2009, banking jobs in London declined from 146,000 to 133,000, a 9 per cent downturn. This reflected the job losses at the London office of Lehman Brothers and other banks that gave rise to headlines about wholesale layoffs. Nevertheless, by 2011 the banking sector headcount was back at 146,000 and it continued at that level. One factor was the post-crisis hiring of significant additional regulatory compliance staff.

Although the banking industry seemed to have weathered the crisis with less damage than might have been expected, there were clouds on the horizon. In 2015, the British Bankers Association, the industry trade body, reported on the challenges to London's wholesale banking sector (BBA 2015a). It drew attention to a worrying 12 per cent decline in assets, compared to rises of 12 per cent in New York and 34 per cent in Hong Kong, and falling returns on equity. It identified four principal challenges: the plethora of post-crisis regulatory reforms at multiple levels—global and EU, as elsewhere, but also unilateral British measures, in particular the structural 'ring-fence'; the British bank levy that was at a much higher level than elsewhere (except France); the business downturn in capital formation activity that was blighting investment banking business; and technology developments that were making wholesale banking activity more internationally 'portable' than ever before. A survey of members, which included a large number of foreign banks with UK oper-ations, revealed that two-thirds had moved some activity and jobs away from the UK since 2010—and that was before Brexit.

A notable post-crisis shift, principally as regards banking, but also other City activities, concerned remuneration. First and foremost, it declined substan-tially, one review estimating that by 2014 total bank pay had fallen 32 per cent since the crisis (9 per cent a year) and that staff compensation was down from 41 per cent of firms' net revenue to 25 per cent (afme 2016). There was a seismic shift in the structure of compensation, with the bonus element plum-meting from 70 per cent to 35 per cent, due partly to pressure on firms to cut costs but also in response to accusations by politicians and regulators that the 'mega-bonus culture' had encouraged excessive risk-taking in the pre-crisis euphoria (BBA 2015a). CEBR estimated that City bonuses had fallen from £12 billion in 2008 to £4 billion in 2014, with £2.5–3 billion pencilled in for 2017; as chief executive Douglas McWilliams put it, 'similar numbers of people employed, but working for a lot less money'. And there were further pay constraints to align risk-taking and reward: deferred bonuses; a significant shift away from cash bonuses to shares; and the potential for the clawback of bonuses for seven years.

Specialist financial legal services featured 118,000 jobs in 2007, while 121,000 worked in 'market infrastructure'—comprising financial 'plumbing' (payments, clearing, and settlement systems), the markets, the regulators, and other financial framework elements (UK International Financial Services 2009). Both activities experienced significant downturns over the crisis, with headcounts in 2010 of 96,000 and 87,000 respectively. By 2011 both sub-sectors had recovered to their pre-crisis headcounts. The jobs headcounts in London's insurance and asset management subsectors were scarcely impacted by the Global Financial Crisis; both increased somewhat between 2007 and 2015, rising respectively from 70,000 to 82,000 and from 24,000 to 31,000. The total headcount of these five activities—banking, legal, insurance, asset management, and market infrastructure—was almost identical in 2007 and 2015, with only small headcount shifts between them.

The 'accounting and management consultancy' subsector was an exception to this pattern of general stability. The subsector is a statistical composite encompassing a broad array of consultancy offerings and other expert services, such as specialist publications and macroeconomic advisory. Employment in the subsector rose from 190,000 in 2011 to 260,0000 in 2015, a 37 per cent increase, which was far more than in any other financial subsector. Possibly this reflects divestment of activities by banks to outsourced provision, notably as regards regulatory compliance, to cut in-house costs and downsize the balance sheet. Experienced in-house City compliance staff cashed in on the acute compliance skill shortage by becoming compliance consultants at higher pay rates; in London no fewer than 220 financial compliance consultancy firms were established in 2013–14 (McGrath and McNulty 2014). But much of the growth was accounted for by the 'big four' global accountancy and management consultancy firms: EY, PwC, Deloitte, and KPMG.

3.4 Chronicling the Downturn, Recovery, and New Challenges: The CBI/PwC Financial Services Survey 2007–17

3.4.1 Downturn and Recovery, 2007–11

Since 1989 the CBI (Confederation of British Industry), Britain's employers' federation, and PwC (PricewaterhouseCoopers), a leading accountancy and consultancy firm, have produced a quarterly Financial Services Survey that provides qualitative and impressionistic indications of trends and 'insights from the industry'. The survey covers financial services business in the whole of the UK, but given the concentration of activity in London there is unlikely to be much discrepancy in the picture portrayed. Soundings are taken every three months from around 100 of the 220 major financial services firms that participate in the survey, focusing especially on two key indicators: business activity—whether it grew or contracted in the quarter—and sentiment—whether firms are optimistic or pessimistic about business prospects in the forthcoming twelve months. Information is also gathered about profitability, costs, hiring, and challenges facing the firm and sector. Besides overall financial services sector commentary, there is specialist commentary on six subsectors: banking, securities trading, asset management, general insurance, life insurance, and building societies.

The first half of 2007, reported CBI/PwC surveys, saw a buoyant financial services sector with growth 'running at an almost eight-year high'. But by the early summer, the sector was becoming cautious about the outlook, though the sentiment was 'uncertainty rather than gloom'. An issue identified as being of concern to the asset management sector of the industry was the cost of spending on regulation and compliance resulting from the EU's Markets in Financial Instruments Directive (MiFID) of 2004 that harmonized the regulation of investment services across the thirty-one countries of the European Economic Area.

The September 2007 survey, conducted in the wake of the onset of the credit crunch in mid-August, reported a 'severe decline' in sector sentiment marking the beginning of eight quarters of negative reports. The December survey reported that financial services activity was falling at the fastest pace since the downturn of the early 1990s and painted a 'grim picture of rising costs and slowing business'. By spring 2008 business and profits were plunging at a 'sharp pace' and it was clear that the financial services sector was in for 'a long siege'. The summer survey stressed intensified liquidity pressures with 'every driver of financial services sector revenues deteriorating'. And then came the September 2008 Lehman Brothers failure and the 'surrounding market turmoil' with 'exceptional market volatility, a collapse in global risk appetite, further sharp falls in equity prices and massive government intervention in banking and financial markets just some of the dominant themes'. In early summer 2009, two years on from the onset of the credit crunch, confidence was reported to be tentatively returning to the sector. However, concern was growing about 'the possible effects of regulation as authorities in the UK and Europe weigh their responses to the financial crisis', which henceforth was a regular refrain of surveys.

The September 2009 survey marked the lifting of the sense of crisis and the onset of eight successive quarters of positive news. Business activity was now on the up, though recovering from a depreciated level, accompanied by an 'unmistakeable increase in confidence'. Cost reduction was a 'dominant theme'. Leading City figures interviewed as part of the December 2009 survey maintained that London's position as a leading financial centre had not been dented by the crisis 'but the economic shift towards the east and the risk of unilateral UK regulatory action posed very serious risks, . . . Further waves of regulation are likely in financial services, posing a bigger potential threat to the sector's competitiveness—if done unilaterally—than any aftershocks from the recent crisis' (Groom 2010). By April 2011 firms reported that activity was at the strongest level since the crisis and 'only slightly below normal', with profitability continuing to improve despite rising costs. And the foremost rising cost was regulation and compliance: 'As so often over the past two years, the threat of regulation emerges as a major preoccupation for the industry.'

3.4.2 *Wavering Recovery and the March of Regulation, 2011–15*

The summer of 2011 saw the onset of five quarters of CBI/PwC reports of declining confidence and activity through to winter 2012, a downturn consistent with the CEBR and Morgan McKinley jobs numbers for 2011 and 2012. The summer of 2011 was a 'torrid few months on global markets', and the mood 'clearly darkened with uncertainty about future demand, worries about the global recovery and shifting regulatory sands weighing on sentiment'. The problems in the Eurozone were an important factor, but so was regulation, with the June 2012 survey reporting that 'Regulation is the other major driver of weaker industry sentiment. This is nothing new, but concern is growing about the impact of regulatory change on every aspect of business. The cost of regulation also continues to mount, with many sectors identifying compliance as a leading driver of capital expenditure and a growing impediment to business development.'

Autumn 2012 saw a 'marked and very welcome improvement in confidence across the industry, fuelled by strengthening profitability and predictions for stronger revenues in 2013'. The upturn lasted for a dozen quarters through to summer 2015. The calming of the Eurozone financial crisis was a key underlying factor. The December 2013 survey reported that confidence in the UK financial services industry was growing faster than at any point in the survey's twenty-four-year history with 'the industry's recovery reaching new heights. Strong growth in activity is driving up profitability, and headcount is climbing fast. Confident forecasts for customer demand are encouraging firms to invest for growth. Strengthening competition and the march of regulation are a concern, but so too is the war for talent.' In summer 2014 a new development was noted, a 'growing willingness to partner with technology firms and emerging rivals'. Rain Newton-Smith, the CBI's director for economics, observed that 'the UK's financial services sector is enjoying its strongest run of growth since 2007, with activity rising across all customer categories and profitability bouncing back'. The banks were benefitting from a steep fall in the value of non-performing loans that suggested that 'much of the fallout from the financial crisis was working its way out of the system'. Nevertheless, worries about the impact of legislation at home and from Europe, such as new capital requirements and the prospect of a financial transactions tax, were 'increasingly weighing on the sector'.

'Looking at the UK's regulatory environment, banks are most concerned about cost and proportionality,' commented Kevin Burrowes, PwC's financial services leader, in spring 2015. 'Even so, the sector currently has a good grip on its regulatory agenda, and regulation is seen as less of an obstacle to growth than at any point last year.' The banking sector's spending priorities were improving IT infrastructure and cybersecurity. The return of a Conservative government in the general election of May 2015 was doubtless welcomed by many of the contributors to the CBI/PwC survey who opined that the new administration's priority for financial services should be 'reducing the cost of regulatory compliance'.

3.4.3 Uncertainty, Fintech, and Brexit

The three years of 'robust expansion' since 2012 petered out in the summer of 2015. 'The winds of volatility blowing through global markets have left a clear mark on the financial services sector impacting business volumes and investment intentions,' observed the CBI's Newton-Smith. 'Slower growth in China and other emerging markets has had a knock-on impact on confidence in the world economy . . . It's interesting to see that the sector is waking up to the impact of fintech. Firms will need to look carefully at their operations and put strategies in place in order to profit from or protect against the impact of new technologies.' 'There is a looming question around how fintech could disrupt the sector,' added PwC's Burrowes. 'Most banks recognise that competition is coming from a new breed of institutions entering the industry but seem unsure of their impact.' Subsequent surveys through to summer 2016 reported waning confidence and lacklustre business growth. The challenge of fintech was a refrain, as were the cost of regulatory compliance—firms reported that it was accounting for more than 10 per cent of operational costs—global macro-economic uncertainty, competition, and Britain's forthcoming referendum on EU membership. 'In such an unpredictable climate,' commented Burrowes, 'the cloud forming across the sector is getting darker.'

The survey following the Brexit vote in June 2016 reported another fall in sector optimism. This was despite healthy growth in business volumes and a resumption of profits growth. Asked about the effect of the vote to leave, half of all financial services firms said it was negative, with market volatility the main cause for concern, though one in ten pointed to a positive impact. 'Add the uncertainty caused by Brexit, technological change and strong competition, and it's plain to see why optimism is falling and pressure on margins remains intense,' noted Newton-Smith. 'Life was busy for UK financial services before the Brexit vote—it just got a whole lot busier as they digest the implications for their businesses,' observed Andre Kail of PwC. 'The big picture agenda of transforming business models to respond to customer, regulatory and technological changes continues apace and now Brexit has added an additional ingredient to the mixture. It's still early days, and there is no real clarity on what future agreements will be reached. Consequently, many of our clients are considering their options, including potential restructuring and relocation of their business.'

Optimism continued to deteriorate through to summer 2017, the span since autumn 2015 constituting 'the gloomiest period for financial services firms since the 2008/09 crisis'. The pessimism was driven by 'external factors', notably the macroeconomic environment, turbulent political landscape, and continued uncertainty around Brexit. The lack of confidence contrasted with the sector's performance both as regards business volumes and underlying profitability. 'The robust performance of financial services firms over the last quarter gives us a good dose of summer cheer,' said Newton-Smith. 'Currently the financial services sector is performing well in both business volume terms and underlying profitability,' observed Kail. 'However, another quarter of falling optimism points to an industry harbouring concerns about the future...The UK will continue to be a leading financial centre, but political uncertainty and the ongoing wait for an agreed Brexit blueprint are fuelling more questions about companies' futures and the performance of the wider economy. More widely, the sector continues to respond to the impact of digital advances in the way they serve their customers and they run their business. We are seeing plans in this area accelerate markedly... Unpacking firms' use of technology reveals a focus on robotics and artificial intelligence, in particular around operational data analysis, risk profiling, customer engagement and process automation,' commented PwC. 'Interestingly, when taken together with the reported increase in hiring, this suggests that firms are currently preparing for long-term change and exploring pilots and prototypes, rather than implementing new processes to help cut costs and remove jobs in the short term. This increasingly technology-driven strategy coupled with a renewed focus on hiring, reinforces the transformational journey that many firms have embarked on' (PwC 2017c).

3.5 Post-crisis Regulatory Tsunami

The CBI/PwC surveys highlighted four principal post-crisis concerns among UK financial services sector firms: the volume and cost of regulatory reform measures, fintech, competition, and Brexit. The financial crisis revealed deficiencies in both British and international regulatory arrangements; central banking authority Charles Goodhart, writing in 2009, identified seven fields where there were 'major issues': (1) deposit insurance; (2) bank insolvency regimes; (3) money market operations by central banks; (4) liquidity risk management; (5) procyclicality in capital adequacy requirements; (6) boundaries of regulation—conduits, SIVs, and reputational risk; (7) crisis management (a) within countries and (b) cross-border (Goodhart 2009). The turmoil triggered an avalanche of new regulation of the financial services sector. There had been nothing like it in the history of the City, with the Big Bang reforms of 1986—essentially an exercise in deregulation—the only comparable upsurge of regulatory change. Wall Street had experienced a regulatory revolution in the early 1930s in response to the 1929 Wall Street Crash and the Great Depression. But regulatory reform in the 1930s was a uniquely American phenomenon; in London it was business as usual. By contrast, the regulatory response to the Global Financial Crisis was both national and international in scope (Davis 2011). It was estimated in 2017 that globally $80 billion was spent on governance, risk, and compliance, with the cost expected to reach $120 billion by 2022 (TPWGF 2017).

Post-crisis financial regulation was distinctly a moving target, with four principal founts of rule-making affecting London financial firms and professionals: the United States government and institutions, the European Commission, the United Kingdom government, and international bodies (gfma 2013). The international nature of the crisis prompted the convening of the first G20 summit on Financial Markets and the World Economy, held in Washington, DC in November 2008, two months after the failure of Lehman Brothers, to enhance international cooperation to promote economic growth and achieve financial reform. The leaders agreed on five principles for reform and a forty-seven-point Action Plan to avoid future crises, mostly moves to strengthen financial markets and regulatory regimes (G20 2009). Progress on the implementation of the Action Plan was reviewed at the London summit in April 2009, hosted by prime minister Gordon Brown, and it formulated an eight-point reform agenda. It also established the Financial Stability Board, charged with responsibility for coordination of the work of national financial authorities and international standard-setters, monitoring compliance with international standards, and addressing developments in financial stability. This involved in particular taking account of macro-prudential risks, specifically excess leverage, hedge funds, and the credit rating agencies, action to tackle tax havens and 'non-cooperative jurisdictions', and the creation of common principles for executive remuneration. The FSB's charter setting out its objectives and mandate was endorsed at the G20's September 2009 Pittsburgh summit, launching it as a key body for the promotion and coordination of international financial regulation; the progress of the regulatory reform bandwagon was reported at subsequent G20 summits. In February 2011 the scope was extended to global imbalances and the regulation of systemically important financial institutions (SIFIs) while enhanced tax transparency was a 'key agenda item' of the G8 summit of June 2013 (HSBC 2016).

First and foremost was reform of the conduct of banking, the epicentre of the crisis. But reform also affected securities, derivatives, commodities, asset management, hedge funds, and insurance. And there were further strands to the tightening of the screws on the financial services industry; these included an intensification of the US post-9/11 'war' on terrorist, criminal, and rogue state financial flows through the international banking system (Zarate 2013), muscularly enforced post-crisis by the imposition of huge fines, largely, though not uniquely, exacted by US regulatory and enforcement agencies, as well as an intensified international focus on tax transparency.

The Dodd–Frank Wall Street Reform and Consumer Protection Act that came into force in the United States in July 2010 was the first major substantive outcome of the post-crisis regulatory reform drive. It was 'the most sweeping financial regulatory reform since the Great Depression', affecting every aspect of the US financial services industry (Federal Reserve Bank of St Louis 2011). At 848 pages, Dodd–Frank was more than twenty times longer than the thirty-seven-page Glass–Steagall Act (1933) passed in response to the 1929 Wall Street Crash; by 2016 Dodd–Frank had spawned 22,000 pages of rule-making. Dodd–Frank rules affected London because most important players were either American or did business in the United States, meaning that they had to conform to US standards.

In the UK the landmark developments were the report of the Vickers Commission in September 2011, which recommended the creation of a 'ring fence' around banks' domestic retail activities, and the Financial Services Act that came into force in April 2013, which comprehensively restructured the framework of British regulatory arrangements. The British Bankers Association observed in 2015 that since 2007 'the banking sector has experienced one of the most intensive periods of regulatory change in modern history, with more than 80 substantial rules and pieces of legislation passed so far' (BBA 2015b). In the decade from 2007 the European Commission proposed more than forty legislative and non-legislative measures 'to create new rules for the global financial system, establish a safe, responsible and growth-enhancing financial sector in Europe, and create a banking union to strengthen the euro' (European Commission 2017). And at the global level there was Basel III on bank capital and liquidity ratios that was agreed in June 2011 with implementation phased in from 2013 to 2019 (Basel Committee on Banking Supervision 2011).

'In the last 5 years, the industry has had to manage almost 50,000 new regulatory documents – a 500 per cent increase in G20 documents,' observed P.J. Di Giammarino, chief executive of JWG, a London-based financial regulation consultancy, in spring 2015 (Groenfeldt 2015). Printed and stacked, the documents would reach to the top of the Eiffel Tower; as the regulatory framework's nuts and bolts were tightened there was the prospect of a pile of paperwork more than three Eiffel Towers tall by 2020 (Lee 2015). And in the wake of the rule-making came implementation—meaning people, systems, and cost. McKinsey estimated that 70,000 new jobs would need to be created in Europe to comply with the requirements of Basel III alone, with Dodd–Frank generating tens of thousands of jobs in the United States.

3.6 Compliance Boom: 'Revenge of the Nerds'

'Revenge of the nerds' was the headline to a Reuters story of November 2012 that reported the onset of a hiring boom in financial services compliance (meeting industry regulations) and risk (ensuring that lending and trading activities are within safe limits). 'It is one of the hottest areas of financial recruitment, according to headhunters. The age of the compliance officer is upon us,' stated the *Financial Times* in spring 2014. 'In times gone by, compliance was seen as a backwater.' One senior bank adviser recalls a City of London firm in the 1980s at which the compliance specialist was also charged with looking after the bosses' wine cellar. 'Now the job of ensuring financial institutions play by the rules is rapidly growing in importance, driven by the tsunami of regulatory initiatives and substantial fines that followed the financial crisis of 2007–09' (Fleming 2014). And not just at the banks, with Ernst & Young reporting an 8 per cent increase in compliance staff at European asset managers.

'It used to be a really tough job to sell as people saw it as boring,' a recruiter told Reuters, observing that some compliance candidates were asking for a pay rise of 50 per cent (Armstrong 2012). 'Compliance Officer: Dream Career?' headlined the *Wall Street Journal* in January 2014 (Millman and Rubenfeld 2014). 'We're in a battle royal for talent in the compliance space,' a risk-and-compliance consultant told the newspaper. 'Hefty fines and other penalties have jolted companies, especially banks, into a compliance hiring spree, as governments at home and abroad tighten business laws and regulations and ramp up their enforcement activity.' It was the same story in London. 'The cost of regulation and compliance is going through the roof and the supply of quality and talented individuals in that space is out of kilter with the demand,' said a City asset manager in June 2014. 'The highest wage inflation that we have is in the assurance functions' (McGrath 2014).

By 2014 it was estimated that compliance- and risk-related roles accounted for four in ten of City hires (Stylianou 2014), with banks' compliance staff headcounts reportedly doubling during the hiring boom. The 'compliance binge' in London was led by HSBC and Barclays. The $1.9 billion fine imposed on HSBC, Britain's biggest bank, for money laundering by the US Justice Department prompted 'massive remedial recruitment' with the bank's permanent and contract compliance staff soaring from 1,600 pre-crisis to a peak of 27,000, a seventeen-fold increase. Rival worldwide megabank Citigroup reached a similar number—26,000 (Moonan 2015). Other banks also hired very actively: JPMorgan Chase added 3,000 compliance staff in 2013–14; Credit Suisse reported that the cost of compliance increased 80 per cent between 2012 and 2015; and Goldman Sachs estimated that most of the bank's 11 per cent headcount rise since 2012 resulted from 'heightened compliance efforts' (Gray 2016).

London's regulatory hiring boom continued in 2015 and into 2016, with recruiter Morgan McKinley commenting that 'compliance is still the City's buzzword' (Morgan McKinley 2015b). But by early 2017 the 'golden era' of compliance hiring was drawing to a close (Gray 2016). 'Panic mode is over now,' a compliance headhunter told Bloomberg (Partington 2017). The initial solution to the post-crisis deluge of compliance requirements was 'to chuck more people at it'. But once firms were up to speed it was possible to replace compliance staff with computers and cut costs while maintaining vigilance. RBS was a case in point. To comply with enhanced requirements it had recruited 2,000 staff to conduct 'know-your-customer' checks, 2.5 per cent of the bank's headcount, but by 2017 it was in the process of automating the function, keeping only a handful of executives 'to deal with issues'. At HSBC by summer 2017 the number of compliance personnel had fallen back to 10,000—still six times the pre-crisis establishment. 'Global banks are paring back staff tasked with detecting wrongdoing for the first time since the financial crisis, ending a hiring boom that accompanied $321bn in fines, as technology replaces employees and penalties wane,' reported Bloomberg. 'The overall number of people in compliance is absolutely reducing,' observed a senior executive. 'Banks are better able to deal with regulatory requirements. They'll always need people to provide judgement, but a lot of monitoring and surveillance activity can be automated.'

3.7 Silicon Roundabout: Regtech and Fintech

The reversal of the compliance hiring boom was attributed to a 'new kid on the block – regtech'. 'It is a blended buzzword, which refers to the new breed of agile regulatory technology that empowers firms to better understand and manage risks, while also streamlining the regulatory compliance process,' explained *Global Treasury News* in April 2017 (Cowburn 2017). 'Past attempts to digitize the compliance and risk process have focused solely on cost reduction and operational efficiency. Instead, regtech has much to offer in terms of mitigating risk across the board – operational, reputational and financial.' But initially, regtech largely focused on 'process automation'—improving inefficiencies within regulatory reporting and using technology to ease the burden of compliance (TPWGF 2017).

Regtech was an aspect of the fintech phenomenon that took off in the aftermath of the crisis. And fintech was a dimension of the broader phenomenon of London's 'Flat White Economy', as consultants CEBR styled London's burgeoning digital sector. The Flat White Economy (named after the type of coffee favoured by the techies) developed in the aftermath of the financial crisis based on three ingredients: dynamic digital technology, demand for digital services, and a supply of digitally skilled labour (McWilliams 2016). It clustered on the run-down 'northern fringes' of the City of London in the vicinity of the Old Street Roundabout—dubbed 'Silicon Roundabout'. Douglas McWilliams, an authority on the Flat White Economy, has counted the establishment of 32,000 new London technology businesses between 2012 and 2014 and estimated that by 2015 more than 100,000 people worked in the overall digital sector. The core of the Flat White Economy is digital retailing and digital marketing, but with the City of London on the doorstep fintech was a natural direction for diversification. Businesses were principally small independents, but there were also at least half-a-dozen 'fintech labs' in London, backed by financial institutions, that provided a mix of funding, training, and development support for high-tech startups. By 2015 it was claimed that London was the fintech capital of the world, employing 44,000 in the sector, slightly more than New York.

UK financial firms surveyed by PwC in 2017 considered consumer banking, payments, and funds transfer to be the areas of business most susceptible to disruption by fintech (PwC 2017a). The disruptors would comprise not only startups but also large technology companies and social media/internet platforms, posing challenges regarding increased price competition, loss of market share, and threats to information privacy; 61 per cent of UK financial services firms believed that up to 40 per cent of their revenues was at risk of being lost to the disruptors. In response to the challenge, 81 per cent said that they planned to initiate strategic partnerships with fintechs, while 47 per cent planned fintech acquisitions. The foremost opportunities provided by fintech were identified as expansion of products and services, the leveraging of existing data sets, increasing the customer base, the development of mobile channels, and also regtech. The survey found that UK financial services firms allocated 9 per cent of annual turnover to IT and fintech, well below the global average of 15 per cent, though maybe Silicon Roundabout was changing that. 'The financial services industry has embraced fintech to help drive change and innovation,' observed Steve Davies, PwC's fintech leader. 'Activity in the UK ranges from partnering with fintech startups, financing in-house incubators, and deploying new solutions, to testing use cases in areas like blockchain. There are few overnight successes and, unsurprisingly, as much perspiration as inspiration' (PwC 2017b).

3.8 Competition and Competitiveness

Respondents to the CBI/PwC surveys regularly identified 'competition' as one of the main challenges facing the financial services sector in the aftermath of the crisis. There were three dimensions to the competition challenge. First, new technology-based ways of providing financial services and conducting financial business—fintech—discussed in Section 3.7. Second, competition from new entrants. And third, competition with London from rival international financial centres, traditionally New York, but now from a wider array of pretenders.

After the financial crisis the British government was keen that new 'challenger banks' should provide competition to the big established banks. Analysts were sceptical about their prospects given the formidable barriers to entry and the looming prospect of greater banking regulation which itself constituted a further barrier to entry. Nevertheless, from 2010 a fair number of challenger banks were established that focused on specialist areas of the market neglected by the majors. By 2017 five of them had entered the upper reaches of *The Banker*'s Top 1000 World Banks league table and were generating impressive profits: Virgin Money in 462nd place; Metro Bank, 782nd; Aldermore, 805th; Shawbrook, 988th; and OneSavings Bank, 993rd. But they were tiny relative to the big banks, and their prospects for growing beyond their niches and constituting substantial disruptive factors were yet to be proved (Dunkley 2017). The asset management industry was also facing competitive headwinds, notably investors' shift from entrusting their money to UK active investment managers to buying passive index-tracking products mostly provided by giant US fund firms, thereby depleting London firms of funds under management. But the London industry was responding creatively by incorporating the commoditized products into new outcome-oriented offerings (Dobson 2016).

March 2007, as the pre-crisis boom approached its peak, saw the publication of the first edition of the Global Financial Centres Index, initially sponsored by the City of London Corporation. The index is based on some complicated mathematics that allows the combination of more than 100 highly varied quantitative and qualitative factors relating to wholesale financial activity into a single index score that the compilers call 'competitiveness'. It is published each March and September.

In March 2007, London was ranked first with New York a close second. Since then, there have been a further twenty-one editions, each headed by London or New York, mostly with London just ahead. The first report featured forty-six financial centres. The report of September 2017 included ninety-two centres, with a further sixteen cities classed as 'associate centres' for which there was not yet sufficient data for inclusion. Thus over the ten years since

March 2007, the number of centres covered by the survey doubled. This reflects two factors. First, the development since the Global Financial Crisis of wholesale financial activity in a host of additional locations. And second, the clamour by cities and governments for inclusion. Does the proliferation pose a threat to London and New York? The March 2017 report observed that 'The historical dominance of the leading centres in Western Europe and North America has been eroded over time. The average assessment of the top 5 financial centres in the Asia/Pacific region is now ahead of the comparable figure for Western Europe and North America. The top centres in other regions are also closing the gap on the leaders.' It appears that the traditional financial centre hierarchy is evolving into more complex structures, with connectivity to other centres a key dimension. Nevertheless, the September 2017 report placed London not only first but ahead of other leading centres by an enhanced margin (Z/Yen 2017).

In spring 2015 HSBC, Britain's biggest and the world's most international bank, instigated a comprehensive review of the location of its headquarters prompted by shareholder discontent about the UK's bank levy that bore disproportionately on HSBC. The bank rigorously evaluated the merits of relocating its domicile to other leading financial centres, including Hong Kong, Singapore, Toronto, and the United States, and sought advice from a pantheon of sages including Henry Kissinger. In February 2016 HSBC announced that it had decided to remain in the UK, describing the decision as 'generational' and likely to mean remaining there for decades to come. 'The UK has got a very developed and internationally-respected regulatory and legal system,' said chairman Douglas Flint. 'It has considerable experience in dealing with complex international matters, because it is the largest and the most international financial centre' (Palmer, Martin, and Wallace 2016). It was an authoritative informed vote of confidence in London's future as a financial centre and constituted a commitment to remain in the UK regardless of the outcome of the forthcoming referendum on Britain's membership of the EU.

3.9 Brexit and Beyond

Britain's vote in June 2016 to leave the EU cast a shadow across London as an international financial centre, though there was much uncertainty as to the spectre's height and depth. A scramble of reports from management consultants envisaged adverse impacts for UK financial services activity and employment with much-qualified estimates of London job losses varying in number: 30,000 by Breugel (2017); 65,000–75,000 by Oliver Wyman (2016); 70,000 by PwC (2016); and 83,000 by EY (2016). A discussion paper from the London

School of Economics concluded that 'Brexit will have negative effects for the City of London . . . such effects will be substantial' (Djankov 2017). However, a survey by Deloitte in spring 2017 reported that the Brexit shock had eased, with expectations of reduced hirings down from 66 per cent to 30 per cent (Deloitte 2017).

The impact of the Brexit vote on London's competitiveness was considered in the GFCI report of March 2017. It noted a decline in London's index score since the previous report, but it still ranked first among the eighty-eight financial centres. New York, in second place, had seen a fall of a similar magnitude to London because of its own new uncertainty—the Trump Administration. The second post-Brexit GFCI report in September 2017 saw London maintaining and even increasing its lead over other top-ten financial centres, with no perceptible Brexit effect on its competitiveness ranking. 'We are going into Europe now,' a venture capital investor based in New York told the study. 'London is the place to be for fintech regardless of what they say about Brexit.'

The twenty-seven other EU countries constituted the UK's largest export market for financial services. The impact of Brexit on this trade was believed to depend on the arrangements that emerged from the Brexit negotiations. A 'soft' Brexit, by which the UK left the EU but remained in the single market, was a lower-risk outcome for the City than other arrangements since it would enable firms to maintain regulatory 'passporting rights' (a single-market member's rights to offer services throughout EU member states). Under a 'hard' Brexit, in which the UK quit the single market, firms might be able to take advantage of the EU's third-country 'equivalence' frameworks for financial services, but they are 'cumbrous and incomplete' alternatives to passporting and UK firms would find it significantly more costly to export to the EU (Armour 2017). If soft Brexit proved politically impossible, the next best outcome would be a suitable bilateral agreement, or, at the least, a transition period of continued EU membership pending completion of equivalence determinations. But all remained to be resolved.

There was much conjecture as to which and how much other European financial centres might benefit from jobs relocated from London as a result of Brexit. The leading contenders, who actively marketed their merits, were Paris, Frankfurt, and Dublin, with the latter pair appearing to prevail despite Paris's allure as a global city. Some in the City speculated that the Brexit impact studies that had been mandated by the Bank of England's Prudential Regulatory Authority in April 2017 had led a number of firms to conclude that there were operations they could conduct from lower-cost locations with Brexit serving as a convenient cover. And it was by no means inevitable that activity would relocate to a European centre. Much of the City's financial services exports to the EU comprised capital market activity conducted by subsidiaries of US-headquartered groups that might well decide that exporting from New York made most sense.

Attention focused in particular on the possible relocation of euro-denominated derivatives clearing from London to the Eurozone in the event of Brexit. The related prize was the relocation of foreign exchange trades involving the euro, of which 43 per cent took place in London compared to just 16 per cent across the whole of the euro area. A little-appreciated factor contributing to the imbalance was London's historic position as a hub of the world's submarine communications cable network. The key role of submarine cables in international communications gives a competitive advantage to financial centres located adjacent to oceans because of their superior (faster, cheaper) direct connections to the spine of the network. By one estimate, the calibre of London's cable connections has boosted its share of global forex turnover by as much as one-third since the advent of electronic trading in the 1990s (Eichengreen, Lafaguette, and Mehl 2016). A comparison of the development of forex business in Singapore and Zurich suggested that the former's more dynamic performance owed much to its littoral direct connection relative to landlocked Zurich. What this means as regards Brexit is unclear, but London's cable superiority and financial centre critical mass, as well as institutional inertia, suggest that any shift of euro forex trading to the Continent will be, at most, gradual.

Brexit, argued a horizon-scanning report published in summer 2017, was a catalyst for the UK financial and related professional services industry to reconsider its future role and competitive positioning. The report, based on 'extensive engagement with leaders across the industry and a rigorous fact-based assessment', provided a vision of the industry and London's role in 2025 (TheCityUK/PwC 2017). It envisaged a sector 'transformed to be highly digitised, innovative and customer-centric'. London would 'still be one of the most important and attractive international centres for financial and related professional services and global business, retaining the full ecosystem of financial and related professional services. It will continue to play an important domestic role and be a leading fintech centre at the forefront of global financial innovation.' Realization of the vision would require a 'coherent response' from the industry, government, and regulators, and 'putting digital at the heart of the industry, driving innovation and transformational change for customers'. There was no looking back to the financial crisis that had erupted exactly a decade earlier or to its legacy impacts—the world had moved on and financial centre London was facing forwards, engaging with its new array of challenges and opportunities.

Acknowledgements

I am most grateful to Douglas McWilliams, president of CEBR (Centre for Economic and Business Research), and Andrew Hilton, chief executive of CSFI (Centre for the Study of Financial Innovation), for discussion of the subject matter of this chapter, to Brahmdev Gohil for research assistance, and to Lilian Roberts for technical assistance.

References

afme (Association for Financial Markets in Europe). 2016. Review of the Reward Environment in the Banking Industry (January).

Armour, John. 2017. 'Brexit and Financial Services'. *Oxford Review of Economic Policy* 33 supplement (March): S54–69.

Armstrong, Rachel. 2012. 'Revenge of the Nerds as Banks see Risk, Compliance Hiring Boom'. *Reuters Business News*, 25 November.

Basel Committee on Banking Supervision. 2011. 'Basel III: A Global Regulatory Framework for More Resilient Banks and Banking Systems' (June).

BBA (British Bankers Association). 2015a. 'Winning the Global Race: The Competitiveness of the UK as a Centre for International Banking' (November).

BBA (British Bankers Association). 2015b. 'Reforms since the Financial Crisis'.

Brown, Gordon. 2004. Speech to Labour Party Conference, 27 September.

Cassis, Youssef. 2006. Capitals of Capital: A History of International Financial Centres, 1780–2005. Cambridge: Cambridge University Press.

CEBR News Release. 2012a. (9 May).

CEBR News Release. 2012b. (12 November).

City of London. 2009. 'London's Place in the UK Economy 2009–10' (October).

Cowburn, Nicola. 2017. 'Regtech: The Route to Mitigating Risk in the Digital Age'. gtnews, 13 April.

Davis, Kevin. 2011. 'Regulatory Reform Post the Global Financial Crisis: An Overview'. Melbourne: APEC Finance Centre (May).

Deloitte. 2017. 'The Deloitte CFO Survey. Brexit Shock Eases' (Q1).

Djankov, Simeon. 2017. 'The City of London after Brexit'. LSE Financial Markets Group Discussion Paper no.762 (February).

Dobson, Michael. 2016. 'The Future of Asset Management'. *FinancialNews*, 27 September.

Draghi, Mario. 2012. Speech at the Global Investment Conference, London, 26 July.

Dunkley, Emma. 2017. 'UK's Challenger Banks Face Fresh Headwinds'. *Financial Times*, 6 August.

Eichengreen, Barry, Romain Lafaguette, and Arnauld Mehl. 2016. 'Cables, Sharks and Servers: Technology and the Geography of the Foreign Exchange Market'. European Central Bank Working Papers Series no.1889 (March).

European Commission. 2017. 'Progress of Financial Reforms'.

Federal Reserve Bank of St Louis. 2011. 'Financial Regulation: A Primer on the Dodd-Frank Act' (May).

Fleming, Sam. 2014. 'The Age of the Compliance Officer Arrives'. *Financial Times*, 24 April.

G20. 2009. 'Declaration on Strengthening the Financial System—London Summit, 2 April 2009'.

gfma (Global Financial Markets Association). 2013. 'Global Regulatory Reform Proposals' (March).

Godby, Robert. 2014. The European Financial Crisis: Debt, Growth, and Economic Policy. New York: Business Expert Press.

Goodhart, Charles. 2009. The Regulatory Response to the Financial Crisis. Cheltenham: Edward Elgar.

Gray, Alistair. 2016. 'Wall St Banks Ease Off on Compliance Hiring'. *Financial Times*, 18 December.

Groenfeldt, Tom. 2015. 'Banking Compliance Paperwork Measured in Eiffel Towers'. *Forbes*, 16 March.

Groom, Brian. 2010. 'Fresh Regulations "Threaten" Financial Services'. *Financial Times*, 19 January.

HSBC. 2016. 'Navigating the New Financial World' (July).

Keegan, William Marsh and Richard Roberts. 2017. Six Days in September: Black Wednesday, Brexit and the Making of Europe. London: OMFIF Press.

Lee, Peter. 2015. 'Banking: Tower of Regulation'. *Euromoney*, 9 November.

McGrath, Joe. 2014. 'Salaries Sizzle'. *FinancialNews*, 2 June.

McGrath, Joe and Lucy McNulty. 2014. 'Compliance Rules Trigger Bonanza for Consultants'. *FinancialNews*, 9 June.

McWilliams, Douglas. 2016. The Flat White Economy: How the Digital Economy is Transforming London and Other Cities of the Future. London: Duckworth Overlook.

Mahate, Ashraf A. 1994. 'Contagion Effects of Three Late Nineteenth Century British Bank Failures'. *Business and Economic History* 23 (1), Fall: 102–115.

Millman, Gregory J. and Samuel Rubenfeld. 2014. 'Compliance Officer: Dream Career?' *Wall Street Journal*, 15 January.

Moonan, Laura. 2015. 'Banks Face Pushback over Surging Compliance and Regulatory Costs'. *Financial Times*, 28 May.

Morgan McKinley. 2015a. 'London Employment Monitor', January.

Morgan McKinley. 2015b. 'London Employment Monitor', June.

Palmer, Kate, Ben Martin, and Tim Wallace. 2016. 'HSBC to Remain in London for at Least "a Generation"'. *Daily Telegraph*, 15 February.

Partington, Richard. 2017. 'Banks Trimming Compliance Staff as $321 Billion in Fines Abate'. Bloomberg, 23 March.

PwC. 2017a. 'Redrawing the Lines: FinTech's Growing Influence on Financial Services'. Global FinTech Report.

PwC. 2017b. 'UK Financial Services Firms Fear up to 40% of Revenue at Risk from FinTech', 6 April.

PwC. 2017c. 'CBI PwC Financial Services Survey', Q2.

Pym, Hugh. 2014. Inside the Banking Crisis: The Untold Story. London: Bloomsbury.

Roberts, Richard. 2008. The City: A Guide to London's Global Financial Centre. London: *The Economist*.

Roberts, Richard. 2014. ' "How We Saved the City": The Management of the Financial Crisis of 1914'. In British Financial Crises Since 1825, edited by Nicholas Dimsdale and Anthony Hotson. Oxford: Oxford University Press, pp. 94–115.

Roberts, Richard. 2016. When Britain Went Bust: The IMF Financial Crisis of 1976. London: OMFIF Press.

Shin, Hyun Song. 2009. 'Reflections on Northern Rock: The Bank Run that Heralded the Global Financial Crisis'. *Journal of Economic Perspectives* 23 (1), Winter: 101–19.

Stylianou, Nassos. 2014. 'City of London Recruitment Drops Despite UK Job Market Boom'. CityAM, 5 July.

TheCityUK/PwC. 2017. 'A Vision for a Transformed, World-Leading Industry: UK-Based Financial and Related Professional Services', June.

TPWGF (Transatlantic Policy Working Group FinTech). 2017. 'The Future of RegTech for Regulators', June.

Turner, John D. 2014. Banking in Crisis: The Rise and Fall of British Banking Stability, 1800 to the Present. Cambridge: Cambridge University Press.

UK International Financial Services. 2009. 'UK International Financial Services—the Future: A Report from UK Based Financial Service Leaders to the Government' (May).

Wojcik, Dariusz and Duncan MacDonald-Korth. 2015. 'The British and the German Financial Sectors in the Wake of the Crisis: Size, Structure and Spatial Concentration'. *Journal of Economic Geography* 15 (5): 1033–54.

Wolf, Martin. 2010. Fixing Global Finance. Baltimore: The Johns Hopkins University Press.

Wolf, Martin. 2015. The Shifts and the Shocks: What We've Learned—and Have Still to Learn—From the Financial Crisis. London: Penguin.

Zarate, Juan C. 2013. Treasury's War: The Unleashing of a New Era of Financial Warfare. New York: PublicAffairs.

Z/Yen. 2017. Global Financial Centres Index 22 (September).

4

Paris

The Possibility of Revival as an International Financial Centre

Laure Quennouëlle-Corre

4.1 Introduction

Much has already been said about the history of international financial centres (IFCs) since the eighteenth century, but the most recent period (i.e. the last twenty years) has yet to be examined in detail.

Since the 1970s, a great deal has been written in an attempt to explain the dynamics of the major centres, from the oldest to the most recent. Among these works, in addition to Youssef Cassis's bestseller *The Capitals of Capital* (2008), we can cite the studies by Paul Einzig (1931), Charles Kindleberger (1974), Richard Roberts (1994), and H. Curtis Reed (1981), which offer a large panel of research seeking to explain and measure the attractiveness of IFCs (Quennouëlle-Corre and Cassis 2011). Reading them gives an idea of the variety of criteria selected by the different authors, and the fact these criteria have changed over time. The subject thus appears inexhaustible and deserves to be re-examined regularly. The 2007 Global Financial Crisis (GFC) and the Brexit perspective make this a very timely moment to look back over the history of international financial centres.[1]

[1] This research is based on data edited by official institutions (Banque de France, the French Ministry of Finance, Bank of International Settlements, OECD, World Federation of Stock Exchanges) or collected by 'Paris Europlace'. Several leaders of Paris's financial ecosystem have been specially interviewed for this research: Anthony Attia, CEO of Euronext, who has occupied key roles in the company since 2000; Jean Eyraud, CEO of the Association française des investisseurs institutionnels (Af2i), and Philippe Haudeville, secretary general of the Af2i; Jean-Pierre Grimaud, CEO of OFI AM, Didier Le Menestrel, president of the asset management company

Although this book focuses mainly on the decade 2007–17, it is also essential to take long-term trends into consideration. The best-known, now considered central, are as follows:

- The financial 'ecosystem': banking system, depth of capital markets, size of savings pool, size of asset management, facilities, and financial services, market infrastructures;[2]
- The internationalization of the economy;
- The skilled labour force (even with the development of advanced automation and artificial intelligence, there is a permanent need for human skills);
- The 'pro-business' environment and government, legal, and fiscal stability;
- Quality of life (culture, security, cost of living, pollution, etc.);
- Urban infrastructure (transport, schools, housing, etc.).

Two kinds of criteria come to light here: those linked to the quality of financial services and those linked to macroeconomics or the quality of the 'environment'—used here in a broad sense. This raises the issue of how to prioritize them in order to explain a financial centre's attractiveness; which of them are essential? What affects the final decision for a location, the financial ecosystem or the macroeconomic environment? How do managers, expatriates, and governments influence the decision?

For instance, does quality of life matter for an IFC's standing? It certainly does, and this needs to be examined, as large banks and funds are likely to move from London after Brexit. The recent report from Deutsche Bank Market Research—a detailed survey of global prices in forty-seven cities—gives some interesting indications: in the 'quality of life ranking' section, Paris (ranked 30) is listed above London (33) but below Zurich (5), Berlin (11), Dublin (21), and New York (28) (Deutsche Bank 2017). However, it is difficult to measure the weight of this criterion in the decision about where to establish firms and services. It is not a top priority, but it still has to be considered. I will study these different factors, but will focus on financial services, the outlines of which are easier to define than the quality of environment, which is, by its very nature, subjective.

In addition to the consequences of the GFC and Brexit on each IFC, the aim of this collective study is to look at the way the financial revolution and the

La Financière de l'Echiquier and director of the French Management Association (Association française de Gestion, AFG).

[2] This includes: stock exchange, clearing business, security settlement system, central securities depositories (CSDs). CSDs play two roles in the national framework: ultimate custody of securities and securities settlement (operating securities settlement systems, SSSs).

second globalization have, in fact, changed their activities, their place in the world, and their role in financial services. The main part of this chapter is therefore divided into three sections. Section 4.2 questions the impact of globalization on Paris from the 1980s until 2007. Section 4.3 focuses on the consequences of the GFC on Paris' financial centre. Section 4.4 searches to evaluate the effects of Brexit on Paris as an IFC.

4.2 What Has Changed since the 1980s? Long-term Trends and New Circumstances

4.2.1 *Paris' Recent Past*

Trying to predict the future of Paris requires looking back over its recent past. Having been a serious competitor to top IFCs such as London and New York in the nineteenth century and the first half of the twentieth century (Quennouëlle-Corre 2015), Paris has struggled to survive as a major European centre over the last hundred years, partly because France was reticent to liberalize its economy, and came late to the second globalization that occurred in the 1980s.

As Ranald Michie analyses in his book on global securities markets, 'Towards the end of the twentieth century, the global securities market reached and probably surpassed the position it had occupied at the beginning' (Michie 2006, p. 297). Globalization involved an unprecedented degree of integration thanks to the technological revolution coupled with the total liberalization of markets and the opening up of monetary and financial borders.

Did this signal the end of geography, as claimed by O'Brien (O'Brien 1992)? There are several indications that location is becoming less and less important for financial activities; the suppression of financial and monetary borders, the development of electronic trading, the expansion of worldwide banking, and the end of stock exchanges' monopoly for trading all contribute to this trend.

The consequences were visible on the stock exchanges and banking systems, and more generally, in the entire financial ecosystem. France, too, was affected by the phenomenon, although somewhat later than other countries when it did succeed in catching up.

This happened in the 1980s when the French 'Big Bang' led to great upheavals in regulation, competition, and technology—as most of the continental financial centres experienced at that time. Since then, 'stability, competition, and security' have been the main principles of France's financial policy, and this has been particularly visible in the stock markets. The MATIF, which was launched in 1985, soon became the major futures market in Europe and the world's third largest market; the end of exchange controls, together with disintermediation, strengthened the growth of French capital markets. In the early 1990s, Paris caught up with European leaders thanks to a determined strategy by French investors, firms, and operators: 'Paris Europlace', an association of French institutions involved in developing Paris as an IFC, was created in 1993. It brought together about 150 members including the Ministry of Finance, the Banque de France, Caisse des dépôts et consignations, the Chamber of Commerce and Industry (CCI), the Greater Paris Regional Authority, commercial banks, insurance companies, investment funds, and brokerage firms. The activity of 'Paris Europlace', which was beginning to stagnate somewhat at the start of the twenty-first century, has been boosted by the announcement of Brexit. The fact that this association already existed has facilitated the recent mobilization of all its stakeholders.

However, Paris requires a certain amount of assistance from French institutions (such as official institutions, professional bodies, and local or national authorities), because it experienced various obstacles for several decades before the 2007 crisis.

The 1990s and early 2000s were buoyant years for Paris, boosted by the arrival of the euro and the fact that European strategies were, at the time, settled by financial institutions, despite the somewhat limited vitality of the Parisian market and its international role (Straus 2005), and the fact that the MATIF was severely hampered by the German futures market's offensive in 1999.[3]

To sum up the situation, as the twenty-first century dawned, Paris enjoyed several major advantages to come back into the race for European leadership, even though its image was suffering from decades of financial protectionism and state intervention. It was about to overcome its fragility. At the time, the bursting of the dot-com bubble tempered the optimistic climate, but it merely postponed the ongoing stock exchange mergers. In this optimistic context in 2000, the creation of Euronext (by the merger of the stock exchanges of Paris, Amsterdam, Brussels, and then Lisbon in 2002) and its location in Paris (but under Dutch law) symbolized the European desire to join the global race, whereas the rapprochement between the London Stock Exchange and Deutsche Börse failed in 2000. In the global context of stock exchange demutualization, Euronext became the first cross-border project to merge stock exchanges ever realized.[4] The merger was completed by the unification of trading and clearing operations (LCH.Clearnet).

In 2006, a new attempt was made to merge Euronext and Deutsche Börse, but this was not approved by some of France's financial institutions that feared the effect of German hegemony on the organization. This partly

---

[3] That was not the only reason. See Pinatton (2006).
[4] The Stockholm Stock Exchange was the first one to demutualize in 1993. But the global wave of demutualization started in the beginning of the 2000s.

explains why some French stakeholders preferred an agreement with the New York Stock Exchange (NYSE) based on a transatlantic strategy, and the desire to export a decentralized organizational model. By 2007, the NYSE Group and Euronext merger could have given Paris its wings, since it would have marked the creation of the world's largest and most liquid exchange group—NYSE Euronext (Bonin and Blancheton 2017). However, the 2007 GFC put paid to this project, and the new private platforms (multilateral trading facilities) now compete with traditional stock exchanges. Five years later, the attempted merger between NYSE Euronext and Deutsche Börse was blocked by the European Union, reluctant to give such a dominant position on the derivative markets to LIFFE (Euronext) and Eurex (Deutsche Börse).

Later, in December 2012, ICE bought NYSE Euronext, and then the American operator separated all its activities, stripped it of its main assets of clearing and futures, and put Euronext back on the market. Paris lost a huge futures market (the LIFFE), while its clearing activities were located in London and owned by the London Stock Exchange, although it retained the Monep (the negotiable options market), the CAC 40 futures market, and several commodity futures markets (e.g. wheat).

It is interesting to examine what several French professional bodies did to defend Paris's role at the time. Institutional investors and asset managers found themselves at the forefront of the battle. They multiplied discrete actions and initiatives to reform French technical regulations and to improve coordination with other European markets. Specializing in retail asset management, they maintained their activities in France, given the depth of the savings pool invested in UCITS. However, the preference for liquid savings encouraged by higher interest rates and regulatory actions is a long-term trend in France that contributes to the low rate of savings invested in shares. Savers gave priority to life-insurance investments and money-market mutual funds.

By contrast, large French banks and insurance companies had a global strategy, and when futures markets increased dramatically and became the most important capital market, most of them delocalized derivative services to Luxembourg. According to several testimonies, some of them tried to save the MATIF in 1999, but they did not play an active role in the Deutsche Börse/ Euronext merger and, more generally, in the defence of Paris as an IFC. The absence of a common strategy including banks and insurance companies disadvantaged Paris in comparison with the collective mindset of the City of London, for instance. Thanks to their huge weight in terms of jobs and activities located in Paris, banks could have tilted the balance in favour of the French capital. In order to compete with the big global banks, they necessarily favoured an international strategy based on a delocalization of profitable activities in London or in Luxembourg.

Nevertheless, the banking industry remains one of Paris's great strengths for its competitiveness, and five French banks are still among the largest banks in continental Europe (see Section 4.3.2). However, the GFC and Brexit may well have changed the banking strategy completely, as we shall see in Section 4.3.

4.2.2 Growing Competition and New Criteria

The recent upheavals have increased the fierce competition between financial centres, and the direction of international capital flows is now based on different criteria. At the start of the twenty-first century, the comparison between IFCs is increasingly focusing on the costs of financial services (listing, taxation, requests for prospectuses, etc.), and on deregulation. This was not the case in the 1960s, when the opening of borders and the suppression of exchange controls were a priority. Tax policies were not really considered a discriminatory factor until the 1980s, since every IFC required more or less the same level of taxation. Similarly, the flexibility of the labour market and the taxation of high wages have become increasingly discriminatory in recent years (while bonuses have grown dramatically) (Godechot 2011). This was a serious obstacle for Paris, considered until then as a centre with a high level of taxation. From another perspective, together with financial liberalization, the capacity for innovation has been a decisive advantage as the rapid development of technology has accentuated competition in processing speed for trading. In the 2000s, innovation capacity remained a key priority for IFCs, which try to stay in the global race by luring highly-skilled labour and fintech firms.

Consequently, the number of IFCs has grown since the end of the twentieth century, and Paris faces new challengers. These days, financial rivalry in Europe is no longer merely a battle between the historical IFCs; London, Paris, and New York are facing new competitors because the attractiveness of financial centres has shifted over the last thirty years. Moreover, the European Union is now a huge potential market for financial services and products, and is becoming increasingly attractive for international operators.

For instance, Luxembourg's financial facilities have made this small country more and more attractive for futures activities and the asset management industry. At the same time, the rapid rise of Dublin and Frankfurt have made them new competitors and changed the entire situation within the EU. With regard to the quality of the financial ecosystem and stability, London, Frankfurt, Paris, and the Swiss IFCs remain the European leaders, while Luxembourg and Ireland have major fiscal advantages. However, for these two countries, being tax havens does not compensate for the lack of infrastructure. For instance, compared to older centres, neither of the two countries can offer a large pool of savings, a comparable size of stock, bond, or derivatives markets, besides the growing activities of asset management and private equity. When taking into consideration the quality of life (culture, security, cost of living, pollution, etc.) and the urban infrastructures (transport, schools, housing, etc.), these competitors cannot rival the major European hubs.

What we can say at this stage of the study is that the global financial landscape is multipolar, especially in the Eurozone. Paris's main competitors are to be found in this geographic and monetary area, as neither the French capital nor any other European centre can rival London's financial cluster and its high degree of internationalization.

4.3 The Consequences of the Global Financial Crisis on the Size and Competitiveness of Paris as an IFC

Historically, financial crises have always been closely intertwined with globalization, and they re-emerged with globalization's second wave with the 1987 crash, which was followed by the Asian financial crisis in the 1990s and the bursting of the dot-com bubble in 2000. Unlike these crises of varying magnitudes, the turmoil in 2007–8, the like of which had not been seen since the Great Depression in 1929, affected every financial centre at the time.

4.3.1 *Paris after the GFC: A Moderate Impact*

Ten years later, it is time to assess the damage and, more generally, the effects on mid-term trends. When reviewing Paris's activities, the assessment is mixed. Depending on the business segment involved, financial services have been more or less affected by the crisis, and their competitiveness does not seem to have changed dramatically. Here we use three criteria to evaluate the effects on the French ecosystem: the number of jobs in the financial sector, capital market activities, and the position of the banking sector.

Firstly, the level of employment in the financial sector has not fallen—on the contrary, it has been increasing steadily after a slight slowdown from 2007 to 2013, as shown in Figure 4.1. These official figures are extracted from the Ministry of Economy and Finance database (INSEE, French National Institute for Statistics and Economic Studies). In 2016, 800,000 direct jobs included 330,000 jobs in Paris and the Greater Paris Region.

Market activities were affected to varying degrees by the crisis. Euronext trading volume has not returned to its pre-crisis level, but its market capitalization has increased since 2008, while its free market and second market rose again in 2012, both indicating the dynamism of the stock exchanges (see figures 4.2, 4.3, and 4.4).

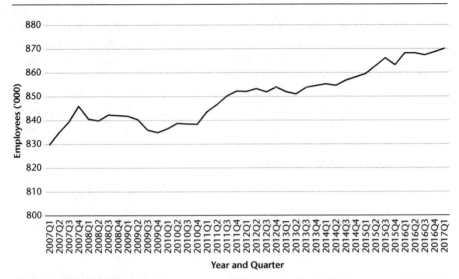

Figure 4.1. Financial sector employment in France, 2007–17

Note: Figures are given by quarter. The number of employees in the financial sector in France are considered as direct jobs. These data are a synthesis of governmental sources and business surveys on employment in the finance and insurance sector. For details see https://www.insee.fr/fr/sta tistiques/serie/001577252.

Source: Author, based on data from INSEE (French National Institute for Statistics and Economic Studies).

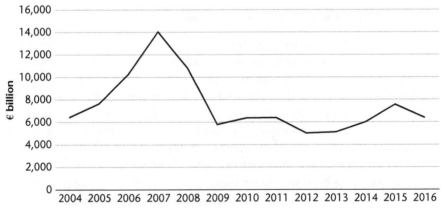

Figure 4.2. Daily trading on Euronext, 2004–16 (€ billion)
Source: Author, based on data from Euronext.

In addition to the Euronext cash market (similar in size to the Deutsche Börse in terms of market capitalization), two other significant capital markets can be taken into consideration. Firstly, the Paris derivative markets offer a diversified range of products such as equity, index, and commodity derivatives. More specifically, supported by the global strength of the French banks,

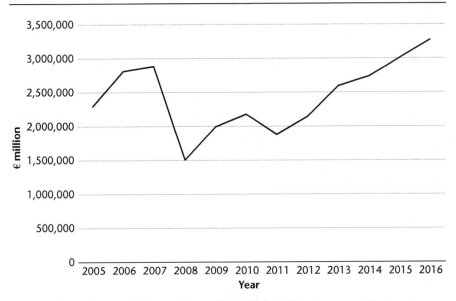

Figure 4.3. Euronext market capitalization, 2005–16 (€ million)
Source: Author, based on data from Euronext.

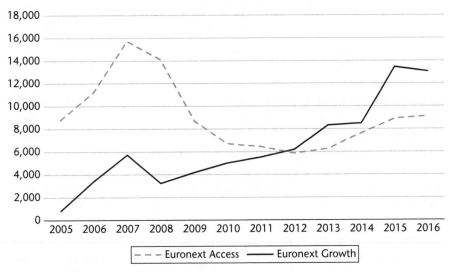

Figure 4.4. Market capitalization of Euronext Access and Euronext Growth, 2005–16 (€ million)
Source: Author, based on data from Euronext.

since 1998 the French OTC derivative market has become the second largest in Europe, behind the United Kingdom and ahead of Germany.

The debt securities markets give another indication of the vitality of Paris's stock exchange. Traditionally, France has always had a strong bond market,

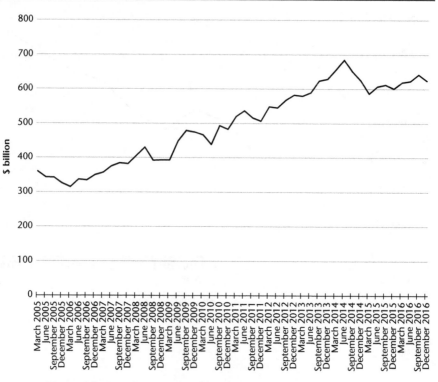

Figure 4.5. French corporate debt securities outstanding ($ billion)
Source: Author, based on data from Paris Europlace. Quarterly figures.

both for corporate bonds and government securities. This is still the case today since France remains the leader in European international corporate bond markets,[5] and Paris's activity on the European government debt securities market has increased steadily since 2005 (see Figure 4.5).

These figures illustrate that the Global Financial Crisis temporarily reduced the share of trading activities for equity markets but not for derivative or debt securities markets. Signs of recovery for the entire marketplace have been visible since 2012. Nevertheless, to get a precise evaluation of a centre's international ranking, it is necessary to compare the volume of activities of all its markets with those of its competitors. Given the various capital markets at stake, a full treatment of the topic is impossible here. The evolution of the turnover of derivatives between 1995 and 2016 can give an idea of the importance of the leading derivatives markets around the world (see Table 4.1). On this evaluation, France arrives in the third position.

[5] 33% of the total outstanding for France, 29% for UK, 10% for Germany, and 7% for Italy. Source: BIS and Association for Financial Markets in Europe (AFME), end 2015.

Table 4.1. Daily turnover in interest rates derivatives (all instruments) in $ billion

Country/Year	1995	1998	2001	2004	2007	2010	2013	2016
USA	32	58	116	317	525	642	628	1,241
UK	59	123	238	563	957	1,235	1,348	1,180
France	19	41	65	151	176	193	146	141
Hong Kong	4	2	3	11	17	18	28	110
Singapore	16	5	3	9	57	35	37	58
Japan	26	32	16	31	76	90	67	56
Australia	3	3	10	13	23	41	66	49
Others	50	79	226	235	341	395	382	193
Total	**209**	**344**	**676**	**1,330**	**2,173**	**2,649**	**2,702**	**3,028**

Source: Author based on data from Banque de France and Bank of International Settlements.

From the same perspective, although France's asset management (AM) industry's growth has been eroded since 2008 compared with other European countries, the sector was not dramatically affected by the crisis. Assets managed on behalf of third parties rose from 1,473 billion euros in 2001 to 2,779 billion in 2007 and amounted to 3,593 billion euros in 2015.[6] In addition to the continued growth in the number of AM firms since 1998 (from 334 in 1998 to 613 firms in 2013, including 4,400 investment managers), Paris's AM industry includes four companies ranked in the global top twenty, and three global custodians ranked globally.

Having been the European leader for many years, the French AM industry is now the second largest in Europe with 20 per cent of market share, far behind the UK (37 per cent of market share). However, when looking at the market share in Europe based on fund domicile, which is our main concern here, the recent and spectacular rise of Luxembourg (27 per cent) and Ireland (15 per cent) explains why France finds itself in fourth place (13.3 per cent), just behind Germany (13.7 per cent). This fall is not a direct consequence of the GFC but is due to the attractiveness of tax-haven centres and their less strict regulations, which are attractive to investment funds. These institutions are by nature highly mobile and are constantly on the lookout for the most profitable location. For this reason, French operators tried to unify French and European laws by means of the 'FROG' initiative (a humorous acronym for 'French Routes and Opportunities Gardens') that they launched in 2016.

4.3.2 *A Resilient Banking Sector*

Banking all over the world was severely hit by the Global Financial Crisis. Overall, the GFC brought to light latent questions about financial and

---

[6] Source: AMF (Autorité des Marchés financiers)/BDF (Banque de France)/AFG (Association française de gestion) calculations.

banking regulation that had not been resolved since the 1987 financial crash. Whereas strict regulation might have been considered a handicap before 2007, this is less valid after the Global Financial Crisis: stable and secure centres are perceived with more interest, whereas before this, the 'financial repression' of several countries was severely criticized by 'neo-liberal' thinking. However, like other European firms, French banks have suffered from the indirect consequences of the GFC, such as the growing weight of regulation (Basel III, MiFID), which reduces their ability to invest their incomes and pursue their activities abroad. Global competition between banks lost impetus after the fall of Lehman Brothers. As Hubert Bonin writes, the 'geobanking map' (Bonin 2017) has been redrawn since the crisis. Could this represent the return of geography in this sector? This is highly unlikely, and it is probable that this is a temporary trend. Moreover, this raises the question of the nationality of big banks and therefore their links to a geographic place, since their employees and managers are of various nationalities and their profits are international, as are their stakeholders.

Until recently, banking stability was not considered as a decisive advantage, but the global crisis cast a new light on the relevance of a healthy banking sector, and this is now regarded as an important factor for an IFC. In the same way, in 2011, the European Banking Authority was set up in London, and the European Union strictly enforced regulation for European banks. This is shown most clearly in the directive of the European Parliament and of the Council of Europe of 26 June 2013, which has been transposed into member states' national law, and which lays down the rules on capital buffers, bankers' remuneration and bonuses, prudential supervision, and corporate governance.

In this respect, its stable banking system could be considered as a strength for France, as few French banks were seriously hurt by the financial crisis and the following Eurozone crisis. In the United Kingdom, the banking sector's profits fell sharply by 4.7 per cent of GNP, and there was a fall of 7.1 per cent in Switzerland. Inside the Eurozone, the change in banking profits represented about 0.5–0.6 per cent of GNP. But the French banks kept on making profits in 2008, whereas significant losses were recorded in the German banking sector (Plane and Pujas 2009). The degree of banks' exposure to securitization made the difference: for instance, the share of Deutsche Bank's profits due to securitization activities amounted to 23 per cent, but the corresponding figure for the income of the three big French banks (BNP Paribas, Société Générale, and Crédit Agricole) was only 3 per cent.

Similarly, the size of French commercial banks may be a key asset during these turbulent times: five French banks are in the global top twenty—compared with only one German bank, for example. While major global banks were scaling back their ambitions to become universal banks, the French BNP Paribas took over the Belgian Fortis in 2009. The three groups,

BNP Paribas, Credit Agricole, and Société Générale are now among the world leaders in custodial services.

While instability remains at the core of the financial and banking systems, the need for security is increasing. The growing influence of the European Central Bank and the European Union in defining new rules and regulations cannot be ignored. Since the GFC, they have been playing a key role in Europe's financial framework. Similarly, transparency in trading and the supervision of offshore centres (tax havens) in Europe has become a priority, and the supervisors have already begun to study the issue, and more information on financial services is being requested. However, even if Luxembourg and Ireland are stigmatized for being tax havens, it will be difficult for the EU to intervene in their domestic taxation systems and the question is still pending.

If a stable financial system and a high-quality regulatory environment are now required,[7] the former criteria—size of the banking system, depth of capital markets, size of savings pool, size of asset management activity, facilities and financial services, market infrastructures, internationalization of the economy, skilled labour force, 'pro-business' environment and government, legal, and fiscal stability—are still crucial to maintaining financial centres' competitiveness. This is the case for the financial ecosystem, the quality of its skilled labour force and its advance in new technologies, in which Paris retains some advantages.

4.3.3 A Dynamic Financial Ecosystem

The French financial 'ecosystem' relies on the diversity and solidity of its actors and a large savings pool. To sum up, Paris offers a complete range of services inside the Eurozone, in equity markets, euro-denominated bond markets, derivative markets, asset management and private equity, banking activities, digital finance and fintech.

In addition, France maintains a high degree of internationalization in financial services. Table 4.2 shows the different kinds of extra-European firms authorized to carry out activities in France, thanks to the European Union financial passport (according to the 2017 Bank de France register).

France's asset management industry, one of the most dynamic and diversified in Europe, belongs to the core of the ecosystem. France offers the second-largest asset management pool in the world with $1,683 billion in assets as French funds, and four asset management firms ranked in the global top twenty. French banks run a large share of AM compared with other countries such as the UK or the United States. Of course, although Paris is well placed in Europe, the size of its independent AM firms cannot be compared with those

---

[7] The 'Autorité des marchés financiers' (AMF) benefits from diversified financial and legal expertise and has recently developed a fast-track process at low cost for funds authorization.

Table 4.2. Type and number of financial institutions in France in 2017

Type of financial services firms	Number of financial services firms
Non-EU investment firms	3,000
Non-EU investment services providers	3,100
Non-EU financial institutions	10
Non-EU credit institutions	540
Non-EU safekeeping and administration of financial instruments for the account of clients	735
Non-EU payments institutions	420
Non-EU electronic money institutions	143

Source: Author, based on data from Bank de France register.

in the United States. For instance, Black Rock—the largest investment manager in the world—had more than $5 trillion assets under management in 2017 (more than the entire French AM sector, including both independent AM firms and banking AM). The situation resembles that of David and Goliath, but for at least twenty years, the AM industry has been the most dynamic element in favour of Paris as an IFC and its lobbying should not be underestimated. It is based on a large personal and institutional savings pool, the latter accounting for 26 per cent of invested institutional assets under management in the EU (not including the UK).

A final criterion for a competitive IFC concerns the importance of a skilled labour force. France is in a strong position with its high level of university education; French business schools and universities are capable of training students to meet the professional needs of the financial industry. The abundant and highly qualified human resources in France can be exemplified by achievements in mathematics (thirteen of fifty-six Fields Medals) and its renowned business schools. According to the Financial Times Business Schools Ranking, four French Masters degree courses in Finance rank among the global top five. The capital city can boast a large talent pool of engineers, data scientists, and computer specialists. And the presence of highly skilled workers could be of importance for local activities in financial innovation. However, the question is beginning to emerge as to how important this is now that skilled workers are increasingly mobile and increasingly attracted by high salaries abroad.

Paris's competitiveness is also linked to its ability to rise to future challenges such as blockchain and fintech in general. Continuing to develop new technologies is an ongoing challenge for any centre. This trend became increasingly marked in the 2000s with the development of private platforms (of which there are now approximately 250 in Europe), competing with official stock exchanges, which became quoted companies at the same time. This multipolar world forced the IFCs to rethink their role and their attractiveness, especially with regard to the development of blockchain a few years ago. Blockchain may well reduce the volume of IFCs' activities. In the long term, it could be of no interest for blockchain providers to be attached to one geographic centre. Nevertheless, according to some operators, even if clearing activities become instantaneous and counterparty risk is partly reduced, they will still be required at the end of the transaction process. Moreover, considering institutional inertia, it will take a long time to reverse these long-standing trends.

In my opinion, the growth of the wider sector of 'fintech' is more promising for the future of financial centres than the single case of blockchain. The 2016 launch of a new 'French Tech Hub' is an illustration of the success of the French 'finance innovation cluster' set up in 2007, where more than 350 projects have been approved. The recent opening in Paris of the world's largest incubator, with over 1,000 start-ups, has enhanced the city's growing reputation in terms of technology. Over 1,200 French fintech companies now have official approval in various sectors such as big data, new financing tools, payment, risk management, and social and sustainable economics. In this particular sector, which has been growing since 2013 due to the leadership of China, France is gaining some advantage in sustainable and responsible development with so-called 'green bonds', and the Parisian market was the second-largest issuer of green bonds in the world in 2015. In the same year, Euronext launched the 'Low Carbon 100 Europe Index', composed of a basket of a hundred stocks having implemented a strategy to reduce their CO_2 emissions compatible with a 2-degree warming trajectory. In 2016, the competitiveness of Paris suddenly became an issue when the British people voted to leave the European Union. Once again, the French capital is harbouring dreams of leadership.

4.4 The Consequences of Brexit: What Changes for Paris?

The effect of Brexit may be important for Paris, but much remains uncertain and depends on the political negotiations for the entire Brexit process. The first consequence has been the unprecedented mobilization of Parisian stakeholders.

'A kind of sacred union has emerged,' said Gerard Mestrallet, President of Paris Europlace.[8] In fact, several initiatives have been launched to push Paris into the spotlight: the recent FROG initiative led to several regulatory changes. For instance, unlike the current regulation in force in France, it is not necessary

---

[8] AGEFI, Special issue, July 2016.

to have a bank account in Luxembourg to invest capital. The 'FROG' initiative aimed to resolve this legal difference.

Two investors' associations—the Association Française des Investisseurs Institutionnels (AF2i) and the Association Française de Gestion (AFG)—are particularly involved in the fight for the European leadership. In addition to public institutions (Autorités des Marchés Financiers, Banque de France, and the French Prudential Supervisory Authority, ACPR), brokers, and medium-sized banks, Euronext and Euroclear are at the forefront of the battle. It is more difficult for big banks and insurance companies, involved in global strategies, to defend a local centre. However, they play an important role in different markets (the debt securities market, for instance), and Brexit has reactivated their involvement. Since 2016, various Paris Europlace stakeholders have been interviewed and regular international meetings have been held in Paris, the United States, and London, mobilizing the majority of key actors. These efforts to attract foreign companies are certainly not enough on their own to convince them, but this collective action is beginning to bear fruit.

4.4.1 *Pending Technical Issues*

Whether or not it will be a 'hard' Brexit, the main discussions are now focusing on two questions: firstly, the essential question of the European financial services passport, and secondly, the location of clearing houses.

In the aftermath of the Brexit vote, the City of London's main actors feared losing the banks that sell their financial products and services within the European Economic Area. The abolition of the European passport is therefore a critical issue for those countries but also for the UK, which is home to over 5,000 financial institutions that benefit from the European passport. Similarly, more than 8,000 firms from the EU operate in the UK thanks to the 'passport of entry'. France has made this its main battle and is hoping to take advantage of it. Furthermore, abolishing the European passport could generate a transfer of highly-skilled jobs to the EU. But again, we can only speculate about the future.

4.4.2 *Where Should Clearing Houses be Located after Brexit?*

The issue of location is vital for the derivative markets as clearing houses provide central counterparty clearing and risk management services for every kind of derivative product. As derivate activities become a major source of income for the financial sector, this challenge is a decisive one. As we have seen in the first section, in 2004, the merger of the British LCH and the French house Clearnet gave birth to the largest clearing house in the EU: LCH.Clearnet, located in London and owned by LSE. ICE Clear Europe, the other major clearing house, is also in London, which thus houses the vast majority of clearing transactions in euros. Brexit has revived the controversy about their location in the Eurozone, and the European supervisor (European Central Bank, ECB) may not accept a situation in which euro clearing does not comply with EU regulation. Therefore, on 4 May 2017, the European Commission declared its intention to relocate clearing houses of systemic size within the European area. And depending on the European Commission's decision, Euronext may be one of the potential purchasers of the subsidiary LCH. Clearnet SA. In addition to the ECB, the Banque de France and French politicians also wish to be engaged in discussions, since this issue involves the EU's independence with regard to financial regulation. Given the major challenge this represents, it could lead to a battle between Clearnet (France) and Eurex (Germany). To complicate matters, Eurex belongs to Deutsche Börse but is located in Luxembourg, whereas LCH.Clearnet is still under British law. Furthermore, the battle for settlement delivery between the two central securities depositories (CSDs), Euroclear (owned by France, Netherlands, UK, Ireland, etc.) and Clearstream (mainly owned by Germany and Luxembourg), confirms that institutional entanglements are complicating the very existence of future financial centres.

Once the Brexit process is launched, the issue of the geographical location of forex trading will also arise because 90 per cent of the forex market in euros is in London (see Table 4.3).

Will Eurozone members accept that the major euro market remains outside the European Union? This question remains unanswered at the moment and will be part of negotiations between the EU and the British government (along with agriculture, trade, and free movement of people). The negotiations are set to be long and tough, and the agenda remains somewhat uncertain; however, there is no doubt that negotiations concerning the EU's role will be followed closely by French stakeholders. For its influence on financial issues may be

Table 4.3. Daily turnover in foreign exchange markets, 1995–2016, (all instruments) in $ billion

Country/Year	1995	1998	2001	2004	2007	2010	2013	2016
UK	479	685	542	835	1,483	1,854	2,726	2,426
USA	266	383	273	499	745	904	1,263	1,272
Singapore	107	145	104	134	242	266	383	517
Hong Kong	91	80	68	106	181	238	275	437
Japan	168	146	153	207	250	312	374	399
France	62	77	50	67	127	152	190	181
Switzerland	88	92	76	85	254	249	216	156
Other	371	491	440	675	996	1,068	1,258	1,157
Total	**1,633**	**2,099**	**1,705**	**2,608**	**4,281**	**5,043**	**6,684**	**6,546**

Source: Author, based on data from Bank de France register.

strengthened when Brexit negotiations begin. But at the time of writing this article, the cascade of events makes it impossible to predict the outcome of negotiations for the financial sector, which are intricately linked with a global agreement.

4.4.3 *The EU's Power in Question*

Since 2007, major new actors have emerged on the international financial scene and their influence has been strengthened by the crisis: the EU's and the ECB's influence has grown because of various directives on crucial issues such as market infrastructure, accounting standards, and regulation (MiFID I and II, Solvency II).

From the start, the EU was not in favour of a monopoly stock exchange for the entire continent (see Section 4.2.1); therefore, it blocked the merger of the NYSE/Deutsche Börse in the name of competition. The question is whether the European Commission will maintain its position in the coming decades in the light of the new political context: will it favour one or several IFCs in Europe, and within or outside the Eurozone? If its aim is to maintain several IFCs, Paris and other major European centres have an opportunity to benefit from Brexit, whether 'hard' or 'soft'. Ultimately, the balance of power between the UK and the EU will evolve with each stage of the negotiation process.

Studying each financial centre must not neglect the role played by international institutions. Strategic matters will be decided by the Commission, which is the only decision-making body along with the central bank. Consequently, EU countries will have less and less influence with regard to regulations and the institutional framework while the Commission's technical experts and civil servants will have a greater say in the final decision—and could possibly be influenced by British and/or American lobbyists, whose power has been underlined by many recent political studies (Laurens 2015; Autret 2007). Whether at the Council of Ministers, at the European Commission, or at the Parliament, the private-interest representatives have played a growing role in the financial sector. For instance, during the talks about the financial service trade at the end of the 1990s, the US Coalition of Service Industry and the British Invisibles played an active role lobbying in the dialogue on trade liberalization (Coen and Richardson 2009). More generally, the associations of lawyers are extremely powerful, as well as the European Banking Federation, European Stock Exchange Federation, and other financial federations. But their main concern is to reach a consensus among the views of their national bodies (Greenwood 2011). Private interests have to combine different channels in order to successfully gain access to the EU legislative process; and individual companies often prefer to establish their own lobbyists at Brussels (Bouwen 2004).

4.4.4 *The Recent French Political Shift*

At the same time, France's influence within the Commission has declined over several decades. French employees at the European Commission represent now less than 10 per cent of the staff (3,193 employees), and at the highest level, there is only one European Commissioner per member state (28).[9] But this may change with the arrival of new players such as France's Michel Barnier, at the head of a task force of thirty experts in charge of Brexit negotiations with the British prime minister. He may promote France's position against the continuance of the European financial passport, and French lobbying is, at last, under way. An example of this is the Capital Markets Union project, a very long and difficult process that has not yet been completed, but which has been progressing far more rapidly since 2016.

French lobbyists are beginning to exert an influence over current issues such as market infrastructure. For instance, France's asset managers have called for a European 'consolidated tape', establishing a central source of post-trade prices from regulated markets (which already exists in the USA). The ESMA (European Securities and Markets Authority) launched this project a few years ago, and it could give a competitive advantage to the Eurozone. In the same way, French operators have applauded the 2009 directive that provided a harmonized legal framework for 'undertakings for collective investment in transferable securities' (UCITS). Similarly, the recent abolition of the UCITS classification, a drawback for foreign operators in France, has made it possible for these French financial products to be marketed freely across the EU.

France is also beginning to shake off its poor reputation as a fiscal regime, which may give Paris some decisive advantages. The Macron Act in 2015 established a tax regime for free shares that is closer to German and British practices, and a *guichet unique* (a one-stop-shop) called 'Choose Paris region' was created in 2016, offering foreign firms assistance and advice in legal, administrative, and social formalities. But Paris still has to make more effort to show its goodwill in the eyes of foreigners: Parliament's decision in December 2016 to extend the area of TFF (a tax on financial dealings) and its abolition six months later reinforced the perception of fiscal and legal uncertainty in France. Since then, recent decisions taken by the new president Emmanuel Macron in July 2017, such as the tax reductions for high earners in the financial sector, as well as the exclusion of bonuses from traders' redundancy payments, have paved the way towards a more business-friendly environment in France. Many reforms have been announced to reduce taxation on capital, particularly through the 'impatriate scheme': this tax scheme

---

[9] As the EU members now number twenty-eight, the influence of the six founder members is logically reduced in comparison with the old fifteen-member Union. And the rotation of powerful staff is nowadays submitted to geopolitical balances.

for expatriate employees provides for partial tax exemption for part of the income, expatriation bonuses, and compensation related to assignments carried out abroad by foreign employees and senior managers taking up positions in France. Thanks to this temporary regime for high earners (applying for maximum of eight years in addition to the year of arrival in France), France has now the lowest effective income tax rate among its European competitors.[10]

Could the election of Emmanuel Macron give Paris a boost in the post-Brexit race? The newly-elected 'pro-business, pro-Europe, pro-finance' president will undoubtedly improve France's poor reputation regarding certain specific issues that have seriously hampered attracting foreign investors. The recent decision to relocate the European Banking Authority from London to Paris before March 2019, when Britain is set to quit the bloc, can be seen as a sign of this shift and will give a competitive advantage to Paris. (The EBA sets rules and regulations that are used by the European Central Bank to carry out tests of the banking sector within the European Union.)

Will the new political context improve the poor reputation of finance in France and therefore France's position in the financial world? Even if this is the case, it will take more than a decade to reverse current trends. Declarations are all very well, but investors are more interested in legal changes to taxation and labour laws.

4.5 Conclusion

In terms of global economic shock, there are many similarities between the 1929 financial crisis and the 2007 financial crash, but the effect of the latter on finance ten years later seems to be less significant, and activity returned to pre-crisis levels more quickly.

Like other IFCs, Paris was hit by the global crisis in terms of trading and banking activities. Nevertheless, France's financial architecture proved to be resilient to the shocks thanks to the strategy of the big banks and its institutional framework for supervision and regulation. From this perspective, Paris is in a favourable position compared with its main competitors in Europe. Moreover, the banks' failures since 2008 have emphasized the importance of a qualified domestic supervisor (Lescure 2016).

The consequences of Brexit for Paris will vary depending on several factors. Firstly, there is France's ability to reform its labour market and reverse its reputation on fiscal policy, which are its main disadvantages. Secondly, the negotiations between the European Commission and the United Kingdom,

---

[10] The 'impatriate scheme' will reduce the French effective income tax rate from 38% to 24%, but only for eight years. Source: OECD, PWC Worldwide Tax Summaries, *Agefi*.

the financial aspects of which are only part of the discussion, and the level of regulation defined by the ECB within the Eurozone are two major issues to be resolved. Following this, there are various scenarios for the redistribution of some of London's financial activity. The most likely scenario seems to be a partial reorientation towards several continental centres such as Frankfurt, Paris, and Luxembourg, not to mention Dublin and Amsterdam. However, none of them matches London's international influence and its worldwide financial networks. Given the importance of legal matters, the decision will be taken not only by big banks but also by policy-making institutions. The European Union will shoulder most of the responsibility for the future of European centres: will it have a clear strategic vision? The EU has not yet dealt with this issue, but new circumstances may prompt Europe to take control of its own destiny, as it did seventy years ago.

The future of Paris, like others IFCs, depends also on the development of technologies which impact delocalization or location of financial services. From this perspective, the international financial firms have to play their game too. Because the disintegration of the production chain is made possible by the technological revolution and the globalization, global firms may have an interest in separating their activities geographically and in moving a part of their production to cheaper locations—offshore centres for instance (Choppin-Ansidei 2000). The growing division of labour in banking and finance is an additional argument in favour of giving a balanced response to the future attractiveness of IFCs.

References

Autret, Florence. 2007. L'Amérique à Bruxelles. Paris: Seuil.

Bonin, Hubert. 2017. 'Geoeconomics and Banking'. In Advances in Geoeconomics, edited by J. Mark Munoz. New York: Routledge, pp. 217–26.

Bonin, Hubert and Blancheto Bertrand. 2017. Crises et batailles boursières en France aux XXe et XXIe siècle. Geneva: Droz.

Bouwen, Pieter. 2004. 'The Logic of Access to the European Parliament: Business Lobbying in the Committee on Economic and Monetary Affairs'. *Journal of Common Market Studies* 42 (3): 473–95.

Cassis, Youssef. 2008. The Capitals of Capital. Oxford: Oxford University Press.

Choppin-Ansidei, Julie. 2000. 'Location of International Financial Activities: Theoretical Finding and Recent Trends'. *Revue d'Economie Financière* (English ed.) 57: 15–28.

Coen, David and Jeremy Richardson. 2009. Lobbying the European Union. Oxford: Oxford University Press.

Deutsche Bank. 2017. Deutsche Bank Market Report, Special Report, May.

Einzig, Paul. 1931. The Fight for Financial Supremacy. London: Macmillan.

Godechot, Olivier. 2011. 'Le capital humain et les incitations sont-ils les deux mamelles des salaires dans la finance ?' ('Are Human Capital and Incentives the Two Breasts of Wages in Finance?'), *Revue d'économie financière* 104 (4): 145–64.

Greenwood, Justin. 2011. Interest Representation in the EU, 3rd edition. New York: Palgrave Macmillan.

Kindleberger, Charles P. 1974. The Formation of Financial Centres: A Study in Comparative Economic History. Princeton: Princeton University Press.

Laurens, Sylvain. 2015. Les courtiers du capitalisme. Milieux d'affaires et bureaucrates à Bruxelles. Paris: Agone. (English version to be published in 2018: Lobbyists and Bureaucrats in Brussels: Capitalism's Brokers. London: Routledge.)

Lescure, Michel. 2016. Immortal Banks: Strategies, Structures and Performances of Major Banks. Geneva: Droz.

Michie, Ranald. 2016. The Global Securities Markets: A History. Oxford: Oxford University Press.

O'Brien, Richard. 1992. Global Financial Integration: The End of Geography. New York: Council on Foreign Relations Press.

Pinatton, Jean-Pierre. 2006. 'A History of the Market, from "agents de change" to Euronext'. *Revue d'économie financière* (English ed.) 82: 17–26.

Plane, Mathieu and Georges Pujas. 2009. 'Les banques dans la crise'. *Revue de l'OFCE* 110 (3): 179–219.

Quennouëlle-Corre, Laure. 2015. La place financière de Paris au XXe siècle: Des ambitions contrariées. Paris: IGPDE/CHEFF.

Quennouëlle-Corre, Laure and Youssef Cassis (eds). 2011. Financial Centres and International Capital Flows in the Nineteenth and Twentieth Centuries. Oxford: Oxford University Press.

Reed, Howard Curtis. 1981. The Preeminence of Financial Centres. London: Praeger.

Roberts, Richard. 1994. International Financial Centres: Concepts, Development and Dynamics, 4 volumes. Aldershot: Edward Elgar.

Straus, André. 2005. 'The Future of the Paris Market as an International Financial Centre from the Point of View of European Integration'. In London and Paris as International Financial Centres in the Twentieth Century, edited by Youssef Cassis and Eric Bussière. Oxford: Oxford University Press, pp. 313–23.

5

Frankfurt

A Tale of Resilience in the Crises

Eike W. Schamp

5.1 Framing the Crises in Frankfurt

By the end of the twentieth century, some experts considered Frankfurt an ambitious European financial centre in the making. However, the dual US subprime crisis that provoked the European banking crisis and the subsequent euro crisis triggered shocks hitherto unknown in Germany's financial sector and its real economy. Between autumn 2008 and spring 2009, orders in the export-oriented sectors were drastically reduced and exports declined substantially. German banks were caught by surprise and began to falter, being either heavily engaged in US subprimes and/or endangered by failing credits, diminishing interbank trust, and a possible run on the banks by their private customers. The consequences of the crises spread rather unevenly across time and space, however. The international financial centre Frankfurt largely withstood the crises due to three prerequisites: its recent historical path, its embeddedness in a particular socio-economic environment (the 'German model'), and the historical situation at the moment when the financial crises happened. I shall discuss these prerequisites briefly first, before examining the crises and their implications in more detail. Frankfurt's rise after World War II has been extensively studied, from the early days when West Germany did not have sovereignty over its own currency to an international centre disposing of one of the strongest currencies in the world towards the end of the twentieth century. In fact, some historians have considered this a renewed rise, as Frankfurt had been a major trade and banking centre from medieval times until Germany became unified in 1871, a move that brought Berlin to the fore as Germany's leading financial centre (Holtfrerich 2005; Cassis 2012). When Berlin became an island in the divided Germany, it took nearly four decades, however, for Frankfurt to evolve as Germany's undisputed financial centre (Grote 2004) and as an important European and international financial location (Holtfrerich 2005). Nowadays, Frankfurt is ranked second among Europe's financial centres.

This chapter takes a geographical perspective on the financial centre in general and Frankfurt in particular. First, the centre is a geographical place where proximities, social relations, and local endowments matter. Second, the centre is a node in financial networks, in areas of jurisdictional application, and, lastly, in political action. In organizational terms, it is a location of headquarters of banks and institutions, which direct the geographical functioning of actors in the financial system. While the first aspect may raise ideas about competition between places, the second one also considers the workings of a spatial division of labour in a network of different financial locations. Also, a second-rank financial centre such as Frankfurt is exposed to a double squeeze of centripetal forces up to the top, London, and centrifugal forces down to regional financial centres. Due to Germany's political history and current federal organization, regional financial centres such as Munich (insurance, venture capital) or Düsseldorf (private banking) still compete in certain financial activities (Klagge and Martin 2005). As Frankfurt plays in a different league nowadays, centrifugal forces might also work in favour of other European financial centres, among them offshore centres.

The international financial centre Frankfurt is strongly embedded into a socio-economic national system that has been characterized as a 'coordinated market economy' (Hall and Soskice 2001). The foundational narrative of the 'German model' in post-World-War-II Germany focuses on the vision of a 'social market economy', based on ordo-liberalism as the special 'ideological edifice' (Dullien and Guérot 2012),[1] that combines the setting and strong control of workable markets with the social responsibility of the economy. This vision still holds today, at least rhetorically, among political agents, the majority of academics in economics, and the media. As a matter of fact, neo-liberalism came rather hesitantly to Germany and its financial sector through deregulation laws ('Finanzmarktfördergesetz') in 1990, 1994, 1998, and, shortly before the crises, in 2002. Ordo-liberalism also resurged when the German parliament agreed upon a general debt brake to public budgeting by changing the constitution, in the crises, and when the German government insisted on national responsibilities in the EU and tried to impose austerity policies upon other Eurozone countries (Steinberg and Vermeiren 2016).

---

[1] Ordo-liberalism was developed as a theory from the 1930s onwards by the Freiburg school on national economy and became particularly powerful in the recovery period of the 'Wirtschaftswunder' during the 1950s and 1960s. Meanwhile, ordo-liberalism has been hybridized with Keynesian ideas, according to Young (2014).

Germany's financial system has also been considered different from that of the Anglo-Saxon world. The bank-based system, focusing on universal banks that provided 'patient' capital to companies and companies preferring finance in the form of bank credits (Krahnen and Schmidt 2004; Wojcik and MacDonald-Korth 2015) might have been considerably eroded since the 1990s, ironically due in part to changing strategies of the then three large private banks, all located in Frankfurt.[2] Yet, the 'three-pillar-banking system' considered 'unique' has nonetheless survived (Krahnen and Schmidt 2004; Behr and Schmidt 2015). It consists of: private banks, including the three big banks functioning on the eve of the crises (Deutsche Bank, Dresdner Bank, and Commerzbank); a strong sector of savings banks governed by local communities, limited to local markets, and backed by the regional Landesbanken and the central Deka-Bank in Frankfurt; and the sector of local cooperative banks backed by the central DZ-Bank, also in Frankfurt. Additionally, a fair number of special banks exist, such as mortgage banks, building and loan associations, and other 'special purpose banks', among them the large governmental bank Kreditanstalt in Frankfurt. The three pillars have been involved in the crises in very different ways.

At the dawn of the financial crises, Germany had recovered from its long recession of the 1990s in a timely manner. Labour-market policies have been highlighted as the backbone of the renewed economic competitiveness of the German industries and the emerging resilience to the crises (Dustmann et al. 2014; Hope and Soskice 2016; Steinberg and Vermeiren 2016). Actually, after having experienced a very short period of collapse in 2008–9, employment grew considerably in the subsequent stages of the financial crises, the German manufacturing sector regained its export strength, and capital exports rose further. Finally, the German economy benefitted from the weakness of the euro, as one of the consequences from the Eurozone crisis.

5.2 The Crises

The global financial crisis has been often described as having developed in two or three steps, starting first with the banking crisis, and turning next into the sovereign debt crisis of the Eurozone (for details, see Lane 2012). The Eurozone crisis then developed into a crisis of monetary policy when the burden of financial restructuring mainly allocated to Southern Europe resulted in a

---

[2] There is an ongoing controversy between scholars who claim that part of the German model has been eroded in the financial sector and the German financial system has converged 'closer' to the Anglo-American one (Dixon 2014), while others confirm the survival of the German model (Engelen et al. 2010). Behr and Schmidt (2015, p. 14) have argued that the German banking system remains relatively stable due to the fact that 'only a minority of German banks, representing not even half of total bank assets, is private and at the same time exclusively profit oriented'.

deflationary period between 2013 and 2015, prompting the European Central Bank (ECB) to increase liquidity by means of a quantitative easing policy (Steinberg and Vermeilen 2016). Banks are still considered the most important 'channels for financial intermediation' in Europe (Reichlin 2014). As a result, banks had to cope with shifting challenges over time, but were exposed in different ways to the crises according to their business models.

5.2.1 *The banking crisis of 2008 and 2009*

Many German banks were caught by the crisis at a moment when they were confident in their growth. In times of increasing deregulation, in the 1990s, the top two large private banks, Deutsche Bank and Dresdner Bank, both located in Frankfurt, had invested in powerful investment banking activities in London. Deutsche Bank had started investment banking in 1989 by acquiring the London-based Morgan Grenfell and became highly involved in international investment banking with the takeover of the New York-based Bankers Trust in 1999. Dresdner Bank, Germany's second large private bank, acquired the London-based Kleinwort Benson in 1995 and the New York-based Wasserstein Perella in 2001. Banks from two contrasting types of locations are considered to have been highly involved in the financial innovation of subprime products in pre-crisis times: banks in the innovative cores such as New York and London; and banks located in less information-rich places and with a weak business model (Engelen 2009). This neatly matches with empirical evidence in Germany where banks predominantly hit by the crisis either had subsidiaries for investment banking in London and New York or were located at regional financial centres such as Düsseldorf (IKB, a bank for small and medium-sized businesses, and the Landesbank WestLB) and Munich (Hypo Real Estate Bank, HRE). However, the most seriously hit bank in Frankfurt was Commerzbank, Germany's third-largest private bank, which had decided to take over the failing Dresdner Bank just at the time when the crisis was unfolding. Obviously, it was not the German mortgage sector that caused the banking crisis in Germany.

When the evolving crisis affected the whole economy rather quickly, it triggered a number of policy measures in an often ad-hoc way. A continuous flow of directives and laws on finance has been adopted in Germany since that time. As early as September 2008, Bafin (Bundesanstalt für Finanzdienstleistungsaufsicht, the Federal Financial Supervisory Authority) banned short-selling.[3] On 5 October of that year, Chancellor Merkel publicly announced that private bank accounts 'are safe', thus assuring the legal deposit guarantee

---

[3] Bafin has been the German supervisory organization for banks, insurance, and securities since 2002 (Allfinanz supervision). It is located in Bonn.

of €100,000 per private client account.[4] Also in October, the government created the Bundesanstalt für Finanzmarktstabilisierung (the financial-market stabilization agency, FMSA),[5] based in Frankfurt, and established a special fund in order to bail out banks quickly (Sonderfonds Finanzmarktstabilisierung, Soffin)[6] by the means of guarantees (up to €400 billion) and equity participation (up to €80 billion), agreed upon only one week later by the EU Commission. However, the government resisted pressures from domestic groups as well as from abroad to enter into a general stabilization policy.

5.2.2 The European Sovereign Debt Crisis of 2010 and After

The European sovereign debt crisis—or the euro crisis for short—erupted in 2010 in countries 'at the economic fringes' of the European Union: Ireland, Greece, Spain, and Portugal, and culminated in a haircut for private investors in Greece in 2012. Here, we do not wish to go into details, neither on the fundamental issues and deficiencies of the creation of a common currency, the euro, nor the subsequent negotiations between European governments, the ECB, and the EU Commission on policy issues regarding how to cope with the crisis. Suffice to say that the German government, on the basis of a newly revitalized economic strength (low unemployment rate, high exportation rate), attempted to minimize the risks from a common European policy on bank and state bailouts.

This crisis has been reported several times as being a consequence of the banking crisis. Banking, sovereign debt crises, and the crisis of the euro have become inseparably interwoven (Lane 2012), and so have policies at the domestic and European level. Steinberg and Vermeiren (2016) carefully analysed the increasing inability of the German government to enforce its ideas (and that of Deutsche Bundesbank) about political responses to the crises. Increasingly, political responses have become European. For instance, the European Finance Stability Fund (EFSF) came into being in 2010 as a temporary anchor and part of the wider European Stability Mechanism that started to work in 2012. Becoming increasingly afraid of deflationary processes from 2013, the ECB started a programme of quantitative easing by buying sovereign debt papers, and from January 2015 also corporate bonds (Steinberg and Vermeiren 2016). With the Single Supervisory Mechanism agreed upon by

---

[4] Savings rates are still rather high in Germany and households still prefer to hold their money in savings accounts, mostly at savings and cooperative banks.

[5] According to FMSA Neuordnungsgesetz of July 2016, FMSA will be integrated into the national financial control organization Bafin by 2018. In 2011, FMSA became responsible for administering the newly created fund for the restructuring of banks to be financed through bank allocations, and, in 2015, for the tasks of the German national resolution authority.

[6] Soffin was closed in 2015, its activities transferred to the Finanzagentur, the state agency for debt sovereignty management in Frankfurt (founded in 2000).

the European financial ministers in December 2012, a focal supervisory unit of large banks had been created under the umbrella of the ECB, starting in 2014. Much could be said about the incremental and conflict-laden way in which European governments strove to get to grips with the crises. As the ECB took an increasing part in saving the euro currency, Frankfurt simply became a metaphor for currency and European banking policies and supervision.

Traditionally, Deutsche Bundesbank was the major backbone of the financial centre before the introduction of the euro. Deutsche Bundesbank remains an important voice in the European chorus, however, not least due to the importance of the German real economy. Deutsche Bundesbank is responsible for the macro-prudential supervision of the German financial system and, together with the Bafin branch in Frankfurt, for the micro-prudential supervision of banks in Germany. The FMSA has also been allocated a role here, and—given that Germany is a federal republic comprised of sixteen federal states (Länder)—the Land of Hesse supervises the stock exchange through a local branch in Frankfurt (the Land capital is Wiesbaden). Furthermore, and following an agreement at the European level, the European Insurance and Occupational Pensions Authority (EIOPA) was established in Frankfurt in 2011.[7] As a result, Frankfurt has become what some recently have called the 'capital of European supervision' or 'supervision metropolis' (Bischoff 2014), mirroring the hope for a rising attractiveness to (foreign) financial institutions— when, at the same time, Frankfurt's private banks were weakening.

5.3 Frankfurt's Major Actors Coping with the Crises

During the last ten years Frankfurt as a financial centre has experienced a mixture of increasing strength of some financial agents, delayed restructuring and continuous weakness of others, and the appearance of new agents challenging traditional business processes and market structures.[8] The IFC Frankfurt can be considered a local financial cluster that brings together a diversity of actors in finance, financial services, and supporting public and private services (Schamp 2009). Nonetheless, large banks and the stock exchange still form the flagships in Frankfurt around which a host of diverse but smaller businesses abound. These are the leading international Deutsche Bank and some other domestic banks such as Commerzbank and DZ Bank,

---

[7] The corresponding EBA and ESMA were allocated in London and Paris, respectively. Interestingly, Frankfurt is not a focal centre of insurance in Germany (Munich, Hamburg, and Cologne fulfilling that role).

[8] Section 5.3 is based on relevant literature and an analysis of documents from leading journals such as Frankfurter Allgemeine Zeitung, Wirtschaftswoche, Die ZEIT, and others, published between 2008 and 2017.

and the Deutsche Börse. All of them are multinationals, hence their strategic interests do not focus on the development of the financial centre per se but have a major impact on it. It seems that government efforts at various levels are more closely oriented to Frankfurt's development, in re-regulating the financial business and improving the competitiveness of the financial centre.

5.3.1 *The Unfinished Restructuring of the Banks*

As mentioned in Section 5.2.1, there were some major takeovers in the sector shortly before or even during the first stage of the crises that exposed the respective banks to extreme risks and even caused some failures. For example, the Munich-based Hypo Real Estate (a mortgage bank), which had integrated Depfa, a sovereign debt finance institution based in Dublin, as recently as 2007, had to be bailed out by the Soffin fund shortly after, with the highest amount ever disbursed to a bank, and was finally dissolved in 2016. In Frankfurt, Commerzbank had taken over Eurohypo, a mortgage bank, among others, and, in an even bolder move, had decided to take over the loss-making Dresdner in 2008. Deutsche Bank had taken over the retail bank Postbank (Bonn) in 2008 and the failed private investment bank Sal. Oppenheim jr. & Cie (Cologne) in 2009.

Deutsche Bank is unquestionably the leading bank in Frankfurt in international terms. In 2016, the G20 committee ranked the bank the sixth most important bank among thirty in terms of its systemic importance for the global financial system and it was considered the leading systematically important bank in the euro area at the end of 2015 (Batsaikhan et al. 2017). The bank, however, has undergone various shifts in its strategy under varying CEOs, was involved in a number of affairs causing tremendous costs in terms of penalties, and has not been profitable over a span of many years. Yet, even after a continuing contraction of activities, the balance sheet total of Deutsche Bank was by far the highest in Germany with €1.6 trillion in 2016, three times more than its closest followers DZ Bank, Kreditanstalt, and Commerzbank (each around €0.5 trillion, in descending order).

While the US and UK authorities were coming to terms with the financial crises, Deutsche Bank, similarly to some other large banks, was blamed for multifarious violations of regulations. Being involved in affairs relating to the US subprime business, in US tax affairs, in manipulating the euro LIBOR in the United States and London, not to mention some 'minor' manipulations in gold and silver pricing or automatic securities trading in dark pools, for which authorities have brought an action and set punishments recently, Deutsche Bank had to bear huge costs in legal services and penalties (approximately €13 billion as of November 2016). Widely considered a systemic risk, the bank needed to substantially increase its capital. Nevertheless, its credit rating was reduced in 2016. In several rounds, 2010, 2013, and 2017, the bank raised up to €30 billion of fresh capital on public and private markets. New major shareholders appeared, such as the state of Qatar (2014) and the private Chinese HNA Group (2017). Furthermore, the bank had considerable problems in developing a new business model in the same period. Still widely anchored in London with investment banking, the bank reduced this activity considerably in 2016 to slightly more than 20 per cent of all its businesses. In retail banking, Deutsche Bank first proposed to integrate, then, in 2015, to sell Postbank, and—in the absence of an acceptable offer—proposed to fully integrate Postbank once again in 2017. In sum, the bank still appears to lack a clear strategy to shape its future after the crises. The corollary of this has been a reduction of employment all over the world and at the headquarters in Frankfurt.

Commerzbank was the smallest among the 'big three' private banks in Germany before the crises, when the second-largest one, Dresdner Bank, experienced a long period of decline, finally taking shelter under the umbrella of the powerful Munich-based Allianz insurance company in 2001. Commerzbank, wishing to take over Dresdner, promised to relieve Allianz of the burden of a loss-making bank and to fulfil the dreams of some observers to create a second bank of international significance in Frankfurt. Commerzbank had focused on real estate, fund management, and Eastern Europe, while Dresdner had been much involved in investment banking. The crises descended upon this takeover endeavour with dramatic effect. The performance of Dresdner became so disastrous that, shortly after the takeover, Commerzbank was one of the first German banks that it had to be bailed out by Soffin. Soffin took a share of 25 per cent (plus one share) of the bank in January 2009. By order of the EU Commission, Commerzbank had to substantially reduce its business activities. The bank subsequently reduced investment banking activities in London, New York, and Tokyo in 2010; it sold its sovereign bonds (in particular the Greek ones) in 2012; it started to withdraw from shipping finance—one of the business fields where German banks have traditionally been world leaders—in 2012, and from real estate funds in 2013; it sold its custodian activities to the French BNP Paribas in 2013; and in 2015 it sold the international private banking division (wealth management) to the Swiss private bank Julius Bär, which decided to concentrate these activities in Luxembourg.

Restructuring a bank is a long-term process, however. Relocation of some investment banking activities from London (to Frankfurt, among others) still continued in 2014 and 2015. And yet, the bank still had to write off parts of Dresdner Bank in 2016. Eurohypo, having emerged as another huge burden to the bank, was finally closed down in 2016 due to a lack of buyers. Although several rounds of raising new capital have taken place, Soffin's stake in Commerzbank is 15.6 per cent and the bank will have to write off some further activities. Commerzbank is currently strengthening its role as a strong domestic bank focusing on 'Mittelstand' finance and private wealth management in Germany.

Not unexpectedly, the two other 'pillars' of the German financial sector, the savings and cooperative bank sectors, have also been exposed to the crises, and so have their central organizations. Landesbanken, which had been heavily engaged in subprime products, had to be restructured, similarly to Dekabank, which had become the savings banks' centre of investment banking and fund management in Frankfurt. The cooperative bank sector was less involved in high-risk financial activities and, hence, suffered less from the crises. The sector's central bank at Frankfurt, DZ Bank (Deutsche Zentralgenossenschaftsbank), can even be considered a winner of the crises. DZ Bank finally integrated the smaller WGZ (based in Essen) in 2016 to become Germany's third-largest bank and the only central bank for Germany's cooperative banks.

It seems that foreign banks in Frankfurt did not suffer in the same way. Foreign banks had come to Frankfurt in several waves, in the 1970s, the 1980s and the 1990s (Grote 2004), making Frankfurt the major centre of foreign banks in Germany and the second-largest centre in Europe after London (Bischoff 2016a). While the number of active subsidiaries or foreign branches remained stable over ten years, standing at 158 in 2007 and 156 in 2016, respectively (see Figure 5.1), some foreign banks closed their representative offices (without a banking licence) in Frankfurt, reducing the total to thirty-three in 2016. According to a Helaba survey conducted in 2010, many foreign banks were also active in other European financial centres, at the top of which was London, and yet the business area of Frankfurt branches extends to the whole continent (Bischoff 2011). Long before the crises, some other banks had become involved in domestic retail banking through takeovers, such as the large Dutch ING-Diba direct bank. Retail banking in Germany, however, has long been a contested field.

Nevertheless, the after-crises consolidation process of banks at the European level had its effects on foreign banks in Frankfurt too. For instance, the Swedish SEB sold the traditionally trade union-related retail bank, Bank für Gemeinwirtschaft, taken over in 2000, to the Spanish Santander Bank in 2011. SEB Germany now focuses on corporate finance, institutional investors, and real estate finance, just as the French BNP Paribas or Credit Suisse do in Frankfurt. The Dutch ABN Amro bank had merged with Bethmann Bank, a traditional private bank[9] in Frankfurt, along with other private banks in 2004 and planned to sell the latter to the Belgian Fortis bank in 2008. Fortis was one of the first victims of the crisis, however, and went bankrupt just at this

---

[9] Bethmann was founded in 1748.

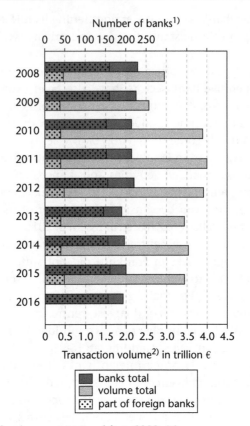

Number of banks[1]

Figure 5.1. Bank development in Frankfurt, 2008–16

Notes: 1) Central banks, banks and exchanges, according to the definition of Deutsche Bundesbank. 2) Transaction volume: balance sheet total + contingent liabilities. Change in balance sheet regulation in 2010, later figures are not comparable to earlier years.

Source: Author, based on data from Deutsche Bundesbank (2017).

moment. When ABN Amro was nationalized by the government of the Netherlands, Bethmann still survived by focusing exclusively on wealth management for the rich. As such, it took over the LGT bank (based in Liechtenstein) in 2011. Wealth management in Frankfurt was recently further strengthened when the Swiss UBS, reorganizing its European wealth management and investment banking in 2016, chose Frankfurt as its European headquarters.

It is obvious that banks active in Germany, with its quickly recovering economy and its ongoing prosperity, have benefitted, while using Frankfurt as a bridge to the European continent. As a consequence, many banks strive to improve access to certain customer groups in Germany, predominantly the German 'Mittelstand' in credit, trade finance, and even the Mittelstand's international investments, as well as wealthy individuals through private wealth management.

5.3.2 *Deutsche Börse*

Another winner of the crises is Deutsche Börse AG, the stock exchange company in Frankfurt. The joint-stock company had come into being as a result of the first deregulation phases in the German financial system,[10] in 1993, and had subsequently grown to a diversified group through mergers with the electronic futures exchange (Eurex) and clearing house as well as through technological innovation. Deutsche Börse was one of the first to introduce electronic exchange trading through Xetra in 1997. Since then, the company has pursued a clear-cut strategy of technological leadership in Europe. As a consequence, Frankfurt dominated the eight regional stock exchanges in Germany. More importantly, the Deutsche Börse emerged as a leading stock exchange on the European continent (Holtfrerich 2005) by the end of the 1990s, competing successfully with London.

Deutsche Börse has developed into a diversified and powerful financial group. With the shift from floor trading to electronic exchange (finalized in May 2011), offering the opportunity to trade 'remotely' (mostly from London), the stock exchange has become a virtual place under high competitive pressure. Grote and others (Grote 2004; Engelen and Grote 2009) have explained the centripetal forces of electronic exchanges by the size of markets providing liquidity, the number of traders providing an information-rich environment, and the opportunities to achieve cost reduction. The competitive squeeze resulted in repeated attempts to take over foreign stock exchanges, and Deutsche Börse participated in this international game actively (Grote 2007). In an interview, the then CEO of the London Stock Exchange (LSE) noted an 'everlasting duel' between LSE and Deutsche Börse (Wirtschaftswoche 2013). In fact, merger attempts with LSE proved unsuccessful in 2000 and 2004–5 (Grote 2007; Engelen and Grote 2009) and failed again in 2017. Other takeover attempts have similarly failed (e.g. of Euronext, Paris, in 2006), while the takeover of the International Securities Exchange (ISE) in New York in 2007 was successful. Such takeovers are highly determined by political power. Take the recent attempt of merging Deutsche Börse with LSE, for instance. Both companies had agreed to the merger and to locating the headquarters of the merged company in London. However, several political institutions had to agree as well. First, the EU commissioner on competition had some reservations concerning the clearing of derivatives. Then, the government of the Land of Hesse, afraid of losing control of the Deutsche Börse, vetoed the planned relocation of the headquarters to London. It seems, however, that the ultimate reason to stop the merger has been the

---

[10] The process of stock exchanges going public, i.e. turning into for-profit enterprises, was widespread in Europe in the 1990s; see Grote (2007).

fact that neither partner foresaw Brexit and its implications for further control by German and EU institutions. In fact, the final blow came with the official request by the British government to leave the EU, formally announced on 29 March 2017. Another attempt to create Europe's largest securities market-place has failed.

Efforts in technology apparently enabled Deutsche Börse to withstand the crises, but produced ambiguous effects as well. On the one hand, electronic trading accelerated the 'speed to market' tremendously, allowing for very short time arbitrage through high-speed trading. Deutsche Börse fostered co-location at Frankfurt in renting computers and delivering data near to their computer centre. Yet, high-speed trading and co-location have recently drawn serious criticism from large customers such as fund management and insurance companies and are treated by Bafin with suspicion. Technological advancement has also encouraged the emergence of alternative trading platforms or so-called 'dark pools', more or less uncontrolled private platforms, which were enabled by the EU's MiFID I directive in 2007. Most of them are located in London and cannot be controlled by Bafin. Subsequently, the share of trade at Xetra was considerably reduced, affecting Xetra's liquidity.[11] Since MiFID II entered into force in January 2017, among other regulations, dark pools and high-speed trading are increasingly being brought under control.

5.3.3 Initiatives in Financial R&D and Innovation

The leading German banks adopted major financial innovations, including derivatives, during the 1990s. However, there was an extremely large gap in terms of public infrastructure in higher education and research for financial innovation in Frankfurt, compared to London and Paris. Various initiatives had emerged to establish a meaningful public knowledge base for the financial sector only shortly before the crises. The Bank Academy, the bank-funded private institution for further education in finance, turned into a business school at university level under the label 'Frankfurt School of Finance and Management', even earning the right to award doctoral degrees in 2004. The then state Goethe University—re-gaining autonomy through its reorganization into a foundation-based yet widely publicly funded university in 2008[12]— established a new school, the House of Finance, which integrated all education and research in economic and legal sciences on financial issues (becoming operational in 2008). Now, multifarious opportunities for collaboration with

---

[11] The German law on high-speed trading of 2013 anticipated the MiFID II regulations (Gomber and Nassauer 2014).

[12] Originally founded as Germany's first foundation-based privately funded university in modern times, in 1914.

the financial sector were arising, such as in applied research projects or by investment in endowed chairs. There are further, more remote institutions of higher education in financial issues such as the private European Business School (in Östrich-Winkel near Wiesbaden) or the Centre for European Economic Research (ZEW) in Mannheim. They attract an increasing number of students from abroad and make available a highly qualified labour force to the financial centre (Bischoff 2016a).

Thus, the human resource base of the financial centre improved considerably while the crises were unfolding. Also, the House of Finance decided to focus its major research on risk management and regulation policies. Given the multifarious attempts to re-regulate financial markets at the European scale, it comes as no surprise that this research is pursued in close collaboration with the proximate regulatory authorities in Frankfurt such as the ECB and the EIOPA (Bischoff 2014). Technology is another research issue that was and still is urgent, given the overwhelming dominance of London in digital innovation. A recent Ernst&Young report (Ernst&Young 2016a) placed the German fintech landscape third in the world, yet far behind the US (New York and California) and the UK (London). The spatial pattern of fintech start-ups closely relates to Germany's decentralized urban structure. Berlin, currently seen as the hot spot of start-ups in Germany, is the leading centre, Frankfurt struggles to catch up, and Munich follows closely behind. A clear division of labour has emerged, with Berlin focusing on B2C activities such as payments and banking & lending, while Frankfurt concentrates on B2B activities (such as enabling processes and technologies) and regulation ('regtech') (Ernst&Young 2016b).[13] Munich is developing in the areas of technology and insurance (Ernst&Young 2016a; 2016b). A number of initiatives to establish a fintech ecosystem in the Rhein-Main-Neckar region have recently emerged, involving various actors such as universities (Goethe University, Technical University Darmstadt), large private firms (Deutsche Börse, Commerzbank, Deutsche Bank), state agencies, and other organizations (Ernst&Young 2016b).

Fintech firms are still small in size. Yet, large players such as the two leading private banks and foreign retail banks (ING-Diba) are active in some B2C fintech segments, and have recently taken over start-ups or collaborate with them, in addition to investing in digital labs of their own. For instance, Deutsche Börse took over the electronic forex trade platform 360T, a fintech firm founded in 2000 in Frankfurt, in 2015. This offers a web-based platform for investors called 'venture network' (for later-stage start-ups and IPOs of all sectors) and provides cost-free space for start-ups (Bischoff 2016a). Deutsche

---

[13] Fintech is a poorly defined innovative part of the financial sector based on digitalization. Market segments are inconsistently defined also.

Bank started its 'digital factory' in 2016 with 400 software engineers, IT and finance experts—expected to grow to 800 by 2018—while the total employment of Frankfurt fintech firms was estimated at a much lower level in the same year (Bischoff 2016a).[14] Another large investor is DZ-Bank, opening its innovation lab in 2016. The rather small but rapidly growing fintech sector is increasingly regulated by Bafin and the EU; some business activities now even require a banking licence. Two consequences seem to be obvious. First, fintech is not emerging as disruptively as some would believe. Second, Frankfurt 'has great potential to become the leading German Fin Tech hub' (Ernst&Young 2016a, p. 8) due to the proximity to headquarters of banks, proximity to regulatory authorities, and, not least, to a particular infrastructural environment, as Frankfurt hosts Europe's, if not the world's, largest Internet node (DE-CIX).

To sum up, the IFC Frankfurt has considerably improved its finance-related education, science, and technological base in the long period of overcoming the crises. And yet, although it has caught up in R&D with the two leading centres in financial research and education in Europe, London and Paris, it still operates on a smaller scale than both those places in this regard. Frankfurt, at least, has a chance to become Europe's second centre in digital technologies in the financial sector, after London.

5.4 Frankfurt, a Resilient Place

The public media have painted an ambiguous picture of the position of Frankfurt as a financial centre over time. Before 2008, the labels 'Bankfurt' or 'Mainhattan' communicated the image of prosperous large banks residing in huge towers. Later, in 2012, the financial centre Frankfurt was named 'Angstfurt', due to the unfolding euro crisis and the emergence of various bank scandals, only to be called a 'silent winner' not much later, in 2013. These short-term narratives uncover the highly emotional, irrational attitudes towards the financial sector, which are nourished by an increasing feeling of uncertainty and opacity. Yet, emotions apart, some factors reveal a considerable resilience of Frankfurt the financial centre.

Resilience is a recently popular concept that describes the structures, agency, and power to resist the impact of and to recover from crises (Martin and Sunley 2015). Resilience of a financial centre can be seen from the perspective of a place or a node. First, there is the impact of the crises on the

---

[14] One must be very cautious in reading these figures. Ernst&Young (2016a) listed about 250 fintech companies and a staff of 13,000 people in Germany as a whole. Frankfurt, called the 'promising second' centre, should have more than a few hundred employees in the sector according to Ernst&Young.

place, its people, and local welfare. In various local dimensions, in particular the labour market, tax revenues, and the office and housing markets, Frankfurt has managed the crises very well. In contrast to continuously declining employment in Germany's banking sector, in line with many other European countries even before the crises, employment in the financial sector in Frankfurt has remained rather stable. Total employment in financial services in the city of Frankfurt was calculated at 73,400 employees in 2008 and 74,400 in 2016 respectively (see also Wojcik and MacDonald-Kurth 2015). Employment in the banking sector per se declined slightly between 2012 and 2016. According to headlines of Helaba publications there was a 'moderate cutback' in 2010, 'unfounded panic' in 2013, and a 'manageable consolidation' in 2014. Service sectors related to the financial sector, such as legal services and accountancy, advertising, and market research, as well as consultancy advanced considerably in the same period (see Figure 5.2). Altogether, Frankfurt has remained a rather small international financial centre compared to London and Paris, where 352,000 and 270,000 people respectively were employed in the financial sector (Batsaikhan et al. 2017).

The local labour market is determined to a considerable extent by banks. In 2012, the six largest banks accounted for more than 60 per cent of total

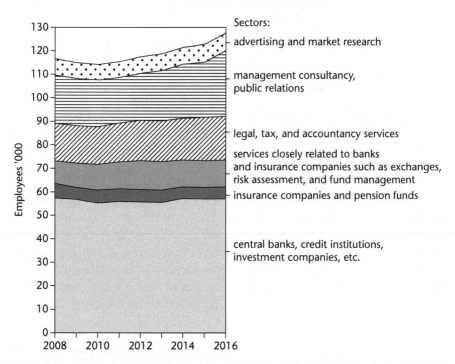

Figure 5.2. Employment in the financial sector and related services in Frankfurt, 2008–16
Source: Author, based on data from Bundesagentur für Arbeit BA Statistik Service Südwest.

Table 5.1. The largest employers in the IFC Frankfurt as of 2012 and 2016

Bank/institution	Type	Employment at the end of 2012	Employment at the end of 2016
Commerzbank AG	universal private bank	13,300	12,700
Deutsche Bank AG	universal private bank	9,700	*
DZ Bank Group	central institute of cooperative banks	5,900	9,300 after merger
Helaba Konzern	Landesbank	5,000	6,090
KfW Bank Group	public bank	3,350	*
DekaBank Deutsche Girozentrale	central institute of savings banks	3,000	3,600
Frankfurter Volksbank	local cooperative bank (retail)	1,400	1,140
ING-Diba AG	online retail bank (Dutch)	1,650	2,000
SEB AG	corporate banking + asset management (Swedish)	950	530
UBS Deutschland	European wealth management (Swiss)	750	600
BNP Paribas	universal bank (French)	750	*
ODDO-BHF-Bank	corporate banking + asset management (French)	600	650
Deutsche Börse	stock exchange	1,600	1,990
Deutsche Bundesbank	German Central Bank	3,650	4,730
European Central Bank	European Central Bank	1,650	3,170
Bafin, Frankfurt branch	local branch of German supervision authority	650	670
FMSA	public authority for bank bailout in Germany	70	125
EIOPA	European supervision of insurance companies	150	139

* data not available

Source: Author, based on Bischoff (2013) and own research.

employment in Frankfurt's banking sector. Restructuring of the two leading German private banks caused increasing fears of cutbacks. Quite the opposite occurred, as rising bank regulation was a major driver of increasing employment at the same time, both internally for the banks and externally at regulatory institutions, in particular the ECB (see Table 5.1).

Yet, limited employment figures signal a continuing disadvantage in economies of scale compared to London and Paris, for instance in the number and variety of professionals in the financial sector. On the other hand, the small spatial extent of the financial district offers closer informal, cultural proximities to those who work on more opaque products.[15] Or, to put it into economic terms: there are considerable economies of speed in Frankfurt (Grote 2002).

[15] When compared to Greater London and Greater Paris, employment figures are underestimated, for several reasons. For instance, financial companies sprawl to the wider Frankfurt-Rhein-Main region because of the small territorial size of the city, such as back offices spreading to Eschborn, insurance companies to Wiesbaden, and fund and bond rating to Bad Homburg.

With increasing innovation in financial products, internationalization, digitalization, and re-regulation in finance, the number and variety of professional services catering to the financial sector have become prominent, at least in business fields such as mergers and acquisitions (M&A), syndicated credits, or large OTC businesses. Hence, Frankfurt has become a main centre of business consulting in Germany, both domestic and foreign, and of international law and accountancy firms. A study on networking in the M&A business in Frankfurt revealed that this was and still is mainly in the hands of American investment banks (the four leading institutions being Goldman Sachs, Merrill Lynch, JPMorgan, and Morgan Stanley) collaborating with international accountants (such as EY, PwC, Deloitte, KPMG), lawyers, and tax consultants (Lo 2003). There is little empirical research on such local networks, not least as data on the number and origin of professional services involved are not available. It seems, however, that the well-known course of the crises is replicated here. While the M&A market of large takeovers quickly collapsed after 2008, American investment banks and international law firms used the opportunity to poach experts from their German competitors. They benefitted by increasing their market share in Europe, including Frankfurt, and by becoming active in mega-deals in Germany such as Bayer, Linde, and Deutsche Börse, since 2015.

Considering a functional perspective on resilience, Frankfurt specialized in financial activities that have been less affected by the crises. Actually, wealth and asset management, as well as lending to small and medium-sized firms (Mittelstand), have become growth activities, alongside other activities in which proximity to the customer matters. Frankfurt only played a minor role in forex trade, the derivatives trade, and investment banking, which were hit most severely by the crises, all activities in which London was and still is the leading player. Frankfurt-based large banks pursued these businesses mainly through their branches in London, indicating strong links between both financial centres (Faulconbridge 2004, Pain 2008). Less researched, however, are linkages to offshore financial centres. Preferred linkages from Germany (and Frankfurt) have been established to nearby offshore locations. Luxembourg, for instance, has emerged as a favourite site for fund administration used by German banks (Walther et al. 2011; Dörry 2015), among them large Frankfurt-based players such as DWS (part of Deutsche Bank Group), the DekaBank, and the Union Invest part of the DZ Bank Group. Luxembourg suffered only briefly from the crises (Walther et al. 2011). Liechtenstein and Zürich, both centres of wealth management for German investors (Merki 2005), faced more pressures from an intensifying international debate on tax havens and the prosecution of German taxpayers by German authorities.[16]

---

[16] Following the US policy on tax havens after 2008.

Professional services such as accountancy and law form the backbone of such networks between financial centres.

5.5 Opportunities and Challenges for Frankfurt's Future Role as the Leading Financial Centre on the European Continent

During the past three decades, Frankfurt has emerged as an important financial centre on the European continent. Since the shock of 2008, Frankfurt has obviously overcome the financial crises well. Although the adjustment of the banking sector lagged behind, Frankfurt strengthened its role as a centre of regulation, improved the knowledge base in both higher education and research, and made increasing efforts in the fintech sector. Much of what enabled Frankfurt to cope well with the crises happened during the crises, but not, however, due to the crises.

Many problems arising with the crises and the way in which authorities such as governments and the ECB have responded to them have not been solved yet. Neither the sovereign debt crisis of Southern European countries nor the requirements for banks to fundamentally change their business models have disappeared. That Frankfurt has been so resilient, then, can be attributed to Frankfurt's role as a leading financial centre on the continent embedded in Europe's most powerful domestic economy based on its exporting strength, in particular beyond the EU borders. In consequence, Frankfurt will continue to be an important financial centre on the continent as long as Germany's economy stays strong and benefits from world trade. Take, for instance, the case of the renminbi. While London remains the focal point of forex trade in this currency, Frankfurt has become China's first choice on the continent for trade finance. In fact, German exports to China doubled between 2009 and 2014, while imports from China have also increased considerably. China's leading public banks, which have offices in Frankfurt, focus on trade-related payment transactions and clearing in a 'follow-your-customer' strategy (Bischoff 2015). Trade in renminbi-based securities has become possible since 2015, when the China Europe International Exchange AG (CEINEX) was founded as a joint venture with Deutsche Börse. Furthermore, the range of business activities of Chinese (and other Asian) banks in Frankfurt is not limited to Germany but extends across the European continent (Bischoff 2015).

In view of these European functions, much has been speculated in recent times on whether Frankfurt could gain from the UK decision to leave the European Union—the so-called 'Brexit'. There are many uncertainties in this regard. The referendum in June 2016 was followed by the official exit notice by the UK government on 29 March 2017. Negotiations between the EU

Commission and governments on how to leave the European Union had just started at the time of writing and are expected to take at least two years. A major issue concerns the future passporting rights, i.e. the rights of UK-based banks (and other non-European banks located there) to be active through branches or subsidiaries across the EU.[17] This applies to some 5,500 financial firms (Sachverständigenrat 2016–17). Reducing passporting rights may imply that most of these firms need to apply for a full EU27 banking licence, which may entail relocating some employment from London into the local EU27 markets.

Wholesale banking, where London is by far the dominant location, is most affected. As the largest non-EU investment banks focus on London in terms of EU turnover (85 per cent to 96 per cent) and employment (70 per cent to 97 per cent) (Batsaikhan et al. 2017), relocation to continental financial centres in the EU27 seems obvious. During the summer of 2017, some American and Japanese investment banks have announced their intention to shift part of their business to Frankfurt. UBS relocated its European wealth management to Frankfurt in 2017. Commerzbank and Deutsche Bank have started to relocate some activities from London, due to the reduction or retreat from investment banking as a consequence of the crises. Altogether, foreign banks are very cautious, however, about reorganizing their business fields in favour of Frankfurt or other competing centres. An obvious, yet unsolved, issue is the future allocation of euro clearing, which has become so important in London since the Global Financial Crisis (Dörry 2017). Nonetheless, experts currently see Frankfurt as being in an advantageous position compared to the other two most attractive centres, Paris and Dublin.

The relocation of European authorities following Brexit, in particular that of the European Banking Authority (EBA) from London, is also unclear. According to recent speculation, the EBA could be either integrated into the ECB or integrated into a larger regulating authority with EIOPA, both of which would favour Frankfurt. Others discuss a reinforcement of ESMA in Paris. Obviously, this is a very political affair among EU27 governments and the EU Commission. Currently everybody, including representatives of local stakeholders, is highly involved in lobbying and negotiating. Political power in the EU still remains widely decentralized. Thus, the possible benefits stemming from a devaluation of London in the course of the Brexit process will probably not focus on only one financial centre on the continent, but will be distributed among several. It seems rather unlikely that the position of one of these centres in the network will change fundamentally.

---

[17] And vice versa, the right of currently about 8,000 EU banks to be active in the UK. Jens Weidmann (2017), the current president of the Deutsche Bundesbank, recently pointed to German banks possibly experiencing problems in doing business with London's financial sector after Brexit.

Summing up the prospects for Frankfurt resulting from Brexit, there seem to be good opportunities to strengthen the role of Frankfurt on the European continent. Some observers estimate that potentially some 10,000 jobs in total will move to Frankfurt within the next five years. This increase would counterbalance the forecast decline of employment in the banking sector (Bischoff 2016b). Thus, while the financial centre Frankfurt might gain in importance in functions such as investment banking and securities trade and cross-border linkages may also change, total employment in the financial sector might only slightly increase in the near future. Again, Frankfurt will remain a small financial centre compared to post-Brexit London, but nonetheless the leading one on the continent.

In the long run, Frankfurt's role as a significant financial centre might be undermined by two threats. With respect to the economic cohesion of the EU, some observers state an increasing paradox that may erode the long-term sustainability of the euro: namely, there is a clash of two different intra-European growth models existing at the same time, the Northern European—mainly German—export-led growth model versus the Southern European demand-led growth model (Johnston and Regan 2016), as long as Germany and other Northern European creditor countries stick to their austerity policies (Steinberg and Vermeilen 2016). The dissolution of the common currency, the euro, would seriously affect the role of Frankfurt as the leading financial centre on the continent. Another threat possibly arises from fundamental shifts in the global trade system that could undermine the successful German export-led growth model. For instance, current tendencies towards mercantilist trade policies of some powerful non-European countries, with the United States in the lead, may endanger global trade as we currently know it. These two macroeconomic and geopolitical issues have the power to fundamentally challenge Frankfurt's role as the leading financial centre on the European continent.

References

Batsaikhan, U., R. Kalcik, and D. Schoenmaker. 2017. 'Brexit and the European Financial System: Mapping Markets, Players and Jobs'. Brussels: Bruegel, Policy Brief 4.

Behr, P. and R. H. Schmidt. 2015. 'The German Banking System: Characteristics and Challenges'. Frankfurt: SAFE Policy Center, White Paper no. 32. http://safe-frankfurt. de/policy-center/policy-publications/policy-publ-detailsview/publicationname/-62520547dd.html, accessed 15 January 2018.

Bischoff, U. 2011. 'Financial Centre Frankfurt: A Magnet for Foreign Banks'. Frankfurt: Helaba Volkswirtschaft/Research. https://www.helaba.de/blob/helaba/55414/b437dfb 0c08ec0aee7f9b0328c18fc5b/report—a-magnet-for-foreign-banks—18-01-2011-data. pdf, accessed 15 January 2018.

Bischoff, U. 2013. 'The Largest Banks in Frankfurt Financial Centre'. Finanzplatz-Fokus 8, Nov. 2013. Frankfurt: Helaba Volkswirtschaft/Research. https://www.helaba.de/blob/helaba/98930/b4dae7cf7571fc52d9abe2e984f2249f/report—the-largest-banks-in-frankfurt-financial-centre—08-11-2013-data.pdf, accessed 15 January 2018.

Bischoff, U. 2014. 'Frankfurt: Hub of Finance and Supervision'. Finanzplatz-Fokus, March 2014. Frankfurt: Helaba Volkswirtschaft/Research. https://www.helaba.de/blob/helaba/130064/0317b85ece415e945af35f2cb897e024/report—frankfurt–hub-of-finance-and-supervision—20-03-2014-data.pdf, accessed 15 January 2018.

Bischoff, U. 2015. 'Finanzplatz Frankfurt: Aufwärts mit China'. Frankfurt: Helaba Volkswirtschaft/Research. https://www.helaba.de/blob/helaba/287234/71a3be332c0328c6a76e1982c4bd7d55/report—finanzplatz-frankfurt–aufwaerts-mit-china—11-03-2015-data.pdf, accessed 15 January 2018.

Bischoff, U. 2016a. 'Finanzplatz Frankfurt bewegt sich weiter. Jubiläumsausgabe'. June 2016. Frankfurt: Helaba Volkswirtschaft/Research. https://www.helaba.de/blob/helaba/391184/167a220da716e20db6d83f726859b099/report—finanzplatz-frankfurt–bewegt-sich-weiter-30-05-2016-data.pdf, accessed 15 January 2018.

Bischoff, U. 2016b. 'Brexit—Let's Go Frankfurt'. Finanzplatz-Fokus. Frankfurt: Helaba Volkswirtschaft/Research. https://www.helaba.de/blob/helaba/407460/ec93e042e5c3bbd7054e77121d7436d7/finanzplatz-fokus-20161103-data.pdf, accessed 15 January 2018.

Cassis, Y. 2012. Capitals of Capital. The Rise and Fall of International Financial Centres 1780–2009, 2nd edition. Cambridge: Cambridge University Press.

Dixon, A. D. 2014. The New Geography of Capitalism: Firms, Finance, and Society. Oxford: Oxford University Press.

Dörry, S. 2015. 'Strategic Nodes in Investment Fund Global Production Networks: The Example of the Financial Centre Luxembourg'. Journal of Economic Geography 15 (4): 797–814. doi:10.1093/jeg/lbu031

Dörry, S. 2017. 'The Geo-Politics of Brexit, the Euro and the City of London'. Geoforum 85: 1–4.

Dullien, S. and U. Guérot, U. 2012. 'The Long Shadow of Ordoliberalism: Germany's Approach to the Euro Crisis'. European Council on Foreign Relations Policy Brief, www.ecfr.eu/publications/summary, accessed 11 April 2017.

Dustmann, C., B. Fitzenberger, U. Schönberg, and A. Spitz-Oerner. 2014. 'From Sick Man of Europe to Economic Superstar: Germany's Resurgent Economy'. Journal of Economic Perspectives 28 (1): 167–88. doi:10.1257/jep.28.1.167

Engelen, E. 2009. 'Learning to Cope with Uncertainty: On the Spatial Distributions of Financial Innovation and its Fallout'. In Managing Financial Risks: From Global to Local, edited by G. L. Clark, A. D. Dixon, and A. H. B. Monk. Oxford: Oxford University Press, pp. 120–39.

Engelen, E. and M. Grote. 2009. 'Stock Exchange Virtualisation and the Decline of Second-Tier Financial Centres—The Cases of Amsterdam and Frankfurt'. Journal of Economic Geography 9 (5): 679–96. doi:10.1093/jeg/lbp027

Engelen, E., M. Konings, and R. Fernandez. 2010. 'Geographies of Financialization in Disarray: The Dutch Case in Comparative Perspective'. Economic Geography 86 (1): 53–73. doi:10.1111/j.1944-8287.2009.01054.x

Ernst&Young. 2016a. 'German FinTech Landscape: Opportunity for Rhein-Main-Neckar', March 2nd. Eschborn: Ernst&Young. http://www.ey.com/Publication/vwLUAssets/EY-FinTech-study-Germany/$FILE/EY-FinTech-study-Germany.pdf, accessed 17 May 2017.

Ernst&Young. 2016b. 'German FinTech Landscape: Opportunity for Rhein-Main-Neckar', Nov. 11th. Eschborn: Ernst&Young. http://www.ey.com/Publication/vwLUAssets/ey-fintech-studie-herbst-2016/$FILE/ey-fintech-studie-herbst-2016.pdf, accessed 17 May 2017.

Faulconbridge, J. R. 2004. 'London and Frankfurt in Europe's Evolving Financial Centre Network'. Area 36 (3): 235–44.

Gomber, P. and F. Nassauer. 2014. 'Neuordnung der Finanzmärkte in Europa durch Mifid II/Mifir'. White Paper Series 20. Frankfurt: House of Finance, SAFE Policy Center.

Grote, M. 2002. 'Frankfurt—An Emerging International Financial Center'. In Emerging Nodes in the Global Economy: Frankfurt and Tel Aviv Compared, edited by D. Felsenstein, E. W. Schamp, and A. Shachar. Dordrecht: Kluwer, pp. 81–107.

Grote, M. 2004. Die Entwicklung des Finanzplatzes Frankfurt. Berlin: Duncker & Humblot.

Grote, M. 2007. 'Mobile Marketplaces—Consequences of the Changing Governance of European Stock Exchanges'. Growth and Change 38 (2): 260–78.

Hall, P. A. and D. Soskice (eds). 2001. Varieties of Capitalism: The Institutional Foundations of Comparative Advantage. Oxford: Oxford University Press.

Holtfrerich, C. L. 2005. 'Frankfurts Weg zu einem europäischen Finanzzentrum'. In Europas Finanzzentren. Geschichte und Bedeutung im 20. Jahrhundert, edited by C. M. Merki. Frankfurt: Campus, pp. 53–81.

Hope, D. and D. Soskice. 2016. 'Growth Models, Varieties of Capitalism, and Macroeconomics'. Politics & Society 44 (3): 209–26. doi: 10.1177/0032329216638054

Johnston, A. and A. Regan. 2016. 'European Monetary Integration and the Incompatibility of National Varieties of Capitalism'. Journal of Common Market Studies 54 (2): 318–36. doi: 10.1011/jcms.12289

Klagge, B. and R. Martin. 2005. 'Decentralized Versus Centralized Financial Systems: Is There a Case for Local Capital Markets?' Journal of Economic Geography 5 (4): 387–421. doi:10.1093/jeg/lbh071

Krahnen, J. P. and R. H. Schmidt (eds). 2004. The German Financial System. Oxford: Oxford University Press.

Lane, P. R. 2012. 'The European Sovereign Debt Crisis'. Journal of Economic Perspectives 26 (3): 49–68. http://dx.doi.org/10.1257/jep.26.3.49, accessed 15 January 2018.

Lo, V. 2003. Wissensbasierte Netzwerke im Finanzsektor. Das Beispiel des Mergers & Acquisitions-Geschäfts. Wiesbaden: Deutscher Universitätsverlag.

Martin, R. and P. Sunley, P. 2015. 'On the Notion of Regional Economic Resilience: Conceptualization and Explanation'. Journal of Economic Geography 15 (1): 1–42. doi:10.1093/jeg/lbu015

Merki, C. M. 2005. 'Der Finanzplatz Liechtenstein: Zürichs attraktive Außenstelle'. In Europas Finanzzentren. Geschichte und Bedeutung im 20. Jahrhundert, edited by C. M. Merki. Frankfurt: Campus, pp. 167–95.

Pain, K. 2008. 'Spaces of Practice in Advanced Business Services: Rethinking London–Frankfurt Relations'. *Environment and Planning D: Society and Space* 26 (2): 264–79. doi:10.1068/d410t

Reichlin, L. 2014. 'Monetary Policy and Banks in the Euro Area: The Tale of Two Crises'. *Journal of Macroeconomics* 39: 387–400. doi:10.1016/j.macro.2013.09.012

Sachverständigenrat (German Council of Economic Advisors). 2016–17. Jahresgutachten 2016/17 'Zeit für Reformen'. https://www.sachverstaendigenrat-wirtschaft.de/, accessed 11 April 2017.

Schamp, E. W. 2009. 'Das Finanzzentrum—ein Cluster? Ein multiskalarer Ansatz und seine Evidenz am Beispiel von Frankfurt/Rhein-Main'. *Zeitschrift für Wirtschaftsgeographie* 53 (1–2): 89–105.

Steinberg, F. and M. Vermeiren. 2016. 'Germany's Institutional Power and the EMU Regime after the Crisis: Towards a Germanized Euro area?' *Journal of Common Market Studies* 54 (2): 388–407. doi: 10.1111/jcms.122555

Walther, O., C. Schulz, and S. Dörry. 2011. 'Specialised International Financial Centres and their Crisis Resilience: The Case of Luxembourg'. *Geographische Zeitschrift* 99 (2–3): 123–42.

Weidmann, J. 2017. 'Herausforderungen für den Bankensektor. Rede zum 21. Deutschen Bankentag, Berlin, 06.04.2017'. http://www.bundesbank.de/, accessed 18 May 2017.

Wirtschaftswoche. 2013. 'Unzufrieden und verärgert', interview with Xavier Rolet. 8 July, pp. 80–1.

Wójcik, D. and D. MacDonald-Korth. 2015. 'The British and the German Financial Sectors in the Wake of the Crisis: Size, Structure and Spatial Concentration'. *Journal of Economic Geography* 15 (5): 1033–54. doi:10.1093/jeg/lbu056

Young, B. 2014. 'German Ordoliberalism as Agenda Setter for the Euro Crisis: Myth Trumps Reality'. *Journal of Contemporary European Studies* 22 (3): 276–87. doi:10.1080/14782804.2014.937408

6

Zurich and Geneva

The End of the Golden Age

Tobias Straumann

6.1 Introduction

According to the Global Financial Centres Index (GFCI) of September 2017, Zurich and Geneva are in a strong position. Zurich ranks ninth, Geneva fifteenth, and they both belong to the group of global leaders. Most importantly, since the GFCI of March 2007, the last survey before the start of the Global Financial Crisis, the Swiss financial centres have managed to maintain their position. In continental Europe, Zurich is still number one, and Geneva, ranking fourth, has only slightly fallen back behind Frankfurt and Luxemburg (GFCI 2017).

Yet, given that Switzerland has abandoned banking secrecy for foreign clients, one of the pillars of its long-term success, the current GFCI appears to underestimate the changes since the Global Financial Crisis. For several indicators suggest that the golden age of Swiss banking is over. In the last ten years, the funds of foreign private clients deposited in Switzerland have more than halved. In the same period, the number of foreign-controlled banks has declined by a third, the number of their staff by a quarter. And as the profit margins of cross-border wealth management have markedly shrunk, half of all Swiss private banks functioning as partnerships have vanished.

This is not to say that Zurich and Geneva are about to disappear as global financial centres. Cross-border wealth management may have declined, but it is still considerable. Secondly, the Big Two, Credit Suisse and UBS, have returned to a more solid way of Swiss banking by shrinking risky parts of investment banking and strengthening their capital and liquidity ratios. The problem of 'too big to fail' is not solved, but less threatening than before 2007, contributing to a better reputation and greater stability. Thirdly, the other pillars of Zurich's and Geneva's success remain strong: infrastructure, human capital, political stability, and monetary stability. Fourth, Zurich still holds an important position as a centre of international reinsurance. Swiss Re has fully recovered from the financial crisis and successfully defended its position as the second largest reinsurer of the world.

But, despite all these advantages, there is no doubt that the age of low-hanging fruit is over. Zurich and Geneva have entered a period of stagnation, and neither a political event like Brexit nor a new trend like fintech is likely to change this scenario. Brexit will provide opportunities for larger financial centres within the EU like Frankfurt or Paris or an English-speaking centre like Dublin. Switzerland, neither a member of the EU nor the Eurozone, is too small a market and lacks the regulatory flexibility to become an international money and capital market. Fintech may provide something of a boost, but, presumably, the big gains will be reaped by international tech companies. And again, size matters. Big financial centres like London are in a better competitive position when new technologies are being developed.

The remainder of this chapter will lay out the arguments sketched above in five sections. Section 6.2 describes how Zurich and Geneva were affected by the global financial crisis. Section 6.3 provides evidence that the golden age of Swiss banking has come to an end. Section 6.4 looks at regulatory and domestic political consequences of the financial crisis. Section 6.5 discusses the most probable effects of Brexit and fintech. The chapter ends with a short conclusion.

6.2 Switzerland's Triple Shock

Switzerland was affected by the Global Financial Crisis in three respects. First, three major financial institutions, Credit Suisse and UBS as well as Swiss Re, suffered from losses on their asset side, forcing them to replenish their capital with funds from foreign investors. In addition, UBS was confronted with a looming liquidity crisis and sought the help of the government and the Swiss National Bank (SNB) in October 2008. Secondly, banking secrecy for foreign clients has been abolished. The steep rise of public debt in the wake of the crisis led the United States and Switzerland's European neighbours to intensify and to coordinate their efforts against tax evasion. The Swiss government, under great pressure from all sides, decided to yield and agree to the system of Automatic Exchange of Information on financial accounts of non-residents which would have been unthinkable before the Global Financial Crisis. Thirdly, the euro crisis unleashed several waves of capital inflows to Switzerland, prompting the Swiss National Bank (SNB) to intervene massively in the foreign exchange market, thus inflating its balance sheet, and to follow the European Central Bank (ECB) in pushing interest rates into negative territory.

6.2.1 *The UBS Crisis*

The size of the write-downs by Credit Suisse, UBS, and Swiss Re and the massive government intervention in favour of UBS came as a surprise to most observers. UBS in particular had enjoyed an excellent reputation before the Global Financial Crisis. No fewer than 3,000 people were employed in risk management and control. The Chief Risk Officer was a full member of the Group Executive Board and head of the Risk Committee. Internal and external audits were conducted at high frequency. In 2005, its Chief Executive Officer was named 'European banker of the year'. In 2005 and 2006, UBS earned record high net profits amounting to more than CHF 10 billion (Straumann 2010).

On the other hand, there had been voices highlighting the thin capital cover of Credit Suisse and UBS for some time. As early as 2000, the parliament debated the stability of the Swiss banking system. The Swiss Finance Minister acknowledged the problem, but opposed higher capital requirements because it would run counter to international coordination measures (National Council 2000). The timing of the debate was conditioned by several events. First, the balance sheet of internationally oriented banks had expanded rapidly since the mid-1990s. Before 1990, they had used their enormous placing power stemming from their off-balance wealth management to internationalize their businesses; now they tapped into global money markets to expand their role in investment banking. Secondly, Union Bank of Switzerland (Schweizerische Bankgesellschaft) had suffered from great losses from the Asian Crisis of 1997–8 and was hit by the LTCM crisis in 1998. The episode showed the new vulnerability of the Swiss banking system. Third, the board of Union Bank of Switzerland agreed to merge with Swiss Bank Corporation (Schweizerischer Bankverein). A new banking giant was formed (Schütz 1998).

In the early 2000s, doubts about the business model of the internationally oriented banks were reinforced by the fact that Credit Suisse First Boston (then part of the Credit Suisse Group) had to absorb great losses in the wake of the stock market crisis. There were also criminal charges against the mergers and acquisitions (M&A) business division that had engineered several IPOs during the dot-com boom. Credit Suisse Group sold the insurance company Winterthur to AXA in order to rebuild its capital basis. At the same time, Credit Suisse and UBS continued to expand at a fast rate. In 2006, their combined balance sheet total amounted to 69 per cent of the balance sheets of the entire banking sector and to nearly 600 per cent of Swiss GDP. Equity as a share of total liabilities was only 3.4 per cent. The contract volumes of their outstanding derivative financial instruments were CHF 43.1 trillion.

The first problems emerged in March 2007 when the UBS hedge fund DRCM suffered from losses caused by its strong exposure in the US subprime market. DRCM was shut down in May 2007 and integrated into UBS. The crisis began in the summer of 2007 when the market for mortgage-backed securities dried up and affected even the top-rated segment. Accordingly, UBS reported enormous losses in the fourth quarter of 2007 and the first quarter of 2008. Credit Suisse fared better, but was hit by the financial crisis, too, suffering from considerable write-downs in the fourth quarter of 2007. To replenish its capital, UBS turned to foreign investors. It received funds amounting to CHF 13 billion from a Middle East investor and the Government of Singapore Investment Corporation Pte, and issued new shares worth more than CHF 15 billion. Credit Suisse believed that it could weather the crisis without additional capital.

In the second and third quarter of 2008, the storm seemed to calm down. But the fall of Lehman in mid-September 2008 unleashed a global scramble for liquidity which targeted the weakest links. UBS was particularly vulnerable because of its huge write-downs in late 2007 and early 2008 and the reluctance of the Swiss government to declare an unlimited guarantee of deposits, in contrast to most other European governments. In October 2008, UBS sought financial support from the SNB and the Swiss Confederation in order to avert a potential liquidity crisis. The SNB bought illiquid assets amounting to several dozens of billions of US dollars and put them into a special stabilization fund (StabFund) financed by a loan from the US Federal Reserve and by equity from UBS amounting to $3.9 billion designed to cover the first 10 per cent of any potential loss of the StabFund. The Swiss Confederation bought notes amounting to CHF 6 billion ($5.2 billion). The notes were to be converted into equity after thirty months, bearing an interest of 12.5 per cent. In addition, the Swiss Federal Banking Commission authorized Credit Suisse to grant a loan to Qatar, which was used by Qatar as capital investment in Credit Suisse in October 2008. As a result of this operation, the Qatar Investment Authority increased its holdings of shares and derivatives of Credit Suisse to a total of 9.9 per cent (Credit Suisse 2009). Altogether, Credit Suisse raised CHF 10 billion from Qatar and two other existing shareholders at the height of the financial crisis (Financial Times 2013).

The rescue operation worked well. The liquidity crisis of UBS came to a halt, and Credit Suisse survived the Lehman shock without reaching out for government help. In December 2008, UBS managed to strengthen its capital by issuing a Swiss covered bond amounting to CHF 2 billion via the Swiss Mortgage Bond Bank. In the aftermath, both the SNB and the Swiss Confederation made a profit. In November 2013, UBS bought back the formerly illiquid assets at a price that was $3.762 billion higher than when it sold them to the SNB, and the Swiss Confederation received more than CHF 1 billion in interest income. Of course, the Swiss rescue operation could only succeed because foreign central banks, notably the Federal Reserve, stabilized the financial system and some large economies such as China, Germany, and the United States provided a fiscal stimulus to sustain global demand.

Why was UBS so strongly affected by the crisis? Evidently, its senior directors and managers, as many others, had underestimated the fragility of the US housing market and its implications for the refinancing markets of the global financial system. As late as spring 2007, both the executive board and the chairman's office believed that it was too early to take measures regarding the funding and liquidity of the investment bank. In the summer of 2007, when they considered a funding freeze, it was already too late to avert great losses (Swiss Federal Banking Commission 2008; UBS 2008). Credit Suisse had been more prudent. Yet, in 2008 the crisis brought the bank the highest annual loss of its history, amounting to CHF 8.2 billion. And possibly, without the emergency capital increase in October 2008 partially financed by a Credit Suisse loan that was sanctioned by the Swiss authorities, the second-largest bank would have had more difficulty in weathering the global liquidity crisis.

The third Swiss financial institution seriously affected by the global financial crisis was Swiss Re, the world's second-largest reinsurer, headquartered in Zurich. The write-downs resulted from investments in asset-backed and mortgage-backed securities (ABSs/MBSs) and two credit default swaps (CDSs). In February 2009, Swiss Re announced that it had made a deal with Berkshire Hathaway (led by Warren Buffet) as an investor to strengthen the capital base. Berkshire Hathaway would buy a subordinated convertible bond amounting to CHF 3 billion and bearing an interest of 12 per cent which could be converted into shares three years after the issue. For its part, Swiss Re had the option of repaying the bond within three years, thus preventing Berkshire Hathaway acquiring a permanent stake. The deal worked well. As early as 2010 Swiss Re managed to prematurely repay the convertible bond issued to Berkshire Hathaway (Straumann 2013).

6.2.2 *The End of Banking Secrecy*

The end of banking secrecy for foreign clients, the second shock triggered by the global financial crisis to Switzerland, came as less of a surprise. Countries suffering from tax evasion and capital flight had protested about the preferential treatment of foreign clients by Swiss authorities for a long time (Guex 2000; Vogler 2006). In the 1920s, when capital flight to the Netherlands and Switzerland took off, France and Germany intervened in the League of

Nations. After the Second World War, the United States and France put pressure on Switzerland to abandon its special regime. In the 1960s Swiss banking and tax secrecy became a popular theme in movies (e.g. James Bond) and in comics (e.g. Astérix). Swiss bankers were drawn as stuffy clerks displaying enormous hidden criminal energy. In 1977, the Schweizerische Kreditanstalt (today Credit Suisse) was shattered by the news that the head of its subsidiary in the southern town of Chiasso had conducted illegal transactions. The Swiss banking community was forced to act and introduced an agreement on the Swiss banks' code of conduct with regard to the exercise of due diligence that would be amended several times.

The crucial event indicating that Swiss banking and tax secrecy would not be tolerated for ever was the conflict over dormant Jewish World War II bank accounts that broke out in the mid-1990s. The World Jewish Congress headquartered in New York, as well as individual members of Congress, the Clinton administration, and lawyers representing some of the heirs demanded a swift and thorough restitution of these dormant accounts. Their determined and concerted effort showed that the Swiss banks could no longer count on the same special relationship with Washington that they had enjoyed during the Cold War. At the same time, the Swiss banking community, not fully aware of the new geopolitical situation, underestimated the moral and political dimension of the claims and eventually had to pay more than one billion US dollars in order to settle the cases.

The Clinton administration also sought a new double taxation agreement with Switzerland and enforced the control of its citizens living outside of the United States by obliging foreign banks to accept the Qualified Intermediary Agreement (QI Agreement). Swiss banks were required to assist in the collection and remittance of withholding taxes on US securities from their US clients who lived outside of the United States. Similarly, the European Union (EU) gained concessions from the Swiss in the context of the Bilateral Agreements II concluded in 2004. Thus, on the eve of the financial crisis, Swiss banking and tax secrecy had already been weakened. However, both the banking community and the Swiss authorities thought they could preserve the nucleus of the secrecy by making minor concession in further negotiations.

Shortly before the UBS crisis Swiss banking secrecy came under strong pressure. As never before, the United States as well as French and German authorities started to criticize Switzerland for not being cooperative when it came to fighting tax evasion. The Swiss authorities always took the view that tax evasion was not considered a criminal offence by Swiss fiscal law and therefore did not justify international exchange of information. Only in the case of tax fraud, that is when the taxpayer deliberately provides false information about his or her income, did the Swiss authorities exchange information with foreign tax authorities (Meier et al. 2013). Now, in the wake of the Global Financial Crisis that drove up the deficits of public finances the US, French, and German governments were running out of patience (Emmenegger 2017).

The process leading to the fall of Swiss banking secrecy for foreign bank clients was set in motion in the spring of 2008. Bradley Birkenfeld, a former UBS banker, was arrested on charges of conspiracy to defraud the IRS and after pleading guilty agreed to cooperate with the US authorities. The IRS then authorized the serving of a 'John Doe' summons to UBS which led to a Deferred Prosecution Agreement of UBS with the US authorities. The US agreed to drop the John Doe summons if UBS was ready to pay a fine of $780 million and hand over information on 285 US clients who had supposedly committed tax fraud. In February 2009, the Swiss Financial Markets Supervisory Authority (FINMA) instructed UBS to provide the IRS with the information. In the summer of 2009, Switzerland agreed to hand over information on 4450 US clients who were under suspicion of tax evasion. With this step, the Swiss government de facto ended banking secrecy vis-à-vis the United States. To make the change formal, Switzerland agreed to a revision of its double tax treaty with the States. From now on, Swiss authorities were obliged to provide information not only in the case of tax fraud, but also in the case of tax evasion.

At the same time, the OECD, with the backing of the G20, put pressure on a number of countries that had some form of banking secrecy, among them Switzerland as well as Austria, Belgium, and Singapore. In March 2009 the Swiss government announced that Switzerland intended to adopt the OECD standard on administrative assistance in tax matters in accordance with Article 26 of the OECD Model Tax Convention and subsequently revised double taxation treaties with a number of countries. As in the US case, Switzerland agreed to provide information in the case of tax evasion. The process was accelerated by the theft by employees of Swiss banks of information on bank accounts of foreign clients that was eventually sold to French and German authorities and used by them to proceed against tax evaders. In June 2013 the Swiss government went a step further by announcing that it was prepared to cooperate actively, within the scope of the OECD, on the development of a global standard for the Automatic Exchange of Information (AEoI) providing for the exchange of non-resident financial account information with the tax authorities in the account holders' country of residence. Participating jurisdictions send and receive pre-agreed information each year, without having to send a specific request. Finally, in December 2015, Swiss parliament adopted the federal law on AEoI. The end of banking secrecy was sealed. Switzerland started collecting data in January 2017 and plans to exchange it for the first time in 2018. Currently, it is looking into widening the new system to countries outside the OECD.

6.2.3 *The Euro Crisis*

The third shock that affected Switzerland was linked to the euro crisis that started in spring 2010. It had two negative consequences for Zurich and Geneva (Baltensperger and Kugler 2017). First, it triggered several waves of capital inflows which put upward pressure on the Swiss franc. In December 2009 the Swiss franc was quoted at 1.50 euro; in August 2011 it approached parity. This dramatic appreciation prompted the SNB in September 2011 to intervene in the foreign exchange market and to introduce a temporary exchange rate floor against the euro, which lasted until January 2015. The result of the SNB's foreign exchange interventions has been that the balance sheet of the SNB has surpassed the size of Swiss GDP. On the asset side, the volumes of foreign securities have become by far the largest investments, and, on the liability side, the sight deposits of Swiss banks at the central bank have reached an all-time high. Secondly, as the European Central Bank (ECB) embarked on a highly expansionary course starting in 2012, the SNB had to follow. In June 2014, the ECB introduced a negative deposit facility rate. The SNB lowered the Swiss deposit facility rate even further in order to maintain the traditional interest rate spread vis-à-vis the Eurozone in two steps in December 2014 and January 2015. The low-interest-rate environment has had negative effects on pension funds that are required to invest a large part of their funds in the domestic market. It has also contributed to a rapid rise of housing prices, as many investors shifted their money from bonds to real estate. Between 2007 and 2016, prices of privately owned apartments and single-family houses rose by nearly 50 per cent. The SNB has repeatedly warned of a hard landing (SNB 2017).

To be sure, it was not the first time that the SNB had to cope with high capital inflows and a rapidly appreciating Swiss franc. There were extended episodes in the early 1920s, the first half of the 1930s, in the 1970s, and in the mid-1990s. Each time, the Swiss exporting and import-competing sectors suffered from a drastic decrease of their price competitiveness, pushing many structurally weak businesses into bankruptcy. The most dramatic episode of recent times was the steep appreciation of the franc between the end of Bretton Woods in 1973 and the stabilization of the US dollar in 1979. Between 1970 and 1980, the industrial sector (excluding construction) lost around 200,000 jobs corresponding to more than 15 per cent of total industrial jobs in 1970. What is new, however, is that the problems of the exporting and import-competing sectors have not left deeper traces in the aggregate economy. The reason is that Switzerland has experienced record-high immigration from EU countries, which stabilized domestic demand. The Swiss economy has thus been in a good state in terms of employment.

6.3 The End of the Golden Age

In the short run, Switzerland's triple shock marked a rupture in the history of Zurich and Geneva as global financial centres. Over the last ten years, however, only the suspension of banking secrecy for foreign clients has had a profound impact. For it has effectively ended the golden age of Swiss banking. The old regulatory regime had provided Swiss banks and foreign banks located in Switzerland with a steady stream of profitable business. Foreign clients were ready to accept a dismal performance of their portfolio, so long as they could evade the taxes of their home country. Cross-border wealth management remains important, since banking and tax secrecy was not the only comparative advantage of Zurich, Geneva, and other minor Swiss centres. But cross-border wealth management does not provide the same margins of profit any more, and that has left deep marks.

Several indicators illustrate the decline of this line of business (see Figure 6.1). The funds of foreign private clients have declined by 55 per cent from 2007 to 2016, and those of foreign commercial clients by 37 per cent. Given that financial markets have boomed since 2009, as captured by the Pictet BVG-25 plus Index (comprising 25 per cent of stocks), the decline has been quite dramatic. According to a new estimate, Switzerland's share in global cross-border wealth management declined from 49 per cent in 2006 to 26 per cent in 2015 (Alstadsæter et al. 2017).

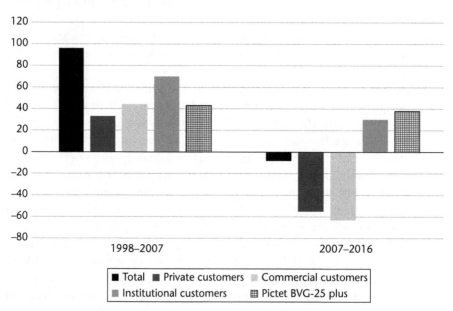

Figure 6.1. Assets of non-resident custody account holders in Switzerland, change in %

Note: Pictet BVG-25 plus Index, a standard benchmark for Swiss pension funds, reflects an investment portfolio comprising 25 percent share of risky assets (mostly stocks).

Source: Author, based on data from SNB.

Another sign that the golden era has ended is the declining interest of foreign banks. Between 2007 and 2016 the number of foreign-controlled banks decreased from 122 to 81, the number of their staff declined from 21,920 to 16,137, thus falling back to the level of the late 1990s. As for branches of foreign banks, the downward trend is also strong. Its number decreased from thirty to twenty-six, and the number of staff from 1,334 to 1,095, which is much lower than in the late 1990s.

Credit Suisse and UBS have suffered not only from the decline of cross-border wealth management located in Switzerland, but also from their costly adventures in the US subprime market. Most importantly, their profitability has come down considerably. From 1998 to 2006, their operating results oscillated between CHF 5 and 10 billion; from 2014 to 2016, the figures remained below CHF 1 billion. Only thanks to extraordinary income did Credit Suisse and UBS achieve a sizeable profit in these last years. Accordingly, their stocks have not performed well. In 2007, the share price of Credit Suisse and UBS had been at nearly 100 and at around 70 respectively; in March 2018 they were both below 20. Another indicator showing that the age of low-hanging fruit may be over is that between 2007 and 2016 the number of staff employed by both banks in Switzerland was reduced from 67,000 to 50,000.

The end of the golden age has affected both Zurich and Geneva. In the greater Zurich area, where nearly half of the value added by the Swiss financial sector is generated, the number of full-time equivalent employees in banks, insurance companies, and financial service providers has stagnated at the level of roughly 100,000 since 2010—between 1995 and 2010, this number had increased by more than a third. Similarly, the nominal value added has not grown since 2010, while it doubled between 1995 and 2010. In the greater Geneva area, which accounts for 20 per cent of the value added by the total Swiss financial sector, the same stagnation has occurred in terms of employment and productivity (Fondation Genève Place Financière 2017b). A comparison with London shows the relative decline of Zurich and Geneva. Compared to other European financial centres, the situation looks much less dramatic. But there is no doubt that the Global Financial Crisis marks a watershed between rapid growth and stagnation.

Yet, the end of the golden age does not mean that Zurich and Geneva are about to disappear from the list of global financial centres. For their strengths have never been exclusively based on banking secrecy. Four other factors have been just as important and have proved resilient since the financial crisis: infrastructure, human capital, political stability, and monetary stability. Since the outbreak of the euro crisis, the strong Swiss currency has played a particularly important role. While before 2010 the Swiss franc was not considered a flight currency anymore, it experienced a comeback as a safe asset after Greece was punished by financial markets. The demand for the Swiss currency was so strong that the ensuing appreciation prompted the SNB to introduce an exchange rate floor against the euro in 2011; after suspending the floor in 2015, it has prevented the currency from a further steep appreciation. In any event, Switzerland's extraordinary monetary stability has been called to mind through this episode.

Accordingly, Switzerland still has a share of 24 per cent in global cross-border wealth management (BCG 2017). Another clear sign that Zurich and Geneva are to remain global financial centres is the growth of funds of foreign institutional investors. Between 2007 and 2016 they increased by 30 per cent. Of course, they do not fully compensate for the loss of foreign private clients, as the management fee is much lower. But, obviously, Swiss banks are still able to attract foreign wealth.

Other indicators demonstrate the resilience of Zurich and Geneva. The operating results of the Swiss banking sector have recovered from the trough of 2008 and rose to CHF 8 billion in 2016 despite a difficult interest-rate environment. The market capitalization of the Swiss All Shares Index amounted to CHF 1,429 billion in 2016—close to the record year of 2006 (CH 1,480 billion). SIX Swiss Exchange ranks twelfth in the world based on market capitalization (World Federation of Exchanges 2017). The foreign exchange turnover amounting to 2.4 per cent of global turnover is still above average relative to the size of the Swiss economy (BIS 2016). Credit Suisse and UBS continue to operate as global banks offering the full set of financial services. At the end of 2016, they ranked tenth and fourteenth in terms of assets (S&P Global Market Intelligence 2017). Zurich and Geneva will remain clusters where the client not only gets financial services, but also the complementary legal, accounting, and advisory support.

Furthermore, the other major pillar of Zurich, the insurance sector, has developed positively since the Global Financial Crisis. In 2016, its contribution to nominal added value was as high as the one generated by Zurich's banking sector, while in 2010 the banking sector contributed nominal added value amounting to CHF 14.5 billion and the insurance sector only CHF 9.7 billion. This trend was reflected in the evolution of employment. The number of full-time equivalents in the banking sector decreased from 55,300 to 48,600, whereas the insurance sector increased employment from 19,800 to 21,200 (Kanton Zürich 2017). Zurich is particularly strong in reinsurance, which has always been a highly international business. Swiss Re is the world's second-largest reinsurer, and all major international insurance and reinsurance companies have subsidiaries in Zurich.

On the national level, too, insurance services have become more important relative to financial services over the last ten years. In 2010, net export of financial services and of insurance services amounted to CHF 18.8 billion and CHF 4.4 billion respectively. In 2016, the corresponding numbers were CHF

15.9 billion and CHF 6.1 billion respectively (SNB 2017). The Swiss insurance sector has never profited from a regulatory advantage as the banking sector has, but nevertheless it has been thriving. This is another indicator that the traditional strengths of Zurich and Geneva still provide a competitive edge.

Moreover, the suspension of banking secrecy for foreign clients has increased the reputations of Zurich and Geneva, and the reduction of proprietary trading by Credit Suisse and UBS has strengthened the resilience of the banking sector. Margins may have come down considerably, but the increased resilience is likely to make large losses less probable in the future. Thus, over the long-term, average earnings may be more stable in comparison with the great volatility during the golden age of Swiss banking.

Finally, Geneva has become a leading global centre of commodity trade finance, which partially compensates for the decline of income from cross-border wealth management (Fondation Genève Place Financière 2017a). Geneva hosts more than 400 companies that have large market shares in the trading of oil, cereals, coffee, rice, sugar, and cotton. As there are reputational risks involved, the Swiss government has pressured banks and commodity firms to adopt strict standards strengthening transparency, corporate social responsibility, accountability, reputation, and cooperation with authorities and stakeholders (Bundesrat 2015). The goal of these recommendations is to avoid Switzerland being targeted for supporting unsound business practices as happened in the case of banking secrecy. Whether these government efforts will be sufficient remains to be seen. But there is a real possibility that Geneva's role as a hub in commodity trade finance is more than temporary.

6.4 Regulatory and Political Changes

In the wake of the financial crisis, Switzerland not only abandoned banking secrecy for foreign clients, but also tightened the regulation and supervision of the financial sector. Furthermore, the crisis affected the reputation of bankers. Political initiatives aimed at reducing the salaries of directors and top managers, and the dominant role of the central bank in managing the crisis exposed its members to higher scrutiny. For the first time in Swiss history, the chairman of the governing board of the SNB was forced to resign.

In contrast to the suspension of banking secrecy, the strengthening of regulation and supervision of the financial sector evolved in an orderly fashion. One major reason was that the domestic pressure for tighter rules was overwhelming. In November 2009, the Swiss government established a commission of experts to develop a new regulatory framework with regard to the problem of 'too big to fail'. In 2011, the Swiss parliament passed a revision of the Banking Act to be effective from March 2012. In February 2015, another commission of experts, after evaluating the new law, recommended a further tightening of regulations. Most recommendations were adopted by the Swiss government in May 2016. The revised framework entered into force on 1 July 2016, and the new requirements will have to be met by the end of 2019.

Of course, Swiss lawmakers and regulators always took the international agreements known by the name of Basel III into account. Yet the Swiss authorities went beyond copying international guidelines. In particular, they adopted stricter capital rules for Credit Suisse and UBS (FINMA 2016, p. 25). For these two banks, required tier-one capital amounts to 5.0 per cent relative to unweighted total assets, consisting of 3.5 per cent of common equity tier-one and high-trigger contingent convertibles (CoCos) of 1.5 per cent which are considered tier-one capital. The Financial Stability Board (FSB) requires only 3.0 per cent of tier-one capital. Possibly, this ratio will be increased during the next revision of Basel III. But so far, there is no consensus.

On top of the 5.0 per cent of tier-one capital, Credit Suisse and UBS are obliged to hold an additional 5.0 per cent of bail-in and capital instruments that are to be used in case of emergency. These are mostly low-trigger CoCos. The current requirement of the FSB amounts to 3.75 per cent. Finally, Credit Suisse and UBS have to present emergency plans. For this reason, they have separated their Swiss business from their international business by creating separate legal entities: Credit Suisse (Switzerland) Ltd and UBS Switzerland AG. The idea of the regulator is to shield the domestic payments system against contagion from an international financial crisis. The three domestic systematically important banks—Postfinance, Raiffeisen group, and Cantonal Bank of Zurich—are also subject to stricter capital and liquidity rules. Swiss Re has higher capital ratios imposed by the Swiss Solvency Test (SST).

In recent years, the Swiss banking community has been pushing back against the regulatory wave in the wake of the financial crisis. In fact, the current framework has become enormously complicated and voluminous, generating rising costs for the banking sector. Citizens and most politicians are incapable of understanding what is at stake. So far, critical voices of bank managers have had little chance to be heard. The public may not understand the regulatory framework, but the majority appears to rather accept the arguments of the government than support a simplification or liberalization of the current regime.

The mistrust of the public is a consequence of the financial crisis. In October 2008, when the Confederation and the SNB supported UBS, the public outrage was enormous, especially because bank and insurance managers had earned record-high salaries before the crisis. At a single blow, the argument that these salaries were justified in the face of the competitive business and the economic importance of the banking sector lost any plausibility in the public debate.

The most outspoken advocates of the free market had to call for the help of the government.

The anger about bank managers strongly contributed to the adoption of the popular federal initiative 'against rip-off salaries' in March 2013. No less than 68 per cent of voters supported the initiative, with a turnout of 46 per cent. The result was sensational as most initiatives have been rejected by the voters since the creation of the right of popular initiative at the federal level in 1891. The aim of the initiative was to ensure a better control of total remuneration by the annual general meeting. The initiative itself was not a product of the Global Financial Crisis. The collection of signatures began in 2007 and was concluded in early 2008, months before the UBS crisis. In addition, the salaries paid out to executives of the pharmaceutical corporation Novartis were stimulating the debate before the referendum just as much as the bonuses of bankers. Nevertheless, it is highly probable that the initiative would have met more opposition if it had not been for the financial crisis. As for the effect of the initiative, the results are mixed. There has been more debate about the remuneration of directors and managers, but the large gap between top and normal salaries has not substantially narrowed.

Six months later, Swiss voters were again called to the booth to decide on a proposal to cap salaries using the 1:12 ratio. The initiative had been launched by the organization of young socialists in October 2009, one year after the UBS crisis, and reached the required number of valid signatures (which is unusual for an initiative of a youth section of a major party). This success can be interpreted as another sign of the ongoing anger about the banking community. To be sure, 65.3 per cent of voters rejected the initiative, with the turnout being 53 per cent. But the fact that a third of voters supported such an extreme intervention into the private sector was remarkable.

The strong appreciation of the Swiss franc resulting from the euro crisis reinforced the political debate about the role of monetary policy. The first public controversy broke out in the wake of foreign exchange interventions by the SNB in the spring of 2010 that failed to stop the appreciation and resulted in a large loss. And as the balance sheet of the SNB continued to grow in 2011, opposition to the SNB's monetary policy gained currency. In August 2011, several deputies of the conservative Swiss People's Party (SVP) launched the initiative 'Save our Swiss gold', forbidding the sale of the SNB gold reserves and stipulating a minimum gold cover ratio of 20 per cent relative to total SNB assets. The referendum held in November 2014 resulted in a clear rejection of the initiative (77 per cent voting no on a turnout of 50 per cent). Nevertheless, it was the first time in decades that an initiative concerning the central bank had been put to a popular vote.

In January 2012, the chairman of the governing board of the SNB, Philipp Hildebrand, resigned after allegations of insider trading. Hildebrand, one of the architects of the UBS rescue in October 2008, was criticized for not preventing his wife from making a currency trade involving the Swiss franc in 2011. In December 2011, the details of this trade were revealed after stolen bank documents were made public by a news magazine close to the conservative Swiss People's Party. Confronted with the evidence, the supervising Bank Council of the SNB found it increasingly difficult to defend Hildebrand's position in public, although the currency trade had neither been illegal nor had it violated internal regulations. In addition, new documents disclosed on the day of his resignation showed that Hildebrand had regularly met his private banker to discuss investment opportunities. Again, this was not illegal under Swiss law, but difficult to reconcile with his role as central banker. It was the first time that the highest executive member of the SNB was forced to leave the institution.

Criticism of the SNB's policy receded in the following years, but re-emerged after the suspension of the currency floor in mid-January 2015. Some leaders of finance and industry felt duped by the sudden change of course after the SNB reaffirmed its commitment to the floor in the days before the decision was taken. On the other hand, it was difficult to communicate such a break with the previous policy in a smooth way. As the SNB prevented the franc from appreciating too steeply, thus cushioning the negative consequences for the exporting industries, criticism slowly receded, although the SNB has continued to intervene in the foreign exchange market. At the end of the second quarter of 2017, total assets amounted to CHF 775 billion, corresponding to nearly 120 per cent of the Swiss GDP figure for 2016. Although the Eurozone has recovered from the crisis, it is hard to see how the SNB will be able to return to a normal interest rate policy anytime soon. In this respect, the financial crisis has not ended yet, and the exceptional state of Swiss monetary policy is likely to remain a political issue. However, it will hardly be a competitive disadvantage for Zurich and Geneva, as most other global financial centres also struggle with uncertainty regarding the normalization of interest rate policy and the political backlash against independent central banks.

6.5 Brexit and Fintech

There is a strong consensus that Brexit will have a considerable influence on the future financial geography of Europe. Yet there is little reason to expect that Zurich and Geneva will be among the financial centres that will profit from Brexit. One problem is that Switzerland is neither a member of the EU nor the Eurozone. Another difficulty is that Zurich and Geneva lack the tradition of a truly international financial centre equipped with a liquid money market and a multitude of financial institutions and services. The Swiss Confederation also lacks the ability to develop optimal regulations for an international financial centre, the reason being that its tradition of direct democracy inhibits a tailored policy in any policy field. Thus, there has never been a majority willing to set up a special regulatory framework for the banking sector. Banking secrecy was a defensive measure to keep hold of a business that had come to Switzerland due to political turmoil in Europe. It did not result from a long-term plan concocted by government officials and banking executives.

A short historical review may serve as an illustration. For there was a period, in the 1950s and 1960s, when Zurich was in a good position to surpass London. Meier and Sigrist (2006) quote an article of Fortune Magazine of 1958: 'The Zurich Stock Exchange is the most cosmopolitan securities market in Europe.—Because it is also the freest. Since Switzerland has no currency restrictions, an investor anywhere in the world can buy securities there with any kind of money he happens to have. More US securities are traded in Zurich than anywhere else outside North America...' Max Iklé (1968), a former senior official of the Swiss National Bank, believed that 'Zurich is an international financial centre that today is ranked third behind New York and London and has perhaps even surpassed London in some respects.' Similarly, though from a different ideological angle, the political economist Susan Strange (1971) wrote: 'In the 1960s, it was generally considered by bankers as second only to London, and some were inclined to believe that by the end of the century, if the flow of foreign funds to Switzerland went on, it would be the major financial centre of Europe.'

But the banking community of Zurich and the federal authorities failed to take advantage of the opportunity. They lacked the vision, but also the political power to provide a liberal framework that would have transformed it into a global money and capital market. On the contrary, Swiss authorities even succeeded in chasing away gold trading by introducing a transaction tax. In contrast, Luxemburg, once a centre of the European steel industry, began to attract financial business by changing its regulations in the 1960s. It attracted parts of the Euromarkets, the mutual funds industry, and cross-border wealth management.

Thus, both Zurich and Geneva lack the fertile ground on which a truly global financial centre can flourish (Cassis 2010). Even in asset management, where Zurich and Geneva have some competitive edge thanks to the high domestic savings rate, the gap with London is rather big. A recent study by the Swiss Finance Institute (SFI) and zeb, a management consultancy specializing in the European financial services industry, observes that the Swiss innovative strength in terms of appropriate asset management solutions and products 'is viewed rather sceptically by the market as a whole, and the quality of internationally accepted investment solutions is regarded as only mediocre' (SFI and zeb 2015).

The relocation of two hedge funds from London to Switzerland in 2010 and back to London and Jersey a few years later is a case in point (Financial Times 2015; Le Temps 2017). When in the wake of the Global Financial Crisis EU regulation of hedge funds was tightened and the British government introduced a capital levy, several hedge funds, among them the heavyweights Brevan Howard and BlueCrest, moved a substantial part of their business and staff to Geneva. But, lacking the stimulating environment of the City, BlueCrest and Brevan Howard abandoned their new home in 2014 and 2015 respectively. Furthermore, as it turned out, the Swiss regulation of hedge funds was not substantially more favourable than the EU regulation. Clearly, Geneva was not able to compete with London. The history of funds in the canton of Schwyz (near Zurich) is another case in point. They flourished from the 1990s to the late 2000s, but lost their critical mass in the wake of the financial crisis.

In a similar vein, it is unrealistic to expect that the Swiss financial centres will reinvent themselves in the context of digitization and fintech. This is not to say that entrepreneurs and authorities are missing out on the trend. There is a 'Crypto Valley' in the small city of Zug (near Zurich), and the Swiss Confederation has tried to create a conducive regulatory framework comprising three elements (SIF 2016). The first element sets a deadline of sixty days for the holding of money in settlement accounts, which is particularly relevant for providers of crowdfunding services. The second element is a so-called 'sandbox' where a provider can accept public funds up to a total value of CHF 1 million without asking for authorization. The third element is a new fintech licence granted for institutions which are restricted to the deposit-taking business (acceptance of public funds) not exceeding the overall value of CHF 100 million. But the positive effect will hardly be big enough to boost Swiss banking in the aggregate.

A new report that thoroughly analyses the state of digitization and fintech in the financial industry in Zurich comes to guardedly optimistic conclusions (Kanton Zürich 2017). Banks and insurance companies are quite advanced in implementing digital front-end services, considering and using fintech tools (e.g. big data, online distribution, personal finance management, blockchain, robo-advisors), and digitizing the value chain. Insurance companies are somewhat more conservative than banks, but they seem to have taken up the challenge, too.

6.6 Conclusion

In the late 1920s, the Austrian economist Felix Somary (1929) observed a great anomaly in European capital markets. 'Never in its history', he wrote, 'has

Europe seen as politically weak creditor countries as today—creditors whose only weapon against defaulting debtors is the omission of further credit.' Somary was talking of three neutral countries with small populations that had not been conquered during the First World War and therefore served as safe havens for frightened investors and taxpayers: the Netherlands, Sweden, and Switzerland. Of the three countries, only Switzerland continued to maintain this role throughout the second half of the twentieth century. The Netherlands was occupied by the Wehrmacht and was never able to re-establish the vital role it had played in the inter-war years, and in Sweden the ruling Social Democrats tightly controlled the financial sector and capital movements after the Second World War.

This era came to an end in the late twentieth century and early twenty-first century. Europe became a continent in which the demand for safe havens became less important and the tolerance towards tax evasion became weaker. The Global Financial Crisis of 2007–9 put the final nail in the coffin. Presumably, Swiss banking secrecy would have lasted longer without this financial shock, but there is no doubt that it had been weakened well before 2007.

Interestingly, however, Switzerland continues to maintain its function as a safe haven—just as in the inter-war and post-war years. The reason is that during global financial turmoil the stable Swiss franc has served as an alternative to the large currencies. From this perspective, Europe's old financial and monetary order still exists, and accordingly, Zurich and Geneva will continue to play a role in cross-border wealth management, even though their competitive advantage has become much smaller since the acceptance of automatic exchange of information. The same is true for Zurich's strong position as an international hub for reinsurance. It will persist. Brexit and digitization are unlikely to change this position in a fundamental way, for better or worse.

Acknowledgements

The author thanks numerous colleagues for their critical comments, especially Peter Kugler and Jakob Schaad.

References

Alstadsæter, A., N. Johannesen, and G. Zucman. 2017. 'Who Owns the Wealth in Tax Havens? Macro Evidence and Implications for Global Inequality'. Cambridge, MA: NBER Working Paper 23805.

Baltensperger, E. and P. Kugler. 2017. Swiss Monetary History since the Early 19th Century. Cambridge: Cambridge University Press.

BCG (Boston Consulting Group). 2017. 'Global Wealth 2017: Transforming the Client Experience'. Boston: BCG.

BIS (Bank for International Settlements). 2016. 'Triennial Central Bank Survey: Foreign Exchange Turnover in April 2016'. Basel: BIS, Monetary and Economic Department.

Bundesrat. 2015. 'Grundlagenbericht Rohstoffe: 2. Berichterstattung zum Stand der Umsetzung der Empfehlungen'. Bern: Schweizerische Eidgenossenschaft.

Cassis, Y. 2010. Capitals of Capital: The Rise and Fall of International Financial Centres, 1780–2009, 2nd edition. Cambridge: Cambridge University Press.

Credit Suisse. 2009. 'Annual Report 2008'. Zürich: Credit Suisse.

Emmenegger, P. 2017. 'Swiss Banking Secrecy and the Problem of International Cooperation in Tax Matters: A Nut Too Hard to Crack?' *Regulation and Governance* 11: 24–40.

Financial Times. 2013. 'Barclays PLC Credit Suisse Gave Qatar Loan During Crisis'. 1 February.

Financial Times. 2015. 'Brevan Howard Abandons Geneva and Returns to London'. 12 July.

FINMA (Swiss Financial Market Supervisory Authority). 2009. Financial Market Crisis and Financial Market Supervision. Bern: FINMA.

FINMA (Swiss Financial Market Supervisory Authority). 2016. Annual Report 2015. Bern: FINMA.

Fondation Genève Place Financière. 2017a. 'Rapport d'Activité 2016'. Geneva: Fondation Genève Place Financière.

Fondation Genève Place Financière. 2017b. 'Enquête conjoncturelle résultats 2017–2018'. Geneva: Fondation Genève Place Financière.

GFCI (Global Financial Centres Index). 2017. Global Financial Centres Index 22 (September 2017). Shenzhen and London: China Development Institute (CDI) and Z/Yen Partners.

Guex, S. 2000. 'The Origins of the Swiss Banking Secrecy Law and its Repercussions for Swiss Federal Policy'. *Harvard Business History Review* 74: 237–66.

Iklé, M. 1968. Die Schweiz als internationaler Bank- und Finanzplatz. Zurich: Orell Füssli.

Kanton Zürich (2017). 'Finanzplatz Zürich 2016/2017'. Zurich: Volkswirtschaftsdirektion (Amt für Wirtschaft und Arbeit).

Le Temps. 2017. 'Le mirage des grands hedge funds étrangers à Genève'. 6 April. https://www.letemps.ch/economie/2017/04/06/mirage-grands-hedge-funds-etrangers-geneve, accessed 30 June 2017.

Meier, H. B., J. E. Marthinsen, and P. A. Gantenbein. 2013. Swiss Finance: Capital Markets, Banking, and the Swiss Value Chain. Hoboken, NJ: Wiley.

Meier, R. T. and T. Sigrist. 2006. Der helvetische Big Bang: Die Geschichte der SWX Swiss Exchange. Zurich: Verlag Neue Zürcher Zeitung.

National Council. 2000. 'Amtliches Bulletin der Bundesversammlung'. 6 March. Bern: National Council, pp. 28–31.

S&P Global Market Intelligence. 2017. 'Data Dispatch: The World's 100 Largest Banks'. http://www.snl.com/web/client?auth=inherit#news/article?id=40223698&cdid=A-40223698-11568, accessed 3 September 2017.

Schütz, D. 1998. Der Fall der UBS: Warum die Schweizerische Bankgeselschaft unterging. Zurich: Bilanz.

SFI (Swiss Finance Institute) and zeb. 2015. 'Swiss Asset Management Study 2015: Swiss Asset Management: On or Next to the Winner's Podium?' Zurich: SFI and zeb. http:// www.swissassetmanagementsurvey.com/SwissAssetManagementStudy.pdf, accessed 30 June 2017.

SIF (State Secretariat for International Financial Matters). 2016. Financial Market Policy for a Competitive Swiss Financial Centre. Bern: Federal Department of Finance.

SNB (Swiss National Bank). 2017. Financial Stability Report 2017. Zurich: SNB.

Somary, Felix. 1929. Wandlungen der Weltwirtschaft seit dem Kriege. Tübingen: Mohr/ Siebeck.

Strange, S. 1971. Sterling and British Policy: A Political Study of an International Currency in Decline. London: Oxford University Press.

Straumann, T. 2010. 'The UBS Crisis in Historical Perspective. Expert Opinion Prepared for Delivery to UBS AG'. Zurich: University of Zurich, Institute for Empirical Research in Economics.

Straumann, T. 2013. 'The Invisible Giant: The Story of Swiss Re, 1863–2013'. In The Value of Risk: Swiss Re and the History of Reinsurance, edited by H. James. Oxford: Oxford University Press, pp. 237–352.

Swiss Federal Banking Commission. 2008. 'Subprime Crisis: SFBC Investigation into the Causes of the Write-downs of UBS AG'. Bern: Swiss Federal Banking Commission.

UBS AG. 2008. 'Shareholder Report on UBS's Write-Downs'. Zurich: UBS AG.

Vogler, R. 2006. Swiss Banking Secrecy: Origins, Significance, Myth. Zurich: Association for Financial History, Switzerland and Principality of Liechtenstein.

World Federation of Exchanges. 2017. WFE Annual Statistics Guide 2016. London: World Federation of Exchanges. https://www.world-exchanges.org/home/index. php/files/52/Annual-Statistics-Guide/453/WFE-Annual-Statistics-Guide-2016.xlsx, accessed 30 June 2017.

7

Hong Kong, Shanghai, and Beijing

China's Contenders for Global Financial Centre Leadership

David R. Meyer

7.1 Introduction

The 1978 reforms of Deng Xiaoping unleashed the extraordinary, sustained growth of China's economy (see Figure 7.1). This expansion underpins the top global rank of its financial centres of Hong Kong, Shanghai, and Beijing. The increasing heft of the country's economy generates an ever-larger demand for financial services that are supplied from these agglomerations. The financiers operate locally in networks of collaboration and sharing expertise, and their most important networks reach across Asia and to Europe and North America. China's much faster growth than the United States from 1980 to 2016, as shown by the steeper slope of its gross domestic product (GDP) curve (vertical axis is log base 10), suggests that China's financial centres are gaining in importance relative to New York. That occurs because the growing domestic economy generates larger demands for financial services from firms in Hong Kong, Shanghai, and Beijing.

Within Asia the other large economies of Japan and India remain far smaller than China's as of the second decade of the twenty-first century. Consequently, their domestic economies provide much less support for their financial centres. Tokyo, Japan's premier financial centre, and Mumbai, India's leading centre, therefore have little prospect of challenging Hong Kong, China's window to global capital; and Shanghai and Beijing will continue to increase in importance relative to Tokyo and Mumbai.

The Global Financial Crisis of 2007–8 ratcheted through China's export-dependent economy, generating a swift fall in industrial production and

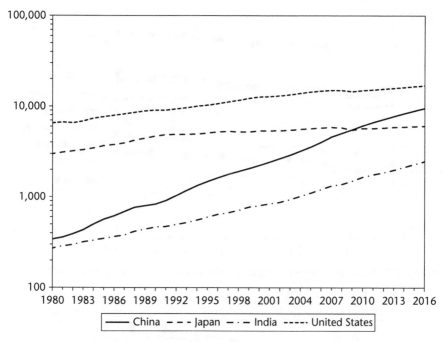

Figure 7.1. Gross domestic product (GDP), billions of constant 2010 United States dollars, 1980–2016

Source: Author, based on data from the World Bank (2017).

slowing GDP growth. Its government quickly responded with a RMB 4.0 trillion stimulus package, and its central bank, the People's Bank of China (PBOC), pursued a massive expansion of bank credit to support fiscal efforts (Yu 2009). China's credit-driven growth continued unabated over the subsequent decade, which partially accounts for its faster rate of increase compared to other Asian economies and the United States (see Figure 7.1).

Asia's economic growth over the past several decades has generated a huge amount of total investable wealth of high net worth individuals (HNWIs) in the region (see Figure 7.2). These wealthy people who have investable assets of US$1 million or more are a market for financial services, such as private wealth management, investments, and personal and corporate finance. Their accumulated capital enters financial intermediation in forms such as stocks, bonds, private equity, venture capital, hedge funds, and fund management; this fuels economic growth and development. Along with other world regions, total investable wealth in Asia dipped during the Global Financial Crisis of 2007–8, but Asia quickly recovered. By 2015, Asia became the global leader of total investable wealth, surpassing North America.

Among Asian financial centres, Hong Kong, Shanghai, and Beijing possess exceptional access to the wealth of HNWIs in the region (see Figure 7.3).

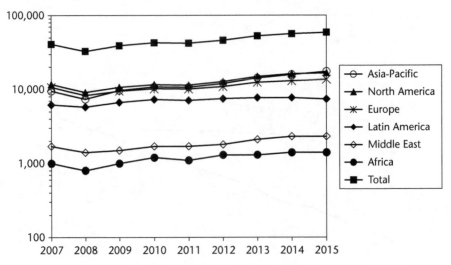

Figure 7.2. Total investable wealth (US$ billions) of HNWIs by region, 2007–15
Source: Author, based on data from Capgemini (2012–2016b).

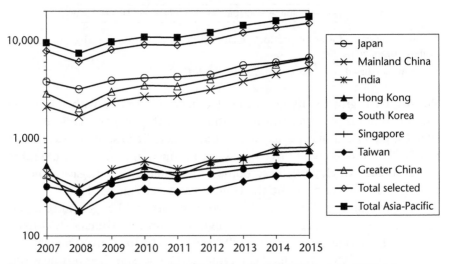

Figure 7.3. Total investable wealth (US$ billions) of HNWIs in Asia, 2007–15
Note: Greater China (Mainland China, Hong Kong, Taiwan).
Source: Author based on data from Capgemini (2012–2016a).

During the Global Financial Crisis, all major economies of Asia witnessed a drop in total investable wealth of HNWIs, and then quickly recovered. By 2015, greater China, comprising mainland China, Hong Kong, and Taiwan, contained total investable wealth of HNWIs slightly below Japan, which previously had been the undisputed leader. Hong Kong's total investable wealth alone is slightly below that of India. The city is the world's fourth-ranked private wealth management centre, after Switzerland, the United Kingdom, and United States, excluding the offshore centres of Panama and Caribbean (Deloitte 2015; Meyer 2014b). China's large state banks headquartered in Beijing, with major offices in Shanghai and Hong Kong, have expanded significantly into private wealth management. These moves enhance the global prominence of China's leading financial centres.

Some observers question the claim that the twenty-first century will be the Asian century (Auslin 2017). While China's and India's growth necessarily will slow down, their much faster growth over the past several decades compared to the United States (Figure 7.1) suggests these observers' views may be misplaced. Hong Kong, Shanghai, and Beijing gain unusual benefits from China's overwhelming heft in the Asian economy. At the same time, its financial centres are playing increasingly significant roles in global financial networks. We now turn to these changes in China's financial centres, identifying the opportunities and challenges, as well as the risks that may emerge.

7.2 Trends in China's Financial Centre Networks

7.2.1 *Hong Kong—China's Window to Global Capital*

Following the Opium Wars, the British established Hong Kong in the 1840s as their key port to access the China trade. Leading trading companies set up offices and warehouses, and other foreign firms soon followed. They agglomerated to utilize the port facilities and, equally important, to participate in knowledge networks of expertise about trade with China and elsewhere in Asia. During the 1850s, major Chinese traders likewise joined the Hong Kong hub, and British and other European exchange banks commenced expansion in Hong Kong. When the top foreign trading companies founded the Hongkong and Shanghai Bank in 1864–5 in Hong Kong, with the most important branch in Shanghai, the city's status as China's window to global capital and premier financial centre of the Asia-Pacific region was secure. The bank's founders offered their global trading offices as representative offices of the bank, thus immediately allowing it to develop networks throughout Asia and reaching to Europe and the Americas. At the same time, exchange banks in Hong Kong possessed networks to branches of the banks within Asia and globally. These ties positioned Hong Kong financiers as pivotal hubs of Asia-Pacific's networks, and they maintained linkages to European financial centres, especially London, where the Hongkong and Shanghai Bank had a major office (Jones 1993; Meyer 2000).

The bank established a formal branch-office network from the 1860s to the 1910s in the leading business centres of Asia (King 1987; 1988). The modern branch network of HSBC (the bank's name today) in Asia bears a close resemblance to the structure that existed by 1920 (Meyer 2014a). During the first several decades of the twentieth century, important Chinese rice merchants founded banks in Hong Kong, thus creating a Chinese financial network radiating from the city throughout Asia (Sinn 1994). By 1940, local Chinese banks had proliferated in the city, and British exchange banks, such as the Hongkong and Shanghai Bank and the Chartered Bank of India, Australia and China, handled their international fund transfers (Schenk 2000; 2002).

During the two decades following 1950, externally headquartered banks significantly expanded their presence in Hong Kong. Their home bases were in the United States, Europe, and Asia, including state banks of China; this pattern remains today (Meyer 2016a; Schenk 2000; 2002). These banks possess branches in major Asian financial centres, solidifying Hong Kong as the premier Asia-Pacific centre. Most of the world's top-ten commercial and investment banks use Hong Kong as their Asia-Pacific management centre; Singapore is their southeast Asia centre (see websites of banks). Financiers across sectors—corporate and investment banking, private equity, hedge funds, fund management, and private banking—share expertise and knowledge and work on deals through the intense internal networks in Hong Kong. They use its superb airline connections to Asian cities for their external meetings with other financiers and clients. They possess the best access to financial opportunities in the Asia-Pacific region, and financiers from outside Asia visit them to access their knowledge and expertise about regional business (Meyer 2015).

The world's largest banks certify Hong Kong's financial community as China's window to global capital (see Table 7.1). Over the twenty-year period from 1997 to 2016, global banks in the top twenty remained committed to Hong Kong, even during the Global Financial Crisis. While some evidence suggests that lesser-ranked banks may have pulled back from Hong Kong during that crisis, overall, a large share of the top 100 banks in the world use Hong Kong as their Asia-Pacific base. Consequently, China possesses access to the world's largest banks for exchanging capital globally.

The close bonds of Hong Kong's financiers with their peers in the cores of the global economy, Europe and North America, remain as they have been since the late-nineteenth century (see Table 7.2). Licensed banks are the premier banks in Hong Kong that can fully operate for deposit-taking and disbursing funds. Actual shares of banks by region and political unit are imperfect measures because domestic bank consolidation leads to fewer large banks in a given political unit. With this caveat, about one-third of Hong Kong's licensed banks come from western Europe (about 25 per cent) and North America (about 10 per cent). Banks from the major economies of western Europe operate in the city, providing network ties for exchanging capital with banks in key financial centres of that region. United States and Canadian banks

Table 7.1. Presence of world's largest 500 overseas banks in Hong Kong, 1997–2016

	Number			% of group		
World ranking	1997	2008	2016	1997	2008	2016
1–20	19	20	20	95	100	100
21–50	26	23	27	87	77	90
51–100	36	26	28	72	52	56
101–200	51	35	32	51	35	32
201–500	83	55	56	28	18	19
Subtotal	215	159	163	43	32	33

Source: Author, based on data from Hong Kong Monetary Authority, Annual Report (Hong Kong Special Administrative Region, 1997–2017).

Table 7.2. Region/political unit of beneficial ownership of licensed banks in Hong Kong, 1997–2016

Region/political unit	% of total licensed banks		
	1997	2008	2016
Asia (total)	57.2	56.6	59.6
Hong Kong	8.9	6.9	4.5
Mainland China	10.0	9.0	13.5
Taiwan	2.2	12.4	12.8
Australia	2.2	2.8	3.2
India	2.2	7.6	7.7
Japan	24.4	7.6	7.1
Malaysia	1.7	2.8	2.6
Philippines	1.1	1.4	1.3
Singapore	2.8	2.8	3.8
South Korea	1.7	3.4	3.2
Western Europe (total)	23.3	26.9	25.0
France	4.4	4.8	4.5
Germany	5.6	4.8	2.6
Italy	3.3	2.8	1.9
Netherlands	1.7	2.8	1.9
Spain	1.7	1.4	1.3
Sweden	1.1	0.7	1.3
Switzerland	1.7	2.1	5.1
United Kingdom	3.9	7.6	6.4
North America (total)	11.1	11.0	9.0
Canada	3.3	3.4	3.2
United States	7.8	7.6	5.8
Selected total (%)	91.6	94.5	93.6
Total number of licensed banks	180	145	156

Source: Author, based on data from Hong Kong Monetary Authority, Annual Report (Hong Kong Special Administrative Region, 1997–2017)

provide network bonds with leading financial centres of North America. Banks from Asia represent close to 60 per cent of licensed banks, and together with banks from Europe and North America, they account for over 90 per cent. The rest of the world—Eastern Europe, Russia, the Middle East, Africa, and Latin America—accounts for a trivial share.

Hong Kong's financial community retains its long-term prominence as the pivot of Asia-Pacific finance. Banks from the major economies of Asia have operations in the city (Table 7.2). Each of the non-locally headquartered banks is involved in intra-organizational and inter-organizational networks within Hong Kong and across Asia. Theoretically, these banks could operate much of their Asian business from their domestic headquarters. To maintain competitiveness, however, they need a significant presence in Hong Kong to participate in the Chinese and foreign social networks of capital that meet in the city (Meyer 2000). Befitting its status as the city's sovereign power, China's mainland banks are consequential members of Hong Kong's financial networks. Network ties with Singapore reveal the close coordination in banking that exists between Asia's top two financial centres.

As China's window to global capital, Hong Kong financiers provide a wide range of intermediary services to the cores of the world economy. Its financial institutions export and import services such as dealing and brokering, asset management, investment advisory, mergers and acquisitions, and corporate finance. Hong Kong financiers are pivotal decision-makers in the allocation of global capital; exports far exceed imports (see figures 7.4 and 7.5). The Global Financial Crisis of 2007–8 had a small impact on the exports of services and no noticeable impact on imports. Exports focus on the United Kingdom (London) and the United States (New York); however, their import shares are closer to the other economies. Exports and imports rose significantly over the 1999–2015 period, revealing increasing integration of China through Hong Kong with London and New York, the pivots of global finance.

Hong Kong operates more as a supplier of financial services to the leading economies of the Asia-Pacific region than as a market for these services; exports far exceed imports (see figures 7.4 and 7.5). Singapore, the southeast Asia financial centre, always looms large in exchanges of financial services, reflecting complementarity between Asia's top two financial centres. As the largest economy of Asia after China, Japan generates sizable demand and supply of financial services. Consistent with Hong Kong's long-term ties to mainland China, it is a major market for the city's services and a modest supplier of services to Hong Kong firms. The reason that mainland China does not dominate as a market for Hong Kong's financial services is that domestic firms supply a large share of these services. Hong Kong's firms focus on the global market.

China gains substantial benefits in access to global capital because Hong Kong's firms are integral members of the global triad which also includes London and New York firms. The strength of Hong Kong's network ties of producer services firms, of which financial services are a subset, to London and New York ranked second and third in the world, after London–New York ties (Taylor et al. 2014). Some of these producer services firms provide specialized

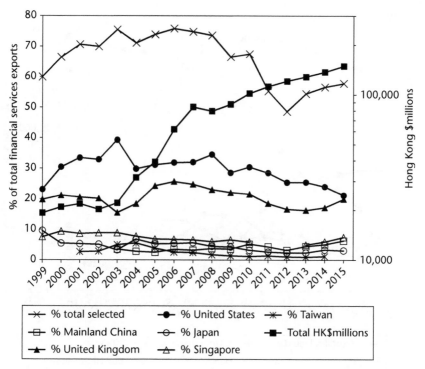

Figure 7.4. Exports of financial services from Hong Kong by total and percentage to selected political units, 1999–2015

Source: Author, based on data from the Census and Statistics Department (2002–17).

expertise in handling currency exchanges and managing currency markets. Hong Kong's participation in these markets offers China a critical avenue to global capital. The city's annual interbank payments by currency rose five-fold from US$12 trillion to US$61 trillion between 2001 and 2015 (see Figure 7.6). The Hong Kong dollar portion has fluctuated, even as it remained the largest currency portion for most of the period. The direct US dollar portion rose about six-fold over the period. Intriguingly, the euro payments portion has declined. The Global Financial Crisis produced a dramatic decline in interbank payments from the peak in 2007; that level was not surpassed until 2013.

Overall, the biggest change in the interbank currency market in Hong Kong is soaring renminbi payments after 2010. Hong Kong banks dominate global offshore renminbi payments, with a share of over 70 per cent (Hong Kong Monetary Authority 1997–2017). China's government enabled that control. In 2003, it chose the city as the first financial centre for executing renminbi trading and delayed extending that permission to other centres until 2012 (Hong Kong Monetary Authority 2015).

133

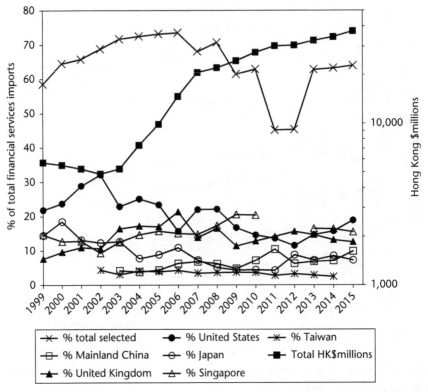

Figure 7.5. Imports of financial services to Hong Kong by total and percentage from selected political units, 1999–2015

Source: Author, based on data from the Census and Statistics Department (2002–17).

7.2.2 The Rise of Mainland China's Financial Centre Networks

The most consequential change in China's financial centre networks in the twenty-first century consists of the growing importance of mainland centres. They have ascended to the upper ranks of global financial centres (see Figure 7.7). The Global Financial Centre Index (GFCI) is a composite of over 100 variables covering six sectors (business environment, human capital, taxation, reputation, infrastructure, and financial centre development) and survey views of over 3,000 financial professionals, as of the latest six-month survey (Z/Yen 2007–17). The wide range of variables and reliance on an opinion survey necessarily mean that the GFCI cannot be used as a precise ranking, but it can serve as a rough indicator of financial centre importance. With these caveats, Hong Kong typically ranks third globally after London and New York, although recent surveys place it fourth, after Singapore. That drop is meaningless because on any measure of scale and scope of financial services and network reach, Hong Kong is third globally (Meyer 2000; 2014a; 2015).

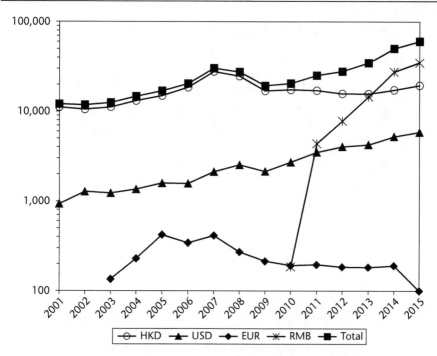

Figure 7.6. Hong Kong annual interbank payments by currency in US$ billions, 2001–15
Source: Author, based on data from the Bank for International Settlements (2017).

Initially, rankings of Shanghai, Beijing, and Shenzhen experienced large swings, probably reflecting data issues and uncertainty among financial professionals regarding how these centres functioned within China and externally (see Figure 7.7). In recent surveys their rankings shifted to a range of 15 to 25 globally. Shanghai and Beijing may be on the verge of moving into the top fifteen. If these levels are sustained, China's financial centre networks will have emerged as key constituents of global networks. Shenzhen's stabilization in the low-20s should be qualified, however. One component of its networks operates internally to the mainland, where its financial firms are highly networked, while Shenzhen's other component, as a satellite of Hong Kong, consists of ties to that city's financial firms (Meyer 2016b). Combining Shenzhen's firm networks with Hong Kong's enhances its financial firms as intermediaries between China and global networks. Shenzhen's firms maintain widespread network relations with firms in China's financial centres through branch offices of the large state banks of China, as well as through domestic venture capital and private equity firms headquartered in the city which have branches in these centres.

China's financial centre networks are embedded in a political-economic milieu which frames their internal and external relations. The leading centres

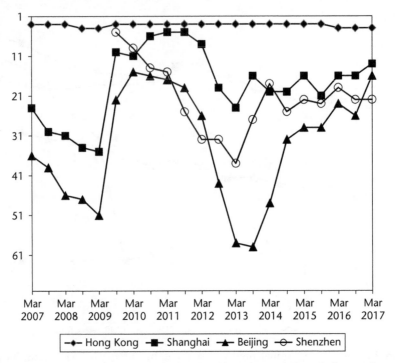

Figure 7.7. Global Financial Centre Index (GFCI) ranking of China's financial centres, 2007–17

Source: Author, based on data from Z/Yen (2007–17).

possess complementarity: Hong Kong is the global financial centre (offshore), Beijing is the political-regulatory centre, and Shanghai is the commercial-financial centre (Lai 2012). The economic growth of China since the 1978 reforms of Deng Xiaoping propelled Beijing as its political-regulatory centre to becoming a major presence in China's networks. Beijing governmental units, from the Politburo Standing Committee down through the ministries and regulatory agencies, engage in policy making and macro planning. The Ministry of Finance (2017), as the national executive agency of the Central People's Government, administers macroeconomic policies and the country's annual budget, as well as managing fiscal policy, economic regulations, and government expenditures. The financial regulatory agencies and commissions, including the PBOC, the China Securities Regulatory Commission (CSRC), the China Banking Regulatory Commission (CBRC), and the State Administration of Foreign Exchange (SAFE), however, impact Beijing more directly as a financial centre.

They exert exceptional influence over decision-making and actions of financial actors in China. The government follows a rule-based approach consisting of laws, orders, regulations, and directives; however, these are expressed in generalities. Implementation and enforcement are left to the discretion of administrative authorities, which leads to non-standardized results. Financial actors, therefore, utilize face-to-face contact to build social relationships. These serve as the mechanism to understand the meaning of rules and to gain favourable decisions for their business. This information asymmetry between market regulators and market participants compels financial firms to establish offices in Beijing to maintain access to financial regulatory agencies and commissions (Zhao 2013).

Beijing also houses the global headquarters of most of the largest state-owned enterprises (SOEs) and of the four largest state banks (Agricultural Bank of China, Bank of China, China Construction Bank, and Industrial and Commercial Bank of China) (Chiu and Lewis 2006). Foreign financial firms, especially investment banks, target SOEs for equity and bond issuance, and collaborate with state banks on financial transactions. Consequently, leading financiers in these foreign banks focus on building and maintaining relationships with government agencies and commissions and with SOEs and large state banks (Lai 2012).

Shanghai's international status as the leading commercial-financial centre of China's networks dates from the late-nineteenth century. Yet this omits the significance of the city in China's domestic financial networks that originated in the early part of that century. Ningpo merchants relocated to Shanghai by the early nineteenth century and founded banks by the 1820s. When foreign merchants and bankers arrived in the 1840s and 1850s, following the Opium Wars, Shanghai merchants and financiers already controlled the lucrative Yangtze Valley business. Over the next decades, Chinese banks headquartered in Shanghai extended their financial networks throughout China. Foreign bank branches that arrived from the late-nineteenth century up to the 1930s primarily served their home-country clients. Whenever they required financial exchanges domestically, they collaborated with Shanghai bankers. Thus, Shanghai was the premier domestic financial centre of China, and foreign bank branches provided the international links (Cheng 2003; Ji 2003; Meyer 2000).

Contemporary Shanghai financial networks retain the relations that emerged from this earlier period. Foreign commercial banks typically place their China headquarters in Shanghai to serve their multinational clients with business in China, especially in the Yangtze Valley. They provide trade finance, working capital, and asset management; therefore, their business relationships are not as focused on relations with governmental agencies and commissions. Whenever they cannot fully supply renminbi financing due to quota restrictions, they utilize their offices in Hong Kong. These foreign banks develop relationships with large state banks that also house their leading commercial bankers in Shanghai to provide loans and credit facilities to their major domestic clients, which likewise have large operations in the Yangtze Valley (Chen et al. 2014; Lai 2012).

Beijing officials recognize that financial networks in Shanghai are more commercially oriented. Consequently, regulatory agencies and commissions, especially the PBOC, CSRC, and CBRC, give their Shanghai offices considerable authority to interpret and implement laws and policies established by the Beijing headquarters. Shanghai offices focus more on market-oriented business and international activities of financial firms, as well as on financial supervision, payments, and credit. They also are empowered to experiment with financial innovations (Lai 2012).

This political-economic milieu that frames China's financial centre networks produces differences in the external and internal relations of the complementary centres of Hong Kong as global financial centre (offshore), Beijing as political-regulatory centre, and Shanghai as commercial-financial centre. Market-based financial exchanges dominate networks between China's financial centres and foreign ones. These external network ties are exhibited in networks of advanced producer services firms. Based on the degree of intra-organizational office connections, Hong Kong ranks first in China and third globally, Shanghai ranks second in China and seventh globally, and Beijing ranks third in China and twelfth globally. Over recent years, Shanghai and Beijing have risen significantly in connectivity, reflecting their growing importance in global financial networks (Derudder et al. 2010; 2013).

As China's window to global capital and Asia-Pacific centre, Hong Kong ranks top worldwide in linkages both to London and New York (see Table 7.3). Shanghai ranks sixth worldwide in linkages to London and tenth to New York. Beijing follows with a world rank of fourteen in links to London and nineteen

Table 7.3. Financial centre linkages of Hong Kong, Shanghai, and Beijing based on advanced producer services in 2010

World rank	Financial centre linkage outside Asia	World rank	Financial centre linkage inside Asia
2	Hong Kong and London	20	Hong Kong and Singapore
3	Hong Kong and New York	31	Hong Kong and Shanghai
6	Shanghai and London	37	Hong Kong and Tokyo
10	Shanghai and New York	39	Hong Kong and Beijing
14	Beijing and London	44	Shanghai and Singapore
19	Beijing and New York	50	Hong Kong and Sydney
32	Hong Kong and Paris	52	Beijing and Singapore
45	Shanghai and Paris	54	Shanghai and Tokyo
46	Hong Kong and Dubai	56	Shanghai and Beijing
47	Hong Kong and Chicago		
57	Hong Kong and Milan		

Note: World rank of the degree of connectivity between the same offices in the city pair.

Source: Author, adapted from Taylor et al. 2014. 'City-Dyad Analyses of China's Integration into the World City Network', Table 2. p. 873.

to New York. Shanghai's position above Beijing's follows from the former's greater market-based financial exchanges. That comports with Shanghai's long-term role as mainland China's most important international financial centre, after Hong Kong. Except for Shanghai's ties to Paris, Hong Kong dominates the remainder of China's financial centre links outside Asia. The high global ranking of Shanghai and Beijing, along with Hong Kong, demonstrates that China's financial centre networks occupy a leading position in global networks.

Within Asia, Hong Kong's extensive intra-organizational linkages to Singapore comports with financial firms' deployment of Hong Kong as Asia-Pacific regional headquarters and Singapore as southeast Asia headquarters (see Table 7.3). This dyad ranks highest among China's financial centres because Hong Kong's financial firms serve as China's Asia-Pacific intermediaries. As the leader of China's financial centre networks, Hong Kong possesses the largest linkages to Shanghai, Tokyo, and Beijing. The greater importance of Shanghai's financial firms than Beijing's in market-based networks is exhibited both in the higher world rank of linkages of Hong Kong with Shanghai than with Beijing and in Shanghai's higher world rank than Beijing's in linkages to Singapore and Tokyo. The Shanghai–Beijing dyad ranks far below either city's linkages to Hong Kong, suggesting that market-based ties between Shanghai and Beijing have lesser importance.

Within mainland China, political-financial networks dominate. China's state banks and insurance companies control most finance on the mainland. Consequently, Beijing's banks and insurance firms possess the largest network connectivity among financial centres (Zhao et al. 2015; Zhen et al. 2013). Shanghai's banking and insurance networks are second most important, whereas Shenzhen ranks third on banking and is less important on insurance. The Shanghai and Shenzhen stock exchanges and local offices of government securities regulators attract securities firms to these cities, making them key nodes in stock exchange networks, whereas Beijing attracts securities firms that deal with regulators.

China's financial centre networks based on all producer services exhibit two complementary features. First, Beijing and Shanghai firms possess linkages almost twice as large as any other city pair, befitting their status as political-regulatory and commercial-financial centres of China (Zhao et al. 2015). Both cities' firms possess their next largest connectivity with firms in Shenzhen and Guangzhou, leading centres of South China and the Pearl River Delta. Firms in these latter cities retain significant intercity network ties. These firms also maintain tight network bonds with firms in Hong Kong, underscoring its firms' positions as China's window to global capital.

Second, the mainland's producer services networks exhibit a distinctive regional structure (Zhen et al. 2013). Beijing is the undisputed national centre of China's networks due to the primacy of political decision-making in finance; firm networks involving Beijing firms radiate across China's centres. Shanghai's firms dominate in the eastern coastal region, especially the Yangtze Delta, a pattern rooted in the nineteenth century. While Shanghai's firms have national ties, these are not as widespread as firms in Beijing. Shenzhen's firms serve southern China and the Pearl River Delta, again intimately related to their proximity to Hong Kong's firms.

In sum, China's financial centre networks exhibit a consistent structure. Hong Kong firms operate as China's window to global capital and leaders in the networks of the Asia-Pacific region. Its firms retain deep connections with firms in the mainland centres of Beijing and Shanghai, and Shenzhen firms, besides their internal domestic linkages, are bonded with Hong Kong firms. Within the mainland, Beijing's firms are prominent in the political-regulatory networks and Shanghai's firms head the commercial-financial networks. China's leaders—Hong Kong, Shanghai, and Beijing—now occupy the upper ranks of global financial centres.

7.3 Opportunities and Challenges

While Hong Kong's financial firms have been China's window to global capital since the nineteenth century, until 1997 colonialism directly impacted that relationship. Since 1997, the city's status as a global financial centre has been supported by its sovereign power. Consequently, financial networks among Hong Kong, Shanghai, and Beijing are strengthening. Dramatic changes in Asia and the global economy raise both opportunities and challenges for these centres.

Fintech, defined as the application of information technology to financial services, offers an opportunity for China's financial centre networks. The Asia-Pacific region has moved into global leadership in fintech investments, and mainland China and Hong Kong accounted for about 90 per cent of the regional total in 2016 (Wozniak and Conway 2017). China's top technology firms—Baidu, Alibaba, Tencent, and JD.com—lead the innovation and adoption of fintech. They focus on consumer and small-to-medium-size firms (SMEs), which traditionally have been poorly served by large state banks. Their businesses make China the Asian leader in customer payments/remittances, lending, personal wealth management, and insurance. Over half of the population now use mobile devices for these activities (McKinsey Greater China FIG Practice 2016; Mittal and Lloyd 2016).

China's top financial centres and their satellites lead its fintech (KPMG China 2016; Mittal and Lloyd 2016). Beijing, arguably home to the largest number of fintech firms, is anchored by Baidu and JD.com. Large state banks of China headquartered in Beijing, including China Construction Bank and Industrial and Commercial Bank of China, also invest in fintech. The PBOC is developing regulatory frameworks to support fintech, and the government funds startups (McKinsey Greater China FIG Practice 2016; Zhang 2017). These internet leaders, fintech firms, banks, and regulators position Beijing as a key node of fintech in China's financial centre networks and globally (Ji 2017).

Shanghai and its satellite of Hangzhou house a large number of top fintech firms, anchored by Alibaba in Hangzhou. Shenzhen, the satellite of Hong Kong, is likewise a major fintech centre. It houses Tencent, a leading funder of fintech startups, and other large technology firms that have entered that sector, such as Huawei and ZTE (KPMG China 2016; Mittal and Lloyd 2016). PingAn, also headquartered in Shenzhen and China's second largest insurance company, runs a US$1 billion investment fund focused on fintech and owns Lufax, its online wealth management and lending platform (Ren 2017). While Hong Kong is not a major technology centre, its financial firms support fintech firms in Shenzhen. Hong Kong's firms comprise a large market for firms working on business-to-business (B2B) products, and they provide access to global capital markets for fintech firms (Financial Services Development Council 2017). Besides close ties to Beijing, Hong Kong's regulators, including the Securities and Futures Commission (SFC) and HKMA, maintain strong relationships with London regulators, especially the Financial Conduct Authority. These ties keep Hong Kong fintech firms, financial firms, and regulators engaged with a leading global centre of fintech (Banking Newslink 2017; McGrath 2017).

China's continued economic expansion and its citizens' growing wealth boost demand for more investment opportunities, and the government aims to strengthen financial markets. Commencement of 'stock connects' between Hong Kong Exchanges and the Shanghai and Shenzhen exchanges is one such effort. Hong Kong–Shanghai connect started in November 2014, and Hong Kong–Shenzhen connect began in December 2016 (Ren 2014; Richards 2016). The connects permit mainland traders to access Hong Kong's market from Shanghai and Shenzhen and permit international traders to access mainland markets through Hong Kong accounts. Traders can have multiple accounts, mainland mutual funds can invest in Hong Kong stocks, and plans are commencing to allow exchange-traded funds to operate as securities. The Hong Kong SFC and China's CSRC coordinate regulations and maintain real-time surveillance monitoring of trading to protect the integrity of markets (Li 2015; Richards 2016; Zhou 2015).

Trading in both directions on each connect has increased, with Shanghai's connect larger than Shenzhen's (Hong Kong Exchanges 2017). Shenzhen's connect allows international investors to access the large number of innovative technology companies listed on that exchange. While total value of trading remains small, these links set the basis for long-term trading. Increased access of institutional investors to China's 'A-shares' (mainland equities) through stock connects encouraged these investors to support the decision of MSCI to include 'A-shares' in their world index beginning in 2018 (Hughes and Bullock 2017). Nonetheless, their proportion of the index will remain tiny, and MSCI warned that continued reform of China's markets is necessary for larger inclusion in the index. Consequently, the impact on China's stock exchanges in Hong Kong, Shanghai, and Shenzhen will remain modest for the foreseeable future.

China's government continues to strengthen its financial centre networks to the rest of the world. At a news conference after the National People's Congress in Beijing in March 2017, Premier Li Keqiang announced that a 'bond-connect' programme would be launched which would allow Hong Kong traders to directly access the world's third-largest bond market in Shanghai. He explicitly framed this as a mechanism to support the city as China's global financial centre (Luo and Lin 2017). The bond-connect programme was officially approved in May 2017, and trading commenced in early July (Chan 2017; Hong Kong Monetary Authority 2017a). Although global bond investors had had access to China's bond market since 2016, trading was difficult and accounts had to be opened on the mainland. With bond connect, foreign investors, including pension funds, central banks, and sovereign wealth funds, can freely trade through Hong Kong dealers without quota restrictions (Hong Kong Monetary Authority 2017b).

In keeping with the growing integration of Hong Kong, Shanghai, and Beijing, the bond-connect programme is managed through coordination among HKMA, Hong Kong Exchanges, PBOC, Shanghai Clearing House, China Foreign Exchange Trade System, and China Central Depository & Clearing (Hong Kong Monetary Authority 2017a). Because Beijing officials chose Hong Kong as the first direct entry point to China's bond market, this gives the city's financial firms a head start over bond dealers and traders in other financial centres in acquiring expertise and knowledge about China's bond market and developing trading strategies and algorithms. This bond trading enhances Hong Kong as a global renminbi payments centre. Expertise and market-making in bonds in Hong Kong may attract more mainland companies to go public in Hong Kong and to issue bonds there (E. Li 2017). A hint at future global networks of China's financial centres emerged with a proposal to establish a London–Shanghai Stock Connect, linking London's and Shanghai's stock exchanges. This proposal remains in the 'study phase', partly because Brexit, the exit of the United Kingdom from the European Union, raises uncertainty and this has made Chinese officials wary (Liu 2016; Price 2017).

China's 'One Belt, One Road' ('Belt and Road') initiative and related Asian Infrastructure Investment Bank (AIIB) have potential to enhance financial centre networks in Hong Kong and Beijing. When President Xi Jinping travelled to central and southeast Asia in September and October of 2013 he broached the idea of building the Silk Road Economic Belt and the 21st-Century Maritime Silk Road. Around the same time, Premier Li Keqiang raised the prospect of building the Maritime Silk Road targeting ASEAN at the China–ASEAN Expo in Guangxi, China. While the core of this grand development initiative revolves around 'Belt and Road', it is aimed more broadly at strengthening the economic development of Asia, the Middle East, Europe, and Africa. The initiative is not exclusive to China; instead, the aim is to bring together many countries, international organizations, and the private sector to cooperate in development projects (National Development and Reform Commission et al. 2015).

From the beginning, President Xi and Premier Li conceived of the AIIB as a key facilitator of the 'Belt and Road' initiative. In October 2014 a memorandum of understanding was signed by twenty-one Asian countries which supported the founding of this multilateral development bank, and by April 2015 the AIIB formally commenced with fifty-seven members (Callaghan and Hubbard 2016; Jin 2015). In March 2017 another thirteen applicants joined, including Hong Kong, bringing the total to seventy members. Elite Communist Party cadres supported Hong Kong's participation in the 'Belt and Road' initiative and in the AIIB. Zhang Dejiang, Chairman of the Standing Committee of the National People's Congress, overseer of Hong Kong and Macau affairs, and third-ranking member of the Politburo Standing Committee, told a 'Belt and Road' summit in Hong Kong in May 2016 that the city had the capacity to contribute significantly to the initiative. Jin Liqun, President of the AIIB, had supported the city's membership of the bank from its inception (Jie 2017; E. Li 2017; Sun and Lau 2016).

The 'Belt and Road' initiative, along with the AIIB, vaults China into a position of leadership in economic development in Asia. Yet, among the bank's senior executives, only the president, Jin Liqun, is from China, and its first set of projects is not dominated by China's SOEs (AIIB 2017). Nevertheless, the long-term infrastructure development process will generate extensive opportunities for China's businesses. The World Bank and IMF are dominated by the United States, which blocks Chinese influence over projects, and the Asian Development Bank, heavily influenced by Japan, has not been a leader in Asian development (Yu 2017).

As an Asia-Pacific financial centre and China's window to global capital, Hong Kong's commercial and investment banks, private equity firms, hedge funds, and fund management firms will have opportunities to provide loans, issue and buy bonds, offer treasury management, and purchase stakes in 'Belt and Road' projects. The local presence of major commercial and investment banking units of the large state banks of China, especially Bank of China, China Construction Bank, and Industrial and Commercial Bank of China, also enhances the participation of Hong Kong financial institutions in the projects. These banks possess direct links to their Beijing headquarters, which in turn have ties to the government ministries and SOEs involved in the 'Belt and Road' initiative. Bank of China International (BOCI), the global investment banking arm of Bank of China (Beijing) is headquartered in Hong Kong. Through its CEO, Li Tong, it has taken a leading role in supporting 'Belt and Road' projects (Meyer 2017).

While the state banks of China in Hong Kong have direct access to Beijing regarding projects, Hong Kong's membership of the AIIB provides its private-sector financial firms with additional access to information about them. Many of the projects will require renminbi financing; Hong Kong's position as global leader in renminbi payments, therefore, will generate substantial financial business (Leung 2017; E. Li 2017). As headquarters for AIIB, Beijing's financial firms will strengthen network ties to Hong Kong financial centre networks, as well as wider network linkages to London and New York financial firms. Thus Beijing's importance in financial centre networks will be enhanced (McCord 2016).

Beijing government officials, agencies, and ministries work closely with their equivalents in the United Kingdom, reinforcing China's financial centre network bonds with London. The PBOC coordinates regulations and procedures with the Bank of England and the British Treasury which cover issues such as renminbi trading, issuing of stock by Chinese companies on the London Stock Exchange, and clearing facilities. These build network bonds between Beijing and London. The Shanghai Clearing House has set up a representative office in London, further reinforcing these ties (Barker 2017).

London's firms aim to work with the AIIB and to be heavily involved in financing infrastructure projects for 'Belt and Road'. This involvement derives from London's financial networks that reach to Europe, the Middle East, Central Asia, and Africa. Expertise of London's firms in risk management, long-term funding, and government finance is seen by Chinese leaders as supporting its 'Belt and Road' (Gui and Neild 2017; Yiu 2017). These projects strengthen financial network bonds between London and Beijing, and because Hong Kong financial firms (many of them with large offices in London) will also be involved in 'Belt and Road' projects, its network ties to London will continue to grow.

Challenges to Hong Kong as the leading financial centre of the Asia-Pacific region have arisen throughout its history, yet its status remains secure (Meyer 2016a). Beijing officials from the President to the Premier to heads of ministries and regulatory bodies such as the PBOC continually express support for the city as the country's window to global capital (Meyer 2014c). They go beyond words to actions, as exhibited more recently when China's government set Hong Kong as its first offshore renminbi payments centre in 2003 and waited eight years to allow other financial centres to have permission, ensuring that the city's firms would dominate offshore renminbi payments. As a related issue, the government's selection of Hong Kong to be the first centre to have direct access through offshore accounts to China's bond market gives the city's firms a head start in dominating the offshore renminbi bond market.

China's determination to protect Hong Kong as its global financial centre colours its approach to recent challenges to its control over the city as a Special Administrative Region, albeit with substantial autonomy to govern itself. The Occupy Central pro-democracy (Umbrella) movement emerged in the second half of 2014 as a challenge to China's authority over the election of the Chief Executive, the most senior government official. Representative constituencies elect that official, but the final appointment is reserved for China's government (Basic Law 2017). Nevertheless, social and economic issues loomed large, including a weak educational system, competition by mainland graduates for the best jobs, large numbers of mainland students in local universities, millions of mainland residents coming each year to shop, and high property prices, driven partly by wealthy mainland residents (Gough 2014). Nevertheless, these protests did not undermine Hong Kong as an Asia-Pacific financial centre (Meyer 2014c). Criminal charges that Hong Kong police brought in March 2017 against nine organizers of the 2014 protests, however, guaranteed that these issues would fester (Wong 2017).

The term 'mainlandization', which conveys the idea that Hong Kong is becoming more like mainland cities, distils these contentious issues. Yet the continued influx of foreigners to work in global businesses and the growing talent pool of young people from the mainland suggests this view is oversimplified (Chen 2016; EJ Insight 2016). In a talk in Hong Kong in spring 2016, Zhang Dejiang, overseer of Hong Kong and Macau affairs, rejected allegations that China has mainlandized the city. He argued that Hong Kong is a pluralistic city and localism, fondness for your home place, is fine. The 'one country, two systems' model is appropriate, but advocating independence is against China and the government (Un and Lau 2016). President Xi and Premier Li, commenting on China's appointment of Carrie Lam as Chief Executive following her election by the constituencies, challenged her to heal social divides and improve the livelihood of the average citizen (Lam and Ng 2017; South China Morning Post 2017). Lam is attempting to forge a bridge to the city's young people, arguing they should be listened to and can take legitimate actions, so long as they adhere to the Basic Law (Yeung 2017).

Controversy erupted with the twentieth anniversary of Hong Kong's return to China's sovereign control, on 1 July 2017. On 27 May, Zhang Dejiang gave a speech at a meeting at the Great Hall of the People in Beijing to commemorate the Basic Law of the HKSAR. Some observers raised concerns that his comments about Beijing's power to supervise city officials and expect loyalty to the HKSAR and China and efforts to improve institutional arrangements for implementing the Basic Law would undermine the city's government (Lau and Chung 2017). The title of Zhang's speech and its content reveal that China's government expected full adherence to the Basic Law under the 'one country, two systems' model, and the central government had authority to interpret the law (China Daily 2017). At the same time, Zhang trumpeted the essence of Article 109, that the government of the HKSAR should maintain Hong Kong's status as an international financial centre.

Arguably, a major challenge to Hong Kong's status as one of the three great global financial centres may emerge as 2047 approaches. That is the endpoint of the guarantee of Article 5 of the Basic Law (2017), Hong Kong's governing constitution which grants it substantial autonomy and judicial independence for its legal system based on English common law. The article states that 'The socialist system and policies shall not be practised in the Hong Kong Special Administrative Region, and the previous capitalist system and way of life shall remain unchanged for 50 years'. That is the principle of 'one country, two systems', which Chinese leaders keep emphasizing as the way Hong Kong is to function as a global business centre.

Recently, several Chinese officials have commented on what will happen after 2047. Song Ru'an, deputy commissioner of Beijing's foreign ministry office in Hong Kong, stated that '...it is too early to talk about what will happen after 2047. We should focus on how to implement "one country, two systems" comprehensively and accurately' (Cheung 2017). At the same time, Song said, 'I believe that the city's high degree of autonomous power will continue.' President Xi Jinping provided endorsement of this theme when he stated that '...we are willing to...look into the future and to ensure "one country, two systems" is stable and has a far-reaching future' (Reuters News Service 2017).

These statements by Chinese leaders are unequivocal. The government is open to maintaining sufficient autonomy for Hong Kong after 2047 under the 'one country, two systems' formula in order to ensure that it remains one of the top three global financial centres. China has demonstrated that this formula works. Since the return of Hong Kong to the country's sovereign control in 1997, global financial firms have maintained their organizational management of the Asia-Pacific region in the city, and it has thrived as a financial centre. The leaders of China recognize the benefits that accrue to the country in prestige and access to global capital. They never cease repeating their support for Hong Kong and implementing policies to ensure its pivotal position as China's global financial centre.

7.4 Risks of Financial Instability

The fiscal stimulus and credit expansion which China's government insti-tuted to mitigate the economic disruption of the Global Financial Crisis of 2007–8 continued over the subsequent decade and now raises risks of finan-cial instability. As a percentage of GDP, nonfinancial-sector debt rose from 80 per cent to 175 per cent and household debt increased from 20 per cent to over 40 per cent between 2007 and 2017 (International Monetary Fund 2017). Swelling intra-financial-sector debt transmitted through opaque instruments such as wealth management products contributes to potential instability. Meanwhile, a substantial share of credit at subsidized interest rates flowed to state-owned enterprises that are less productive than private-sector firms.

The outpouring of credit (loans) far exceeded the economy's growth, and these loans sit as assets on swollen bank balance sheets. China, therefore, is revisiting the non-performing loan (NPLs) problems of the 1990s, which it had resolved by removing bad loans from bank balance sheets and recapital-izing banks. Most assets of China's banking system are in state-owned banks. These banks are pressured to give loans to support local employment, prevent social unrest, and spur economic growth, and these pressures contribute to weak credit assessment. As NPLs rise, banks attempt to cope by providing riskier loans, hoping they can cover losses (Levy and Meyer 2012; Zhang et al. 2016). Officially, NPLs in the Chinese banking system average about 2 per cent, but this figure is highly suspect. Even a government newspaper called atten-tion to the rising NPL problem (X. Li 2017). The real-estate sector is a major source of these NPLs. Its share of China's GDP rose from about 10 per cent a decade ago to almost one-third by 2016. Many property developers could face bankruptcy (PR Newswire Asia 2017; Wei and Fong 2017).

Nonetheless, claims that China faces growing financial instability and this may contribute to a new global financial crisis are disputed (Ma 2017; Tinker 2017). China's rate of annual percentage growth of GDP plummeted from an extraordinarily high rate immediately prior to the Global Financial Crisis (see Figure 7.8). Still, this slowing rate of growth took it to a level of between 6 per cent and 7 per cent by 2016, a rate that is high by global standards on an economy that almost doubled in size (see Figure 7.1). China's high savings rate provides banks a large deposit cushion to prevent illiquidity problems, and government control of most banks and the closed capital account offer policy levers to mitigate external financial threats.

Hong Kong, Shanghai, and Beijing will be impacted by a new global finan-cial crisis. Based on Hong Kong's multiple experiences with such crises over the past century, likely results will include contraction of financial activity, shrinkage of the number of financial firms, and declines in employment. Yet, based on past experiences, recovery from a financial crisis will be swift. The

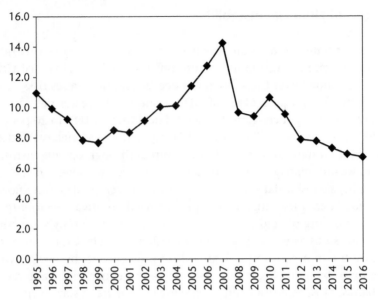

Figure 7.8. Real annual % growth of gross domestic product (GDP) in China, 1995–2016
Source: Author, based on data from the World Bank (2017).

position of China's financial centres in global networks will not be disrupted. Hong Kong has never lost its status as the leading centre of the Asia-Pacific region because its financiers are the network hubs of expertise, knowledge, and relationships in the region; this strength will fuel the city's rebound. Shanghai financiers, likewise, have never lost their pivotal position in mainland business networks. After any crisis, external financiers will need to collaborate with Shanghai financiers to access mainland business. Finally, Beijing's rising importance in global financial networks will not be disrupted. As the political-regulatory centre of China, its future prominence is secure. China's financial centres are buttressed by the world's second-largest economy, whose growth rate will probably exceed any other large economy, including the United States, during a recovery from the crisis.

References

AIIB. 2017. 'Approved Projects'. https://www.aiib.org/en/projects/approved/index.html, accessed 9 February 2018.
Auslin, Michael R. 2017. The End of the Asian Century. New Haven, CT: Yale University Press.
Bank for International Settlements. 2017. www.bis.org.

Banking Newslink. 2017. 'FCA and SFC Sign Fintech Co-Operation Agreement 2017'. 16 May.

Barker, Peter. 2017. 'China, Britain to Boost Financial Cooperation'. Xinhua News Agency, 22 March. Basic Law of the Hong Kong Special Administrative Region of the People's Republic of China. 2017. Hong Kong: Constitutional and Mainland Affairs Bureau.

Callaghan, Mike and Paul Hubbard. 2016. 'The Asian Infrastructure Investment Bank: Multilateralism on the Silk Road'. *China Economic Journal* 9 (2): 116–39.

Capgemini. 2012–16a. 'Asia-Pacific Wealth Report 2016'. www.asiapacificwealthreport. com.

Capgemini. 2012–16b. 'World Wealth Report 2016'. www.worldwealthreport.com.

Census and Statistics Department. 2002–17. 'Report on Hong Kong Trade in Services Statistics'. Hong Kong Special Administrative Region.

Chan, Norman T. L. 2017. 'Remarks by the Chief Executive of HKMA at the Bond Connect Launch Ceremony 3 July 2017'. Hong Kong Monetary Authority, 3 July. http://www.hkma.gov.hk/eng/key-information/speech-speakers/ntlchan/ 20170703-1.shtml, accessed 9 February 2018.

Chen, Frank. 2016. 'More Mainlandized? HK is Also More Internationalized Than Ever'. EJ Insight, 29 June.

Chen, Ke et al. 2014. 'Agglomeration and Location Choice of Foreign Financial Institutions in China'. *Geojournal 79* (2): 255–66.

Cheng, Linsun. 2003. Banking in Modern China: Entrepreneurs, Professional Managers, and the Development of Chinese Banks, 1897–1937. Cambridge: Cambridge University Press.

Cheung, Tony. 2017. 'Too Early to Discuss Post-2047 Future'. *South China Morning Post,* 24 May.

China Daily (Hong Kong). 2017. 'Reaffirming "One Country, Two Systems" and Guaranteeing Full Enactment of the Basic Law'. 29 May.

Chiu, Becky and Mervyn K. Lewis. 2006. Reforming China's State-Owned Enterprises and Banks. Cheltenham: Edward Elgar.

Deloitte. 2015. The Deloitte Wealth Management Centre Ranking 2015. Zurich: Deloitte.

Derudder, Ben et al. 2010. 'Pathways of Change: Shifting Connectivities in the World City Network, 2000–08'. *Urban Studies* 47 (9): 1861–77.

Derudder, Ben et al. 2013. 'Measurement and Interpretation of Connectivity of Chinese Cities in World City Network, 2010'. *Chinese Geographical Science* 23 (3): 261–73.

EJ Insight. 2016. 'Hong Kong Becoming China, Veteran Mainland Journalist Laments'. 9 December.

Financial Services Development Council. 2017. 'The Future of Fintech in Hong Kong'. FSDC Paper No. 29, Hong Kong Special Administrative Region.

Gough, Neil. 2014. 'Hong Kong Wealth Gap on Display in Protests'. *New York Times,* 5 October.

Gui, Tao and Larry Neild. 2017. 'UK Can Share China's B&R Initiative to Build Prosperity'. Xinhua News Agency, 7 March.

Hong Kong Exchanges. 2017. https://www.hkex.com.hk/Mutual-Market/Stock-Connect/ Statistics/Historic-Monthly?sc_lang=en#select1=0&select2=0, accessed 9 February 2018.

149

Hong Kong Monetary Authority. 1997–2017. Annual Report. Hong Kong Special Administrative Region.

Hong Kong Monetary Authority. 2015. 'Hong Kong: The Premier Offshore Renminbi Business Centre'. Hong Kong Special Administrative Region.

Hong Kong Monetary Authority. 2017a. 'Joint Announcement of the People's Bank of China and the Hong Kong Monetary Authority', 16 May. http://www.info.gov.hk/gia/general/201705/16/P2017051600781.htm, accessed 9 February 2018.

Hong Kong Monetary Authority. 2017b. 'BCCL and HKMA Promote Bond Connect', 3 July. http://www.info.gov.hk/gia/general/201707/03/P2017070300951.htm, accessed 9 February 2018.

Hughes, Jennifer and Nicole Bullock. 2017. 'China Stocks Hit 18-Month High on MSCI Inclusion'. *Financial Times*, 22 June.

International Monetary Fund. 2017. 'People's Republic of China'. Staff Report for the 2017 Article IV Consultation, July 13. http://www.imf.org/en/publications/cr/issues/2017/08/15/people-s-republic-of-china-2017-article-iv-consultation-press-release-staff-report-and-45170, accessed 9 February 2018.

Ji, Ming. 2017. 'Fintech—An Untapped Source of Grade A Office Demand in Beijing', 28 March. http://www.joneslanglasalle.com.cn.

Ji, Zhaojin. 2003. A History of Modern Shanghai Banking. Armonk, NY: M. E. Sharpe.

Jie, Gao. 2017. 'HK Capable of Contributing to AIIB's Success'. Xinhua News Agency, 12 April.

Jin, Liqun. 2015. 'Financing for the Future: The Vision for the Asian Infrastructure Investment Bank'. *Horizons* (4), Summer: 54–61.

Jones, Geoffrey. 1993. British Multinational Banking, 1830–1990. Oxford: Oxford University Press.

King, Frank H. H. 1987. The Hongkong Bank in Late Imperial China, 1864–1902: On an Even Keel. The History of the Hongkong and Shanghai Banking Corporation, Vol. 1. Cambridge: Cambridge University Press.

King, Frank H. H. 1988. The Hongkong Bank in the Period of Imperialism and War, 1895–1918. The History of the Hongkong and Shanghai Banking Corporation, Vol. 2. Cambridge: Cambridge University Press.

KPMG China. 2016. '2016 China Leading Fintech 50'. https://home.kpmg.com/cn/en/home/insights/2016/09/2016-china-leading-fintech-50.html, accessed 9 February 2018.

Lai, Karen. 2012. 'Differentiated Markets: Shanghai, Beijing, and Hong Kong in China's Financial Centre Network'. *Urban Studies* 49 (6): 1275–96.

Lam, Jeffie and Joyce Ng. 2017. 'Chinese Premier Li Keqiang Sets Out To-Do List for Carrie Lam to Take Hong Kong to New Level'. *South China Morning Post*, 11 April.

Lau, Stuart and Kimmy Chung. 2017. 'Beijing's Latest Move Threatens HK Civil Servants' Neutrality'. *South China Morning Post*, 28 May.

Leung, C. Y. 2017. 'HK Embracing Belt & Road'. *Hong Kong Government News*, 7 April.

Levy, Tal and David R. Meyer. 2012. 'Challenges of Network Governance at the State Banks of China'. *Journal of Contemporary China* 21 (75): 481–98.

Li, Eddy. 2017. 'Bond Connect, AIIB Membership a Double Blessing for Financial Industry'. *China Daily* (Hong Kong), 12 April.

Li, Xiang. 2015. 'Multiple Stock Accounts Allowed'. *China Daily*, 14 April.

Li, Xiang. 2017. 'Set for Rebound'. *China Daily*, 22 May.

Liu, Cecily. 2016. 'London Pushes for Shanghai Stock Link'. *China Daily*, 6 August.

Luo, Weiteng and Wenjie Lin. 2017. 'Premier Says Mainland–HK Bond Trading Link on the Way'. *China Daily* (US edition), 16 March.

Ma, Jingling. 2017. 'China's Level of Debt Remains "Under Control"'. *Global Times*, 7 August.

McCord, Steven. 2016. 'OBOR Putting Beijing en Route to Becoming a Global Nerve Centre', 10 November. www.joneslanglasalle.com.cn.

McGrath, Joe. 2017. 'Canary Wharf Imperiled by New London Fintech Hub'. *Institutional Investor Magazine*, 10 April.

McKinsey Greater China FIG Practice. 2016. 'Disruption and Connection: Cracking the Myths of China Internet Finance Innovation'. https://www.mckinsey.com/~/media/mckinsey/industries/financial%20services/our%20insights/whats%20next%20for%20chinas%20booming%20fintech%20sector/disruption-and-connection-cracking-the-myths-of-china-internet-finance-innovation.ashx, accessed 9 February 2018.

Meyer, David R. 2000. Hong Kong as a Global Metropolis. Cambridge: Cambridge University Press.

Meyer, David R. 2014a. 'The Banking Networks of Asian Financial Centres'. In Handbook of Asian Finance: Financial Markets and Sovereign Wealth Funds, Vol. 1, edited by David Lee Kuo Chuen and Greg N. Gregoriou. Oxford: Academic Press, pp. 37–52.

Meyer, David R. 2014b. 'Private Wealth Management in Asia'. In Handbook of Asian Finance: Financial Markets and Sovereign Wealth Funds, Vol. 1, edited by David Lee Kuo Chuen and Greg N. Gregoriou. Oxford: Academic Press, pp. 17–36.

Meyer, David R. 2014c. 'No Need to Fret, Hong Kong's Financial Centre Status is Not Under Threat'. *South China Morning Post*, 23 December: A11.

Meyer, David R. 2015. 'The World Cities of Hong Kong and Singapore: Network Hubs of Global Finance'. *International Journal of Comparative Sociology* 56 (3–4): 198–231.

Meyer, David R. 2016a. 'Hong Kong's Enduring Global Business Relations'. In Hong Kong in the Cold War, edited by Priscilla Roberts and John M. Carroll. Hong Kong: Hong Kong University Press, pp. 60–91.

Meyer, David R. 2016b. 'Shenzhen in China's Financial Center Networks'. *Growth and Change* 47 (4): 572–95.

Meyer, David R. 2017. 'Bank of China International in Hong Kong: Social Status and Network Access'. In Business Networks in East Asian Capitalisms, edited by Jane Nolan, Chris Rowley, and Malcolm Warner. Oxford: Elsevier, pp. 43–67.

Ministry of Finance. 2017. http://english.gov.cn/state_council/2014/09/09/content_281474986284115.htm, accessed 9 February 2018.

Mittal, Sachin and James Lloyd. 2016. 'The Rise of Fintech in China: Redefining Financial Services'. http://www.ey.com/Publication/vwLUAssets/ey-the-rise-of-fintech-in-china/$FILE/ey-the-rise-of-fintech-in-china.pdf, accessed 9 February 2018.

National Development and Reform Commission et al. 2015. 'Vision and Actions on Jointly Building Silk Road Economic Belt and 21st-Century Maritime Silk Road'. Beijing: National Development and Reform Commission, Ministry of Foreign Affairs, and Ministry of Commerce of the People's Republic of China, with State Council Authorization.

PR Newswire Asia. 2017. 'Critical Debt Levels of Chinese Property Developers Threaten Domestic Financial Stability and Global Growth', 21 August.

Price, Michelle. 2017. 'Shanghai-London Connect Talks Moving to Second Phase-London Official'. Reuters News Service, 17 February.

Ren, Daniel. 2017. 'Former Citigroup Retail Banking Head Larsen Joins Ping An to Head US$1 billion Fintech, Health-Care Fund'. *South China Morning Post*, 4 May.

Ren, Shuli. 2014. 'Hong Kong-Shanghai-Just-Barely-Connect'. Barrons Online, 21 November.

Reuters News Service. 2017. 'Xi Tells Hong Kong He Seeks Far-Reaching Future for its Autonomy', 29 June.

Richards, Hannay. 2016. 'Move to Attract More Global Investors'. *China Daily*, 6 December.

Schenk, Catherine R. 2000. 'Banking Groups in Hong Kong, 1945–65'. *Asia Pacific Business Review* 7 (2): 131–54.

Schenk, Catherine R. 2002. 'Banks and the Emergence of Hong Kong as an International Financial Centre'. *Journal of International Financial Markets, Institutions and Money* 12 (4–5): 321–40.

Sinn, Elizabeth. 1994. Growing with Hong Kong: The Bank of East Asia, 1919–1994. Hong Kong: Hong Kong University Press.

South China Morning Post. 2017. 'The Challenges That Lie Ahead for Lam', 13 April.

Sun, Nikki and Stuart Lau. 2016. 'Zhang Cites City's Four Key Roles'. *South China Morning Post*, 19 May.

Taylor, Peter et al. 2014. 'City-Dyad Analyses of China's Integration into the World City Network'. *Urban Studies* 51 (5): 868–82.

Tinker, Mark. 2017. 'Why the Crisis Calls are Wrong on China'. *Australian Financial Review*, 24 July.

Un, Phoenix and Kenneth Lau. 2016. 'You Won't be Mainlandized'. *The Standard*, 19 May.

Wei, Lingling and Dominique Fong. 2017. 'China Can't Control Runaway Home Buying'. *Wall Street Journal*, 13 July.

Wong, Alan. 2017. 'Hong Kong Arrests Democracy Advocates in 2014 Protests, Raising Wider Concerns'. *New York Times*, 28 March.

World Bank. 2017. 'World Development Indicators'. http://data.worldbank.org/.

Wozniak, Lara and Sean Coneay. 2017. 'Blockbuster Deals in China Make Asia-Pacific the Leader in Global Fintech Investments, Accenture Analysis Finds'. Accenture News Release, 27 February.

Yeung, Raymond. 2017. 'Hong Kong's Next Leader Carrie Lam Promises Bigger Part for Youth to Play in Making Policies'. *South China Morning Post*, 7 June.

Yiu, Enoch. 2017. 'London's Green Finance Options Target Chinese Firms'. *South China Morning Post*, 8 May.

Yu, Hong. 2017. 'Motivation Behind China's "One Belt, One Road" Initiatives and Establishment of the Asian Infrastructure Investment Bank'. *Journal of Contemporary China* 26 (105): 353–68.

Yu, Yongding. 2009. 'China's Policy Responses to the Global Financial Crisis'. Richard Snape Lecture, November 25. Melbourne: Productivity Commission.

Zhang, Dayong et al. 2016. 'Non-Performing Loans, Moral Hazard and Regulation of the Chinese Commercial Banking System'. *Journal of Banking & Finance* 63: 48–60.

Zhang, Maggie. 2017. 'PBOC Sets Up New Committee to Oversee China's Burgeoning Fintech Industry'. *South China Morning Post*, 15 May.

Zhao, Miaoxi et al. 2015. 'Mapping Producer Services Networks in Mainland Chinese Cities'. *Urban Studies* 52 (16): 3018–34.

Zhao, S. X. B. 2013. 'Information Exchange, Headquarters Economy and Financial Centers Development: Shanghai, Beijing and Hong Kong'. *Journal of Contemporary China* 22 (84): 1006–27.

Zhen, Feng et al. 2013. 'An Empirical Study on Chinese City Network Pattern Based on Producer Services'. *Chinese Geographical Science* 23 (3): 274–85.

Zhou, Wa. 2015. 'Stock Price Gap Drives Mainland Funds to HK'. China Daily, 15 April.

Z/Yen. 2007–17. Z/Yen Global Financial Centre Index. http://www.zyen.com.

8

Singapore

Connecting Asian Markets with Global Finance

Karen P.Y. Lai

8.1 Introduction

Founded as a British trading colony in 1819, Singapore took its first substantive steps towards becoming an international financial centre soon after independence from Malaysia in 1965. Today it is arguably the world's fastest-growing centre for private wealth management. A WealthInsight report (2013) predicts that Singapore will overtake Switzerland to become the largest offshore wealth centre by 2020. Singapore's significance as an international financial centre (IFC) has been evident since 1968 with the formation of the Asian dollar market (ADM). Since then, the financial services industry has grown both in terms of size and scope with currently more than 700 financial institutions participating in banking, fund management, treasury operations, insurance, equity markets, debt issuance, commodities trading, and more. Over the years, the GDP contribution of financial services has risen from 4.6 per cent in 1965 to 12.25 per cent in 2016 (see Figure 8.1). In terms of employment, finance and insurance services employ 5.56 per cent of Singapore's resident population in 2016; this figure rises to 20.69 per cent if business services (which would count finance and insurance services as major clients) are included. Singapore now ranks amongst the top IFCs in the world, behind only London and New York and generally on a par with Hong Kong (Z/Yen Group 2017).

This chapter examines the emergence and contemporary development of Singapore as an IFC by investigating the multiscalar processes of financial markets and activities. Taking a financial geography perspective, financial markets and actors are understood as being firmly rooted in IFCs as the physical locations where the production and exchange of financial services

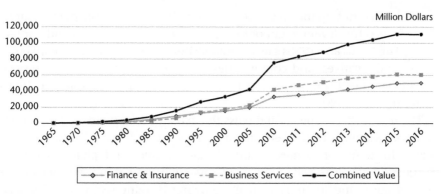

Figure 8.1. Contribution of financial services sector to Singapore's GDP, 1965–2016
Source: Author based on data from the Singapore Department of Statistics.

take place. Markets are not just abstractions that exist 'out there' and operated by 'invisible hands'; they are spatially embedded and socially constructed. While finance appears to be global in operations and impacts, the *location* of financial activities, i.e. the 'capitals of capital' (Cassis 2010), is crucial in explaining and understanding financial markets, products and services. In this vein, this chapter unravels the spatial and temporal dynamics that have influenced the development of financial markets and activities to account for the rise of Singapore as an IFC, and highlights some contemporary challenges and future growth sectors, particularly those arising in the ten years following the 2008 Global Financial Crisis. Some portions of the analysis will also reflect on the preceding 1997 Asian Financial Crisis, as industry changes and policy response back then set the stage for subsequent industry shifts and have shaped the responses and impacts of firms, regulators, and consumers following the 2008 Global Financial Crisis.

Singapore's significance as an IFC is often traced to the late 1960s when the government made a strategic decision to develop the ADM in 1968. Albert Winsemius, a Dutch economic adviser to the then prime minister Lee Kuan Yew, contacted an official at the Bank of America in London for advice on setting up a financial centre, specifically regarding an offshore 'Eurodollar' financial market for Asia to be based in Singapore (Woo 2016). The rapid expansion of the Eurodollar market during that time created demands for an Asian location to broaden the time zone coverage. With special regulatory and tax treatment for commercial banks to set up separate Asian Currency Units (ACUs) in their Singapore banking operations, the Asian dollar business mushroomed, focusing mainly on South Asian business and buoyed by large US dollar spending in the region during the Vietnam War. Singapore thus acquired a first-mover advantage over Hong Kong, which was also developing an ADM at the same time (Emery 1975). The establishment of the Monetary Authority of Singapore (MAS) followed shortly after, in 1971, as the country's central bank and finance regulator. The flotation of the Singapore dollar in 1973 fuelled the development of foreign exchange (FX) products and transactions. The 1970s and 1980s saw the establishment of new financial markets in equities, derivatives, and commodities, while fund management, corporate financing, and insurance sectors become more prominent from the 1990s onwards (Tan 2005).

The rest of this chapter will discuss the major developments in Singapore's financial sectors and markets and how they are reshaping Singapore's IFC status in terms of domestic shifts, regional role, and global networks. Section 8.2 details the changing regulatory environment in terms of banking liberalization and its impact on the growing banking sector and financial consumption in Singapore. Section 8.3 focuses on selected financial markets that have become increasingly prominent over the past decade, namely Islamic banking and finance (IBF) and the offshore renminbi (RMB) market. Finally, amidst new disruptive technologies and new financial actors in the global system, the emergence of fintech and its growing importance for Singapore's role as an IFC is considered in Section 8.4. The chapter concludes with some forward-looking remarks regarding Singapore's outlook as a premier financial hub in Asia and the long-standing debate regarding competition with Hong Kong for this accolade.

8.2 Regulatory Shifts and Liberalization

Since the 1990s, substantial regulatory attention in Singapore has been directed at liberalizing financial markets and banking sectors to attract more international financial institutions, covering market segments such as fund management, treasury operations, insurance, the equity market, debt issuance, and corporate financing. The internationalization of the finance sector in Singapore was a strategic shift that was mooted following the 1985 economic recession and more actively implemented after the 1997 Asian Financial Crisis. Special committee reports commissioned following those two crises were aimed at assessing the state of the economy and highlighting future growth sectors; the financial services industry featured prominently and consistently in all recommendations. The responses by the Singaporean government to the 1997 Asian Financial Crisis, in particular, reconfigured the structure of the Singaporean banking system in ways that shaped the impacts of and responses to the 2008 Global Financial Crisis and subsequent developments in banking and financial markets in Singapore.

In 1985 Singapore faced its first economic recession and its first government deficit since independence due to depressed demand for manufactured goods and the petro-dollar debt crisis. A review by the Sub-Committee on Banking and Financial Services (1985)[1] highlighted the desirability of deregulation (with particular reference to the United States, UK, Japan, and Australia) for creating greater efficiency, while the securitization of debt and the integration of loan and capital markets were regarded as favourable and necessary in order to develop deep capital markets and a fully-fledged IFC. The report also called for the MAS to 'take on a more developmental role' (Sub-Committee on Banking and Financial Services 1985, p. iv), like that of the Economic Development Board,[2] in order to boost the financial services industry and to contribute to long-term economic growth. This marked a distinctive role for the finance sector in terms of Singapore's economic development, and a departure from Singapore's export-led manufacturing strategy that had prevailed since the 1970s (see Rodan 1989). From that point onwards, the MAS also took on a distinctive promotional role for Singapore's banking and finance sector in addition to its regulatory function.

The focus on banking and finance as a key pillar of growth re-emerged in the 1998 report of the Sub-committee on Banking and Finance following the Asian Financial Crisis (Committee on Singapore's Competitiveness 1998). Singapore's GDP had experienced an even sharper decline than during the 1985 recession (see Figure 8.2). The 1997 Asian Financial Crisis shook the banking systems of Asian economies and the confidence of foreign investors and domestic enterprises in Asia (Arndt and Hill 1999). Although Singapore was among those least affected in Asia, the contagion effects from Asian neighbours meant that weak incomes, restricted bank liquidity, labour retrenchment, and reduced regional trade culminated in Singapore's second economic recession since independence. Alongside economic stimulation measures such as higher tax rebates and increased public expenditure, recommendations of strategic sectors for government-led investment included advanced engineering, chemicals, and aerospace industries but also highlighted a broad swathe of financial sectors (Committee on Singapore's Competitiveness 1998). Areas such as fund management, risk management, equity markets, debt insurance, corporate finance, insurance and reinsurance, and cross-border banking, were identified as strategic for developing the international capacities of Singapore as a financial centre.

The change in spatial framing is significant as these sectors targeted for growth would expand the economic and financial space of Singapore well beyond its national space-economy into regional and global financial networks. The regionalization policy was meant to develop an 'external wing'

---

[1] Part of the ad hoc Economic Committee set up for post-crisis recovery and policy recommendations.

[2] The Economic Development Board is a statutory board that coordinates the industrial policy of the Singaporean government and acts a promotional agent to facilitate foreign direct investment into Singapore.

SGD Million

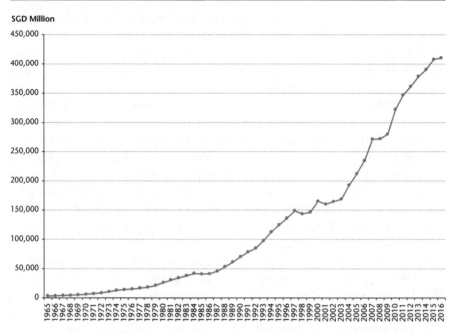

Figure 8.2. Singapore's annual GDP, 1965–2016

Source: Author, based on data from the Singapore Department of Statistics.

and overcome the limitations of Singapore's small domestic economy through the overseas expansion of domestic firms and establishment of industrial parks in other Asian countries (Yeung 1999). The regionalization of domestic firms included a plan for banks not only to facilitate the regionalization of manufacturing and other service firms but also to become wealth-creating enterprises in their own right. The rest of this section therefore focuses on the liberalization and regulatory changes specific to banking in order to examine their impacts on the changing roles of banking firms, new actors in the market, and changing consumer practices within the broader reframing of finance in Singapore's economy and society.

8.2.1 *Banking Liberalization*

The transformation of the local banking industry into a robust globally oriented financial services industry was a developmental goal deemed vital to Singapore's long-term competitiveness and economic success. This involved substantial reorganization of the businesses from traditional loan intermediation into financial services corporations embedded in capital markets. This move also reflects wider trends in global banking since the 1980s whereby banking activities in Europe and the United States have shifted from interest-based banking to fee-based banking for both retail and investment banks. Sources of funds for banks have also changed from traditional loan intermediation to more securitized modes in order to fuel business segments and geographical expansion. Official speeches during the early 2000s emphasized the growing role of non-bank capital to complement bank financing as means by which Singaporean banks could position themselves in the region. This shift from 'bank-based finance' to 'market-based banking' was seen as the way forward for Singaporean banks to grow and become substantial enough for regional leadership and global competition.

The liberalization programme started shortly after Singapore joined the Bank for International Settlements (BIS) in 1996, which was then followed by membership on the Basel Committee on Banking Supervision (BCBS) in 2009. While Singapore was reconfiguring its role on international regulatory platforms, it also had to find solutions for building more robust financial institutions in the wake of the 1997 Asian financial crisis. A key policy shift was towards a more consultative 'risk-based' model of regulation rather than the previous 'one size fits all' supervisory approach, which was in line with Basel II requirements (Ong 2004). This enabled individual firms to exercise greater freedom in expanding into new markets and sectors but also required them to put in place internal risk-control measures that comply with broader regulatory guidelines (such as minimum capital ratios, reporting requirements, etc.) (Hamilton-Hart 2002). This explains the subsequent changes in banking ownership, business strategies, and corporate governance that swept through the industry in what became known as Singapore's 'Big Bang'[3] in the late 1990s and early 2000s (Ngiam 2011).

Therefore, while debates following the 2008 financial crisis have highlighted the systemic risks to national economies and global finance presented by banks that are deemed 'too big to fail', this was not the case two decades ago in Singapore. Instead, banks were challenged to grow bigger in order to extend their extraterritorial reach and secure long-term competitiveness, not only for themselves as business entities but also to strengthen the banking sector and financial centre status of Singapore. A series of banking liberalization measures was implemented during a five-year period from 1999 to 2004, which had the dual impact of increasing the number of foreign banks in Singapore (which were permitted to engage in a wider range of financial activities) and the consolidation of local banks into just three large entities. These 'Big Bang' reforms in Singapore included issuing a new category of Qualifying Full Bank (QFB) licences to encourage foreign banking presence, increasing the number of restricted banks, giving offshore banks greater flexibility in Singapore dollar

---

[3] The use of the term 'Big Bang' reform by Singaporean authorities and policymakers is particularly evocative of the deregulation of financial markets that swept through the City of London in the 1980s.

wholesale business, and lifting the 40 per cent foreign shareholding limit in local banks. All these created competitive pressures on local banks in securing domestic and regional market positions. As pointed out by then deputy prime minister Lee Hsien Loong (Lee 1998):

> Size matters in international banking... [The local banks] need to grow large enough to enjoy the economics of scale, and to have the reach and resilience to go regional, and eventually make a mark in global markets. This is why MAS has encouraged local banks to consider mergers.

The sale of Post Office Savings Bank (POSB) to Development Bank of Singapore (DBS) (both state-owned at that time) by the Singapore government in 1998 also made headlines as it made DBS the largest bank in Singapore and sent a clear message to the industry regarding a push towards consolidation in the local banking sector. These competitive pressures and state signals pushed the other local banks into seeking mergers and acquisitions. When the dust settled in 2002, only three large local banks were left—DBS, United Overseas Bank (UOB), and Oversea-Chinese Banking Corporation (OCBC).

Other than bank mergers, the banking liberalization policies also included divestment requirements and changes in corporate governance. The consolidation and merger of local banks significantly increased deposit bases, deemed vital by the state for promoting extra-territorial competitiveness. The enlarged banks were also supposed to expand their non-deposit-taking business, transforming themselves from traditional banks into more complex financial institutions offering an extensive and sophisticated array of products and services to an expanded regional and global customer base. In 2000, local banks were required to divest themselves of their non-financial businesses and unwind cross-shareholdings within three years. This not only complied with Basel II requirements, but also allowed local banks to rebuild their financial position following the 1997 Asian financial crisis. Rules regarding the management of financial and non-financial divisions of banking firms and limitations on cross-shareholding structures also reshaped corporate governance and management structures, especially for formerly family-owned banks (Lai and Daniels 2017).

These liberalization measures, regulatory changes, and increased competition in the banking sector prompted significant shifts in business strategies for many banks. New bank licensing schemes enabled more foreign banks to engage in a wider range of banking activities, strengthened their product offering and capabilities in Singapore, and created a stronger commercial and retail banking sector. On the other hand, after mergers and business restructuring, the three local banks shifted from traditional loan intermediation into financial services embedded in capital markets, especially in the areas of equity and debt issuance, mergers and acquisitions, asset management, and advisory services. The outcome has been an overall push towards securitization as well as increased emphasis on consumer markets for fee-based activities. This emphasis on consumer markets is particularly strategic given the increasing affluence of the domestic population and particularly growing wealth in the region (e.g. in Indonesia, Thailand, China, and India), both of which have significantly increased demands for financial products and services over the past two decades. This emphasis on developing Singapore as a premier wealth management centre in Asia is reflected in the launch in April 2011 of the Private Banking Code of Conduct, aimed at enhancing the competency of private banking professionals and fostering high market conduct standards (Menon 2011).

8.2.2 Changing Financial Consumption

The development of Singapore as an IFC involved not only banking firms and regulatory bodies but also everyday consumers. Banking liberalization since 1999 has led to greater participation of foreign banks and increased competition in the domestic market. In response, local banks (as well as foreign banks with QFB status) started to diversify their product offerings aimed at the growing middle class in Singapore and the region. Banks shifted their business focus towards fee-paying activities in addition to deposits and loans services, especially in the area of unit trusts and investment solutions either through the banks' own asset management divisions or joint development with other financial institutions. During this same period, the Central Provident Fund (a national compulsory savings scheme for pensions)[4] was liberalized in the 1990s, which allowed members to use portions of their pension savings to invest in commercial funds for potentially higher yields (Lai 2013). This was also part of the strategic plan following the 1985 economic recession and the 1997 Asian financial crisis to develop the wealth management sector in Singapore and boost its IFC capabilities (Tan 2011). Even as domestic banks have transformed themselves from banking firms (focusing on traditional loan intermediation) to more complex financial services corporations (with greater engagement with securities and derivatives markets, and enlargement of non-bank financial investments in insurance and asset management), households and individuals have also increasingly been exhorted to be self-reliant and 'responsible' in taking care of their financial futures and, as a result,

---

[4] The Central Provident Fund (CPF) is a mandatory state-run savings scheme for all working Singaporean citizens and permanent residents, with a portion of gross monthly salary being transferred to individuals' CPF accounts by both employers and employees. Withdrawal can only be made for retirement needs, public housing, medical care, tertiary education, and, since the 1990s, approved investment products.

generate demand for insurance and investment products (Lai 2018). In this way, financial consumers not only perform the role of self-reliant and disciplined subjects responsible for their own financial future (see Langley 2006), but are also framed as citizen subjects who would build a stronger and more competitive national economy through their changing financial practices.

The changing role of consumers in Singapore's financial-centre aspirations is reflected in the organizational change and business strategies of POSB (Lai and Tan 2016). POSB had humble beginnings as a public savings bank with strong social objectives of encouraging principles of saving and thrift, and providing home loans for public housing ownership. After its acquisition by the government-backed DBS bank as part of consolidation and regional expansion plans, POSB underwent a distinctive makeover into a profit-based and fee-driven financial institution. Whereas POSB advertisements used to encouraged savings and thrift, with special tax-free incentives for savings accounts, school visits, public campaigns, and televised lottery draws to encourage high savings rates, advertisements over the past decade have turned towards a model of financial investment whereby anyone could drop into their 'neighbourhood bank' and invest in blue-chip companies. The appeal to social memories and extensive neighbourhood branch networks of POSB has been instrumental to DBS's business strategy in marketing a growing range of insurance and investment products. The enlarged DBS recorded a dramatic increase in sales of investment- and insurance-related products mainly due to referrals from the POSB customer base (Tan 2002). DBS annual reports showed that total sales of wealth management and investment-related products skyrocketed between 1998 and 2003 (see Figure 8.3). A similar trend could also be observed in the business orientation of other Singaporean banks during this period (Lai and Daniels 2017).

This emphasis on investment and fee-paying activities became problematic during the 2008 Global Financial Crisis. While the financial crisis had limited systemic impact on the banking sector in Singapore, the bankruptcy of Lehman Brothers on 15 September 2008 led to the default or early redemption of several credit-linked structured notes (collectively known as Minibonds) that had Lehman Brothers as a swap guarantor or reference entity. The affected products included Minibond Notes issued by Lehman Brothers, High Notes 5 from the DBS, Jubilee Notes from Merrill Lynch, and Pinnacle Notes from Morgan Stanley. The Minibonds were distributed by ten financial institutions in Singapore, including a number of domestic banks and their securities subsidiaries (see Table 8.1). Almost 10,000 investors were affected; a significant portion of them were either retired, elderly, or middle-aged individuals in late-working life who had invested most or all of their life savings (Lai 2013). The impact of financial losses and accusations of misconduct by distributors prompted public outrage and a level of social activism uncommon in

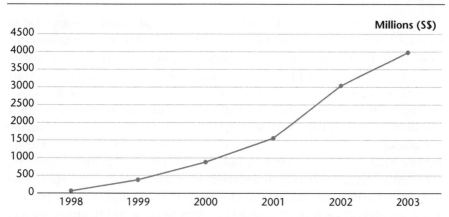

Figure 8.3. DBS bank's increased sales of investment products (excluding bancassurance) following the acquisition of POSB

Source: Author, based on data from DBS Annual Reports, 1998–2004.

Table 8.1. Distributors of Lehman Minibonds in Singapore

1.	ABN AMRO Bank N.V. Singapore Branch[1]
2.	DBS Bank Ltd[1]
3.	Malayan Banking Berhad Singapore Branch[1]
4.	Hong Leong Finance
5.	CIMB-GK Securities Pte Ltd
6.	DMG & Partners Securities Pte Ltd
7.	Kim Eng Securities Pte Ltd
8.	OCBC Securities Pte Ltd[2]
9.	Phillip Securities Pte Ltd
10.	UOB Kay Hian Pte Ltd[2]

1 Retail banks
2 Securities arms of Singapore retail banks
Source: Author, based on data from MAS (2009).

Singapore with public rallies and signed petitions to the MAS for strong action against the distributors. Accusations of banks targeting and mis-selling to retirees became a common theme of discussion, alongside poor documentation and explanation of product features and risks to investors. Findings from the MAS investigation (MAS 2009) regarding banks' due diligence on Notes, sales procedures, assessment of customers' risk profiles, and training and supervision of financial representatives supported media reports of negligence and misconduct. Distributors did not fully understand the nature of the Minibonds, bank representatives were inadequately trained on the products, there were inconsistencies in how products were matched to customers' risk profiles, and wrong information was given to investors. As a penalty, all ten distributors were banned from selling structured notes for periods ranging from six months to two years depending on the severity of offences.

Following this event, MAS regulatory reviews and policy revisions led to changes in operational requirements of banks, including improving information disclosure through compulsory product highlight sheets, new assessment frameworks for matching customers' risk profile, and improving the training of bank representatives. Regulatory frameworks were further refined through amendments to the Securities and Futures Act, Financial Advisers Act, and a Financial Advisory Industry Review (aptly dubbed 'FAIR') aimed at improving the quality of financial advice to retail investors (Financial Advisory Industry Review 2013; MAS 2012). These regulatory changes provide more safeguards for retail investors and closer supervision of securities business in retail banks to ensure due diligence and fair disclosure in the sales and advisory process. These are seen as particularly important steps to safeguard the integrity and reputation of Singapore's financial regulation, especially given the focus on wealth management and high net worth clientele in Singapore and the wider Asia region (WealthInsight 2013).

8.3 New Financial Markets

Over the past decade, Singapore has also actively developed new financial markets to cater to demands from different geographical and market segments. Two of the most significant developments in terms of market participation and government involvement are Islamic banking and finance (IBF) and the offshore RMB market. Both of these have been positioned by the MAS as part of a broader government strategy to foster financial innovation for building a broad-based IFC.

8.3.1 Islamic Banking and Finance

Islamic banking and finance (IBF) had a slow start in Singapore in the 1990s and picked up momentum in the early 2000s with increasing investment flows between the Middle East and the growing economies of Asia. IBF is a form of banking and finance rooted in Sharia law. A key characteristic relates to certain prohibitions such as the injunctions against *riba* (interest), *gharar* (excessive risk, uncertainty), *maysir* (gambling), and 'making money from money' (e.g. currency speculation or financial derivatives). IBF covers a range of products and services from deposit accounts and project financing to insurance (*takaful*) and Islamic bonds (*sukuk*). The ideal forms of transactions are rooted in 'equity-financing' or 'profit-sharing' (respectively *musharaka* and *mudarabah*), but a dominant form of contract remains cost-plus financing (*murabaha*). Whether a certain product or service is deemed Islamically acceptable depends on the interpretation of Sharia scholars of a given Sharia Supervisory Board (Bassens 2012).[5]

A handful of *takaful* products were launched in Singapore in the 1990s, with support from government-owned banks and insurance cooperatives, as test cases to gauge the market (AMPRO Holdings 1995). The interest in IBF products proved rather limited amongst both Muslim and non-Muslim financial consumers, owing to a general lack of awareness about them, and the government took a back seat to observe how the IBF market might develop organically (Gerrard and Cunningham 1997). This started to change in the early 2000s with growing potential for increased trade and financial ties with the Middle East. With a smaller domestic market for IBF compared to neighbouring Malaysia and Indonesia, the focus has been on leveraging the infrastructure currently in place to offer wholesale market activities in the areas of capital market activities and wealth management, and persuading financial institutions to add IBF products and services to their existing suite of activities (Lai and Samers 2017).

Since the early 2000s, the MAS has become particularly active in the development of IBF in Singapore through regulatory reviews, greater participation in international bodies and, later on, tax incentives for IBF products (Vernados 2012). As a prudential regulator, the MAS does not prescribe what constitutes Sharia compliance nor endorse specific Sharia rulings; the responsibility lies with Islamic banks (or conventional banks offering IBF products) to take into account Sharia compliance and to manage this compliance risk as part of their overall risk management process, since they would be generally exposed to the same types of risk, such as credit risk, liquidity risk, and operational risks, with many similar prudential and supervisory issues as conventional banks. Folding IBF within a common regulatory framework allows for greater flexibility in financial innovation and future market development, as it keeps the doors open for potential intersections between Islamic and conventional finance in terms of financial expertise, business reorganization, and potential investors. Subsequent years saw accelerated regulatory developments in opening up greater scope for IBF activities in Singapore (Heng 2009). Other than remitting additional stamp duties and opening up *murabahah* financing, the MAS also joined the Kuala Lumpur-based Islamic Financial Services Board (IFSB) as a full member in 2005, after two years as an observer. Through active participation in the various working groups and task forces in areas such as supervisory review, Islamic money markets, capital adequacy, liquidity management, and solvency requirements for *takaful* operations, the MAS acquired technical

---

[5] Many of these Sharia scholars are based in the Middle East, although Malaysia is also developing significant capacities in Sharia interpretation and governance (see Lai and Samers 2017).

knowledge and built professional networks within the international IBF community (MAS 2011). At the same time, Singapore's experience with global financial governance bodies is advantageous as developing IBF regulatory expertise could be combined with the MAS's experience in other international regulatory working committees such as the Bank for International Settlements, International Organization of Securities Commissions, and International Association of Insurance Supervisors (Ong 2005). In 2006–8, another series of tax policies was implemented to boost the IBF market, such as tax clarification on *murabaha* financing and *sukuk*, which gave participants the same regulatory protection under Singapore's Bank Act as conventional depositors. Further tax concessions were granted on qualifying Sharia-compliant financial activities (e.g. lending, fund management, insurance and reinsurance).

While the 2008 Global Financial Crisis led to a credit crunch that reverberated through global financial markets, particularly in the United States and Europe, the IBF sector remained relatively strong and has been growing at double-digit rates over the past decade (Bin Ghalaita 2015). With different business models and guiding principles for investments, IBF appears to be more resilient during financial crises compared to conventional financial institutions (Hasan and Dridi 2010). This is also reflected in the buoyant activities in Singapore's IBF sector, particularly as new regulations in 2009 permit banks to conduct an even wider range of new IBF activities (e.g. *murabaha* interbank placements, *ijara*, and spot *murabaha*), which sends clear signals to market participants concerning financial innovation. Cross-border financing has also become particularly prominent over the past decade, particularly in terms of *sukuk* (insurance) and Sharia-compliant REITs, leveraging existing financial infrastructure and expertise in Singapore. Issue managers of *sukuk* from Pakistan and the Malaysian state of Sarawak have held road shows in Singapore to reach out to the established pool of institutional investors. Building on the critical mass of reinsurers based in Singapore is also deemed beneficial for *takaful* participants seeking to collaborate with reinsurers in Singapore to provide *retakaful* capacity. In 2009, the MAS even backed a *sukuk* facility in Singapore (the first such move by a conventional central bank) by issuing *sukuk* to be priced against the liquid Singapore Government Securities market, which then provided a transparent price discovery mechanism and also improved stability and confidence in a new financial market. The encouragement of financial innovation has also led to the issue of RMB-denominated *sukuk*, such the RMB 1 billion (US$158.06 million) *sukuk Wakalah* by the Axiata Group, which was then the largest yuan-denominated *sukuk* issued. The listing in RMB denomination was also aligned with Singapore's growing status as an offshore RMB centre for trading and settlement (Islamic Finance News 2014). Singapore has an established role as the largest REITs market in Asia outside Japan and is expected to capitalize on that expertise to dominate the Islamic

REITs market even ahead of larger IBF markets such as Malaysia (Saeed 2011, Suhana et al. 2012).

Listing these *sukuk* and Islamic REITs products in Singapore enables issuers from both within and outside of Singapore to capitalize on a wide range of existing expertise such as legal, accounting, and financial knowledge for the creation of special purpose vehicles, and to tap into potential investors who tend to cluster in an established IFC. While increasing trade with the Middle East provided initial strategic reasons for developing IBF in Singapore, the appeal of this emerging financial sector is also set against the growing interest of investors based within and outside of Singapore in various forms of ethical investment (Šoštarić 2015). The orientation for the IBF market in Singapore is distinctively outward-looking, with the objective of building up IBF activities alongside existing financial market segments and the attraction of both Muslim and non-Muslim investors.

While there has been significant development in IBF in Singapore particularly over the past decade, the Singapore market still has relatively few Islamic financial institutions (especially in comparison with neighbouring Malaysia), in terms of conventional banks offering IBF services.[6] It also suffers from the lack of a domestic market, with no Islamic pension funds and little business demand for Sharia-compliant financial vehicles. Although Singapore seems to lack a critical mass of IBF expertise, institutions, products, and investors, the MAS is banking on a wider neo-liberal strategy that has driven its international financial centre development, which is to create more diverse financial sectors and deeper capital markets within a regulatory climate that welcomes financial innovation and new financial institutions. The enmeshing of global financial networks, national economic development strategies, and Islamically-inflected modes of market making (see Lai and Samers 2017) therefore continues to unfold in the formation of a small but distinct IBF market in Singapore.

8.3.2 *The Offshore RMB Market*

Following from the Global Financial Crisis of 2008, the fiscal and current account woes in the United States, the Eurozone economic crisis, and the long-term stagnation of the Japanese economy have all highlighted the problems associated with the world's traditional reserve currencies: the US dollar, the euro, the British pound, and the Japanese yen. China's rising global power

---

[6] There was a full-fledged Islamic Bank in Singapore but the Islamic Bank of Asia announced in September 2015 that it will be closing over the next 2–3 years and transferring its business over to its majority shareholder DBS bank, which will continue to operate an IBF 'window'. HSBC has also closed its Islamic banking divisions in Singapore in 2013 as part of its global consolidation of Islamic banking business.

since the end of the twentieth century is also hinting at an increasingly multipolar world and fuelling speculations regarding the renminbi (RMB) as a global alternative to the US dollar as the world's dominant reserve currency. However, RMB international recognition and usage has only begun to gain traction recently due to the slow and limited liberalization of the currency. China came out of the 1997 Asian Financial Crisis relatively unscathed, which reinforced the Chinese government's view that a liberalization of its foreign exchange regime and capital markets could introduce too much instability and uncertainty in the longer term. The internationalization of the RMB has therefore been very gradual, building on the wider economic reforms of China under the Open Door Policy of 1978 and China's membership of the World Trade Organization since 2001. This gradual and managed process of capital account liberalization, alongside the maintenance of exchange rate controls, has resulted in a distinct separation between onshore RMB markets (in which controls on interest and exchange rates remain), and the more liberalized component of offshore RMB markets (He and McCauley 2010).

An offshore RMB centre is a financial hub outside of China that conducts a variety of RMB-denominated financial transactions. Hong Kong was appointed as the first offshore RMB centre due to its special status within the Chinese polity and its historical role as a gateway between mainland China and global capital. Yuan-denominated[7] transactions started in 2003 with personal banking services, followed by bonds and equities over the past decade. Other major IFCs followed, such as London and Singapore, as well as smaller financial centres such as Taiwan, Luxembourg, and Toronto. Singapore was amongst the first to be selected for offshore RMB centre status after Hong Kong. This builds on long-standing trade, FDI, and diplomatic relationships between Singapore and China, which then turned towards financial cooperation and linkages over the past decade under the China–Singapore Free Trade Agreement (MAS 2017a). Six out of the top ten Chinese banks now operate in Singapore, with Bank of China (BOC) and Industrial and Commercial Bank of China (ICBC) having QFB status, using Singapore as a hub for southeast Asian markets. At the policy level, close discussions between the MAS and People's Bank of China (PBOC) led to the launch of RMB currency products and services in Singapore. On 8 February 2013, PBOC appointed the Singapore branch of ICBC as the RMB clearing bank in Singapore. On 27 May 2013, ICBC started RMB clearing services in Singapore, with fifty-three transactions valued at more than 1.6 billion yuan (US$240 million), and opened clearing accounts for forty-nine banks during its first clearing day (Wang 2013). This was swiftly followed by the MAS opening its representative office in Beijing (the first in

---

[7] China's currency is officially called the renminbi (RMB). The yuan is the unit of account.

Asia) one day later. Within the first month of the launch of clearing services, four banks issued a total of 2.5 billion yuan of RMB-denominated bonds in Singapore (also known as 'Lion City' bonds).

In October 2013, China announced a further suite of measures to promote the internationalization of RMB through Singapore, including granting of an RMB qualified foreign institutional investor (RQFII) quota to Singapore (which allows foreign investors to invest in mainland China's bond and equity markets) and listing Singapore as an investment destination under the RMB qualified domestic institutional investor (RQDII) scheme (which permits qualified domestic Chinese investors to purchase overseas RMB-denominated products) (see Table 8.2). The strong utilization of the RQFII quota in Singapore and positive outlook led to the doubling of Singapore's quota from 50 billion to 100 billion yuan in 2016 (see Figure 8.4). Direct currency trading between the yuan and the Singapore dollar also commenced on 28 October 2014 (Today 2014), with a daily SGD–CNY benchmark published by the PBOC, which is expected to promote

Table 8.2. Approved RQFII quota list in Singapore, February 2017

RQFII Name	SAFE ApprovalDate	Accumulative Quota (RMB 100 million)
Fullerton Fund Management Company Ltd	30/06/2014	12.00
NIKKO Asset Management Asia Limited	30/06/2014	10.00
APS Asset Management Pte Ltd	26/08/2014	15.00
New Silk Road Investment Pte Ltd	26/08/2014	15.00
Aberdeen Asset Management Asia Limited	28/11/2016	73.00
DBS Bank Limited	30/10/2014	30.00
Lion Global Investors Ltd	27/11/2014	10.00
The Bank of Nova Scotia Asia Limited	30/01/2015	15.00
Schroder Investment Management (Singapore) Ltd	30/01/2015	10.00
KKR Singapore Pte Ltd	26/03/2015	35.00
JPMorgan Asset Management (Singapore) Limited	26/03/2015	20.00
Neuberger Berman Singapore Pte Limited	26/03/2015	8.00
Aviva Investors Asia Pte Limited	28/04/2015	10.00
Target Asset Management Pte Ltd	28/04/2015	2.00
UOB Asset Management Ltd	28/04/2015	12.00
GIC Private Limited	28/04/2015	50.00
CSAM Asset Management Pte Ltd	29/05/2015	7.00
Allianz Global Investors Singapore Limited	29/05/2015	10.00
Oversea-Chinese Banking Corporation Limited	29/06/2015	10.00
Amundi Singapore Limited	29/10/2015	28.00
UBS Asset Management (Singapore) Ltd	28/04/2016	25.00
BlackRock (Singapore) Limited	30/05/2016	200.00
Avanda Investment Management Pte Ltd	30/05/2016	7.00
PIMCO Asia Pte Ltd	29/06/2016	18.00
Phillip Capital Management (S) Ltd	27/07/2015	4.20
ST Asset Management Ltd	30/08/2016	6.50
Harveston Asset Management Pte Ltd	27/10/2016	6.50
Soochow Securities CSSD (Singapore) Pte Ltd	28/11/2016	15.00
Total approved quota under Singapore RQFII scheme		**664.20**

Source: Author, based on data from HSBC Securities Services, 2017.

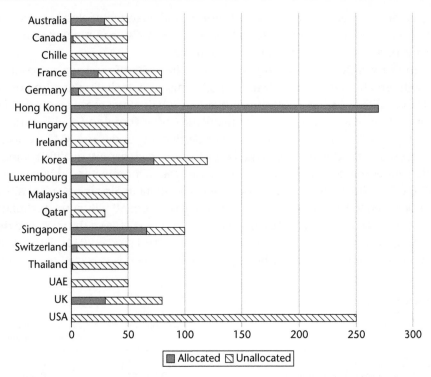

Figure 8.4. Allocated RQFII in approved markets, as of December 2016 (in RMB billion)
Source: Author, based on data from HSBC Securities Services (2017).

transparency, lower foreign exchange transaction costs and improve the currency risk environment. This development should also boost the appeal of offshore RMB in the region, given Singapore's role as a financial centre and the increased trade and investment linkages between ASEAN and China (IE Singapore 2013). Another distinctive feature of the offshore RMB market in Singapore is its connections to wider Singapore–China economic projects. The measures to allow cross-border flows between Singapore and two industrial parks in China (the Suzhou Industrial Park and Tianjin Ecocity, which are joint ventures between Singaporean and Chinese companies and governments) is unique to Singapore (IE Singapore 2013). This will allow companies operating in the two business parks to raise working capital in RMB directly from Singapore, and create a cheaper funding environment for businesses with lower interest rates.

These milestones constitute significant steps towards future RMB trading and settlement activities in Singapore, particularly given the rapid progress achieved over a short time frame, and signal Singapore's commitment to the internationalization of the RMB. The commitment towards economic and financial cooperation between Singapore and China is also evident in the MAS's continuing relationships with key banking, securities, and insurance regulators in China, with annual meetings to exchange views on regulatory cooperation and market development (Shanmugaratnam 2013). Thus far, Singapore consistently ranks amongst the two largest RMB transaction centres after Hong Kong, and overtook London in 2014 as the number one offshore RMB centre after Hong Kong (ASIFMA 2014).

The IMF announced in November 2015 that it would include the RMB in the Special Drawing Rights currency basket, marking a key milestone in RMB internationalization. The use of the RMB has increased significantly over the past few years, not only in cross-border transactions with mainland China but also in offshore market activities. As mainland China's economy grows and becomes even more globally integrated, the RMB will be more widely used internationally and mainland China's capital account liberalization is expected to continue. Within this context, Singapore's early move in establishing itself as an offshore RMB centre is strengthening its position as a regional financial hub. Given the close bilateral ties between the two countries and the continued growth of the Chinese economy during a time when other Asian economies are also moving up the curve of development, Singapore is well placed to leverage its financial expertise and hub status in furthering the internationalization of the RMB. This development of RMB trading and settlement in Singapore will in turn have significant impact on Singapore's future IFC development. This is particularly important as traditional financial services such as foreign exchange trading and capital market activities have declined in volume and significance in global financial markets, marking a need for new engines of growth and to develop distinctive competencies in new or emerging financial markets and services.

8.4 Fintech

Fintech, a shorthand for 'financial technology', has been making waves in the headlines recently, particularly in terms of its potential to severely disrupt the landscape of not just banking but also a range of financial institutions, intermediaries, and technology and e-commerce companies (Bassens et al. 2017, Economist 2015). Fintech encompasses a new wave of companies that are developing products, systems, and platforms to change the way businesses and consumers make payments, lend, borrow, and invest. The most disrupted sectors, or at least most frequently highlighted in the news, are payments and fund transfers, crowdfunding, and peer-to-peer lending. Between 2013 and 2014 alone, global investment in fintech ventures tripled from US$4.05 billion to US$12.21 billion, outstripping the growth in overall venture capital investments (Accenture 2015). While there are ongoing debates about whether the future of financial services would be characterized by ruptures (due to displacement or obsolescence) or redistribution (as existing players grow and enrich the market or simply acquire new fintech firms and technologies), fintech is embraced in Singapore as yet another opportunity for capturing new market trends and developing new capabilities that would bolster Singapore's IFC status.

On 27 July 2015, the MAS announced the formation of a FinTech and Innovation Group (FTIG) that would be formally responsible for regulatory policies and developmental strategies to encourage the use of innovative technology in ways that would better manage risks, enhance efficiency, and strengthen competitiveness in the financial sector. This move came together with the appointment of a Chief FinTech Officer to lead the FTIG, a high-profile position that signalled a clear commitment to developing and harnessing the potential of fintech for Singapore's financial services industry. As highlighted by the Managing Director of MAS:

> The formation of FTIG is a serious commitment by MAS towards our vision of Smart Financial Centre, where technology is applied pervasively to create new opportunities and improve people's lives. [The Chief FinTech Officer] and his team will work closely with the financial industry and technology community to promote a culture of innovation in the industry while ensuring safety and security. (MAS 2015)

In addition, a FinTech Office was established on 3 May 2016 to serve as a one-stop virtual centre for all fintech related matters and with the explicit task of promoting Singapore as a fintech hub (MAS 2017b).

While fintech is a global movement that has gained significant traction in recent years, there are different drivers in different geographical markets (Gnirck and Visser 2016). In developed markets, such as the United States and Europe, fintech comes from the basis of improving efficiency, reducing transaction costs, and adding value, while fintech in developing economies tends to be driven by other critical needs such as financial inclusion and access to business working capital (building on earlier history of microlending programmes). Given that there is a healthy mix of developed and developing markets in Asia, Singapore's combination of financial maturity, technological infrastructure, and sound regulatory framework makes it an ideal launch pad for fintech companies tapping into Singapore's agglomeration of funds and expertise while reaching out to larger potential markets in the region such as Indonesia, Malaysia, Thailand, and Vietnam. A key driver of fintech in Singapore is the strong support of entrepreneurship and innovation by government-linked organizations. The FinTech Office, for example, is coordinated by the MAS, EDB, SPRING Singapore,[8] and Info-communications

---

[8] SPRING Singapore is an agency under the Ministry of Trade and Industry responsible for grooming Singaporean enterprises.

Table 8.3. Grants and schemes available for setting up fintech business in Singapore

Grant/Scheme [Administrator]	Description
Startup SG Accelerator [SPRING Singapore, Startup SG]	• Startup SG Accelerator supports partners, primarily incubators and accelerators, in strategic growth sectors that take on the role of catalysing growth opportunities for high potential start-ups through their programmes, mentorship, and provision of resources. • Startup SG Accelerator will provide funding and non-financial support for these partners to further enhance their programmes and expertise in nurturing successful start-ups.
Startup SG Equity [SPRING Singapore, Startup SG]	• As part of the Startup SG Equity scheme, government will co-invest with independent, qualified third-party investors into a start-up. This scheme aims to stimulate private-sector investments into innovative, Singapore-based technology start-ups with intellectual property and global market potential.
Startup SG Founder [SPRING Singapore, Startup SG]	• Startup SG Founder provides mentorship support and a start-up capital grant to first-time entrepreneurs with innovative business concepts. The scheme provides up to $30,000 by matching $3 to every $1 raised by the entrepreneur. • SPRING will fund the start-ups through Accredited Mentor Partners ('AMPs'). These appointed partners will select applicants based on the uniqueness of business concept, feasibility of business model, strength of management team, and potential market value. Upon successful application, the AMP will assist the start-ups with advice, learning programmes, and networking contacts. • The AMP will decide on appropriate milestones together with the applicant. Their recommended application and milestones will be surfaced to SPRING for vetting and approval. The grant will be disbursed in two tranches based on agreed project milestones over twelve months.
Startup SG Talent [T-UP, STP]	• Startup SG Talent fosters a more conducive environment for promising global talent to set up innovative businesses in Singapore. Schemes under this pillar include: (a) EntrePass, which allows eligible foreigners to start and operate a new business in Singapore (b) T-Up, which allows businesses to access the pool of talent from A*STAR's Research Institutes and build in-house R&D capabilities in their business operations (c) SME Talent Programme (STP) Internship, which will facilitate internship matching between students and technology-based local start-ups.
Startup SG Tech [SPRING Singapore, Startup SG]	• Startup SG Tech is a competitive grant in which proposals are evaluated based on both technical and commercial merits by a team of reviewers, and the best are funded. Applicants may apply for either the Proof Of Concept (POC) grant or the Proof Of Value (POV) grant, depending on the stage of development of the technology or solution/concept.

(continued)

Table 8.3. Continued

Grant/Scheme [Administrator]	Description
Capabilities Development Grant (CDG)—Technology Innovation [Info-communications Media Development Authority]	• The Capabilities Development Grant (CDG) is a financial assistance programme designed to help SMEs build their capabilities across ten key business areas. SMEs can use the CDG to defray up to 70 per cent of qualifying project costs (e.g. consultancy, training, certification, equipment, and software costs) for upgrading initiatives in areas like increasing productivity, process improvement, product development, and market access.
Financial Sector Technology and Innovation (FSTI) [MAS]	• The FSTI scheme was launched to provide support for the creation of a vibrant ecosystem for innovation. MAS has committed SG$225 million over a five-year period, for the following four purposes: (a) Innovation Centres: To attract financial institutions to set up their innovation labs in Singapore; (b) Institution-level projects: To catalyse the development of innovation solutions that have the potential to promote growth efficiency or competitiveness; (c) Industry-wide projects: To support the building of industry-wide technology infrastructure or utility that is required for the delivery of new, integrated services; (d) POC scheme: The POC scheme provides support to both FIs and non-FIs for early-stage development of innovative projects in the industry.

Source: Author, based on data from MAS (2017c).

Media Development Authority. Table 8.3 shows various government grants and schemes available for supporting fintech companies in Singapore. Other organizations such as International Enterprise Singapore (IE Singapore) have also been active in facilitating Singapore companies in their internationalization efforts, including fintech companies.

The proactive stance of Singapore's financial regulator is also reflected in the establishment of a special sandbox environment for fintech companies as a way to delicately manage the tension between innovation and regulatory requirements (see Figure 8.5). State support has also been directed at organizing fintech industry conventions as platforms for pitching sessions, networking events, talent recruitment, and bringing together start-ups, incubators, and investors searching for opportunities and innovation.

8.5 Conclusion

The development of Singapore as a financial centre has a relatively short history compared to other IFCs of similar standing. Its rapid growth, especially over the past three decades, in the increasing breadth and depth of financial

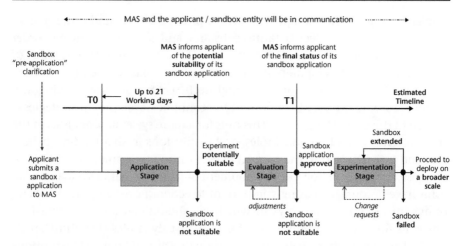

Figure 8.5. Examples of flexibility around regulatory procedures for the fintech sandbox

Source: Author, based on data from MAS (2016).

markets and institutions, and increased prominence and participation in global and regional financial governing bodies, has mirrored the intense industrialization of other sectors of its economy since independence. The 'Big Bang' reforms starting in the late 1990s and transformations in the banking landscape in the 2000s led to the proliferation of industry players and new consumer markets. Singapore has also developed a growing reputation as a wealth management centre and private banking centre. High net worth individuals choose Singapore for their private banking needs due to strong fundamentals such as economic and political stability, high regulatory standards, a robust legal framework, and a critical mass of financial players offering ready access to global and regional financial markets. Through the development of new financial markets in terms of IBF and offshore RMB products and services, Singapore is also creating market niches for itself within global financial networks. The recent but aggressive foray into fintech reflects the consistent efforts of state agencies, financial institutions, and related economic sectors towards product innovation and staying ahead of the curve in a rapidly changing global financial landscape.

Throughout the developments detailed in this chapter, the state has clearly played a vital role in Singapore's development as an IFC. The role of the developmental states in shaping East Asian economies has been well documented (Amsden 1989; Haggard 1990; Johnson 1995), referring to the core idea that the productive structure of a nation could be improved as a result of active economic policy. This includes identifying economic activities that are deemed more conducive to generating economic growth, tight relationships between the state and business sectors to facilitate policy shifts, and implementing policies designed to distort price structures and other market signals (e.g. through selective tariffs, subsidies, and access to finance) in order to induce changes in the pace and direction of capital accumulation. Much of the literature on developmental states in East Asia has focused on strategic investments in manufacturing and high-tech sectors, but the banking and finance sector is also clearly important in economic development strategies—as seen in the case of Singapore. This calls for a more systematic analysis of the state in terms of its functions, roles, and institutions in shaping firm behaviour and activities within the context of economic development strategies. In this case, focusing on how the development of financial markets and financial firms have become increasingly important to economic development policies brings into question the ways in which we should consider the state–firm nexus in finance and implications for capitalist dynamics (Lai and Daniels 2017). The flurry of bank bailouts and nationalization of financial institutions (in effect, if not in name) in the United States and Europe following the 2008 Global Financial Crisis has certainly demonstrated the vital role of the state in finance. More recently, the events of Brexit have also triggered heated debates, as supporters of the 'Leave' campaign proposed a vision of 'Singapore-on-Thames', with Brexit offering an opportunity to recast the City of London as an agile, low-regulation hub for global capital, defined by a unilateral free-trade approach and low-tax regime. Although this proposal has already been met with scepticism from the finance sector and downright hostility from EU leaders, it highlights the need for a rethinking of the state–finance nexus in terms of how we analyse IFC development as being market-led, state-led, or some shifting configuration that is sensitive to temporal-spatial dynamics.

In terms of future development, Singapore's long-standing rivalry with Hong Kong as IFCs, discussed also by David Meyer in Chapter 7 of this book, will probably continue to dominate business headlines and the attention of policymakers in both economies, as they are both positioned as the premier financial hubs of the fastest-growing economic region in the next few decades. In terms of practice, firms in Singapore and Hong Kong have distinctive specialization in geographical and business segments. While Hong Kong benefits from its special status and close economic ties to the enormous economy of mainland China (with some limited coverage of other East Asian economies such as South Korea and Taiwan), Singapore is much better positioned for the diverse and fast-growing economies of southeast Asia and the other Asian giant—India. In terms of business segments, Hong Kong has a much larger equity capital market while Singapore leads in terms of foreign exchange, interest rates derivatives, and insurance business. Both financial centres, therefore, are necessary for comprehensive coverage in the control and coordination of regional economic activities for both financial and non-financial firms in Asia.

Developments in fintech, however, could introduce new opportunities and dynamics for financial centre development in Asia. Both Singapore and Hong Kong have clear ambitions to become the region's leading fintech hub. Will fintech reshape financial ecologies in ways that move Hong Kong and Singapore into different tiers or realms of products and services? On the one hand, Singapore's combination of financial maturity, technological infrastructure, and sound regulatory framework makes it an ideal launch pad for fintech companies tapping into Singapore's agglomeration of funds and expertise while reaching out to larger potential markets in the region such as Indonesia, Malaysia, Thailand, Vietnam, and India. It also has a more established knowledge economy in advanced manufacturing, systems science, IT, and media and related innovative sectors that arguably provides a more robust ecosystem to support economic innovation. On the other hand, Hong Kong has the advantage of the enormous mainland Chinese market, which already has a substantial pool of expertise and capital with rise of fintech giants such as Alibaba, Baidu, and Tencent. On a larger scale, how might the rise of Asian fintech reshape structures of power and hegemony for global finance if new forms of financial products, services, structures, and organizations emerging from Asia acquire particular forms of power over certain markets and systems? This is especially pertinent given that fintech has the potential to reshape existing divisions between production, finance, and consumption through new modes of production and service delivery in ways that might leapfrog or bypass existing firms or structures, which tends to be dominated by Anglo-American firms and institutions at present.

Acknowledgements

Parts of this chapter draw upon research supported by a National University of Singapore (NUS) faculty research grant [R-109-000-127-133]. The author would also like to thank Jieyu Zhou for her research assistance.

References

Accenture. 2015. 'The Future of Fintech and Banking: Digitally Disrupted or Reimagined?' http://www.fintechinnovationlablondon.co.uk/media/730274/Accenture-The-Future-of-Fintech-and-Banking-digitallydisrupted-or-reima-.pdf, accessed 2 June 2017.

AMPRO Holdings. 1995. 'Regional Conference 1995 on Tapping a New Market: Islamic Finance, Insurance & Banking in Singapore'. 8 July. Singapore.

Amsden, A. 1989. Asia's Next Giant: South Korea and Late Industrialisation. Oxford: Oxford University Press.

Arndt, H. W. and H. Hill (eds). 1999. Southeast Asia's Economic Crisis: Origins, Lessons, and the Way Forward. Singapore: Institute of Southeast Asian Studies.

ASIFMA. 2014. 'RMB Roadmap: May 2014'. Hong Kong: Asia Securities Industry & Financial Markets Association. http://www.asifma.org/uploadedFiles/Resources/RMB%20Roadmap.pdf, accessed 1 June 2017.

Bassens, D. 2012. 'Emerging Markets in a Shifting Global Financial Architecture: The Case of Islamic Securitization in the Gulf Region'. *Geography Compass* 6 (6): 340–50.

Bassens, D., R. Hendrikse, and M. van Meeteren. 2017. 'The Appleization of Finance: Reflections on the FinTech (R)evolution'. Financial Geography Working Paper. Global Network on Financial Geography (FinGeo). http://www.fingeo.net/wordpress/wp-content/uploads/2017/07/WP2_The-Appleization-of-Finance_i-1.pdf, accessed 12 September 2017.

Bin Ghalaita, Jamal. 2015. 'The Rise of the Islamic Economy'. World Finance, 8 March. https://www.worldfinance.com/banking/the-rise-of-the-islamic-economy, accessed 30 May 2017.

Cassis, Y. 2010. Capitals of Capital: The Rise and Fall of International Financial Centres, 1780–2009, 2nd edition. Cambridge: Cambridge University Press.

Committee on Singapore's Competitiveness. 1998. Report of the Sub-Committee on Finance and Banking. Singapore: Committee on Singapore's Competitiveness.

Economist. 2015. 'The Fintech Revolution'. 9 May. http://www.economist.com/news/leaders/21650546-wave-startups-changing-financefor-better-fintech-revolution, accessed 5 June 2017.

Emery, R. F. 1975. 'The Asian Dollar Market'. International Finance Discussion Papers. Washington, DC: Federal Reserve.

Financial Advisory Industry Review. 2013. 'Report on Recommendations of the Financal Advisory Industry Review Panel'. 16 January. Singapore. http://www.mas.gov.sg/~/media/resource/news_room/press_releases/2013/Annex%201%20%20Report%20on%20recommendations%20of%20the%20Financial%20Advisory%20Industry%20Review%20Panel.pdf, accessed 12 September 2017.

Gerrard, P. and J. B. Cunningham. 1997. 'Islamic Banking: A Study in Singapore'. *International Journal of Bank Marketing* 15 (6): 204–16.

Gnirck, Markus and Gerben Visser. 2016. 'Singapore, the FinTech Hub for Southeast Asia'. In The FINTECH Book: The Financial Technology Handbook for Investors, Entrepreneurs and Visionaries, edited by Susanne Chishti and Janos Barberis. Chichester: Wiley & Sons, pp. 58–60.

Haggard, Stephan. 1990. Pathways from the Periphery: The Politics of Growth in Newly Industrialising Countries. Ithaca, NY: Cornell University Press.

Hamilton-Hart, N. 2002. Asian State, Asian Bankers: Central Banking in Southeast Asia. Ithaca, NY: Cornell University Press.

Hasan, Maher and Jemma Dridi. 2010. 'The Effects of The Global Crisis on Islamic and Conventional Banks: A Comparative Study'. IMF Working Paper WP/10/201. https://www.imf.org/external/pubs/ft/wp/2010/wp10201.pdf, accessed 30 May 2017.

He, Dong and Robert N. McCauley. 2010. 'Offshore Markets for the Domestic Currency: Monetary and Financial Stability Issues'. BIS Working Papers No. 320. http://www.bis.org/publ/work320.pdf, accessed 30 May 2017.

Heng, S. K. 2009. 'The Future of Islamic Financial Services'. Welcome address at the 6th Islamic Financial Services Board Summit, Singapore. 7 May. http://www.bis.org/review/r090512e.pdf, accessed 11 September 2017.

HSBC Securities Services. 2017. 'RMB Qualified Foreign Institutional Investors (RQFII) Scheme'. 1 February. https://www.bbhub.io/board/sites/2/2017/02/HSBC-HSS-China-Product-Decks-RQFII-CFO-Advisory-Council-01Feb2017.pdf, accessed 11 September 2017.

IE Singapore. 2013. 'S'pore Banks Embrace Slew of China Financial Pacts'. October. Singapore. https://www.iesingapore.gov.sg/Partner-Singapore/Singapore-Industry-Capabilities/Infrastructure-Hub/Singapore-Asia-s-Infrastructure-Hub/Technical-and-Engineering-Services/Energy/Singapore-Sector-Folder/Success-Stories/mc/News/2013/10/Spore-banks-embrace-slew-of-China-financial-pacts, accessed 1 June 2017.

Islamic Finance News. 2014. 'Singapore: Opportunities for Islamic Finance'. Volume 11, Issue 38. http://www.eurekahedge.com/NewsAndEvents/News/1267/Islamic_Finance_News_Singapore_Opportunities_for_Islamic_Finance, accessed 5 June 2017.

Johnson, Chalmers. 1995. Japan: Who Governs? The Rise of the Developmental State. New York: Norton.

Lai, K. P. Y. 2013. 'The Lehman Minibonds Crisis and Financialisation of Investor Subjects in Singapore'. *Area* 45 (3): 273–82.

Lai, K. P. Y. 2018. 'Financialisation of Everyday Life'. In The New Oxford Handbook of Economic Geography, edited by G. L. Clark, M. Feldmann, M. Gertler, and D. Wójcik. Oxford: Oxford University Press.

Lai, K. P. Y. and J. A. Daniels. 2017. 'Financialization of Singaporean Banks and the Production of Variegated Financial Capitalism'. In Money and Finance After the Crisis: Critical Thinking for Uncertain Times, edited by Brett Christophers, Andrew Leyshon, and Geoff Mann. London: Wiley-Blackwell, pp. 217–44.

Lai, K. P. Y. and M. Samers. 2017. 'Conceptualizing Islamic Banking and Finance: A Comparison of its Development and Governance in Malaysia and Singapore'. *The Pacific Review* 30 (3): 405–24.

Lai, K. P. Y. and C. H. Tan. 2016. '"Neighbours First, Bankers Second": Mobilising Financial Citizenship in Singapore'. *Geoforum* 64: 65–77.

Langley, P. 2006. 'The Making of Investor Subjects in Anglo-American Pensions'. *Environment and Planning D: Society and Space* 24: 919–34.

Lee, H. L. 1998. 'Making Singapore Asia's Premier Banking Centre'. Speech by DPM Lee Hsien Loong at the 25th Anniversary Dinner of the Association of Banks in Singapore, 8 June. Singapore: Monetary Authority of Singapore. http://www.mas.gov.sg/news-and-publications/speeches-and-monetary-policy-statements/speeches/1998/making-singapore-asia-s-premier-banking-centre–08-jun-1998.aspx, accessed 12 September 2017.

MAS. 2009. 'Investigation Report on the Sale and Marketing of Structured Notes Linked to Lehman Brothers'. 7 July. http://www.mas.gov.sg/~/media/resource/news_room/press_releases/2009/INVESTIGATION%20REPORT_7%20JUL%2009.pdf, accessed 11 September 2017.

MAS. 2011. 'Islamic Finance in Asia: Singapore'. http://www.mas.gov.sg/~/media/resource/fin_development/manpower/MAS%20Islamic%20LR.pdf, accessed 11 September 2017.

MAS. 2012. 'Consultation Paper on Proposed Amendments to the Securities and Futures Act and the Financial Advisers Act'. 23 May. http://www.mas.gov.sg/news-and-publications/consultation-paper/2012/consultation-paper-on-proposed-amendments-to-the-sfa-and-faa.aspx, accessed 11 September 2017.

MAS. 2015. 'MAS Sets Up New FinTech & Innovation Group'. 27 July. http://www.mas.gov.sg/news-and-publications/media-releases/2015/mas-sets-up-new-fintech-and-innovation-group.aspx, accessed 2 June 2017.

MAS. 2016. 'FinTech Regulatory Sandbox Guidelines'. 16 November. http://www.mas.gov.sg/~/media/Smart%20Financial%20Centre/Sandbox/FinTech%20Regulatory%20Sandbox%20Guidelines.pdf, accessed 11 September 2017.

MAS. 2017a. 'Regional Gateway for RMB'. http://www.mas.gov.sg/Singapore-Financial-Centre/Overview/Regional-Gateway-for-RMB.aspx, accessed 16 November 2017.

MAS. 2017b. 'MAS Role'. http://www.mas.gov.sg/Singapore-Financial-Centre/Smart-Financial-Centre/MAS-Role.aspx, accessed 16 November 2017.

MAS. 2017c. 'Setting up your FinTech Business in Singapore'. http://www.mas.gov.sg/Singapore-Financial-Centre/Smart-Financial-Centre/Setting-up-your-Business.aspx, accessed 16 November 2017.

Menon, R. 2011. 'A Competent, Trusted and Clean Financial Centre'. Keynote Speech at the Wealth Management Institute Connection Dinner, Singapore. 27 October. http://www.mas.gov.sg/news-and-publications/speeches-and-monetary-policy-statements/speeches/2011/a-competent-trusted-and-clean-financial-centre-welcome-address-by-mr-ravi-menon-md-mas-at-the-wmi-connection.aspx, accessed 25 October 2017.

Ngiam, Tong Dow. 2011. Dynamics of the Singapore Success Story: Insights by Ngiam Tong Dow. Singapore: Cengage Learning Asia.

Ong, C. T. 2004. 'Opening Address at the 2004 ISDA Regional Conference: "Basel and Beyond"'. 26 October. http://www.mas.gov.sg/news-and-publications/speeches-and-monetary-policy-statements/speeches/2004/2004-isda-regional-conf-basel-and-beyond.aspx, accessed 22 May 2017.

Ong, C. T. 2005 'Singapore's Perspective on Islamic Finance'. Opening keynote address at the Asian Banker Summit 2005. 16 March. http://www.mas.gov.sg/news-and-publications/speeches-and-monetary-policy-statements/speeches/2005/opening-keynote-address-by-dmd-ong-at-the-asian-su.aspx, accessed 30 May 2017.

Rodan, G. 1989. The Political Economy of Singapore's Industrialisation. London: Macmillan.

Saeed, M. 2011. 'The Outlook for Islamic REITs as an Investment Vehicle'. Gulf One Lancaster Centre for Economic Research. Lancaster University Management School. http://www.lancaster.ac.uk/media/lancaster-university/content-assets/documents/lums/golcer/i6.pdf, accessed 30 May 2017.

Shanmugaratnam, Tharman. 2013. 'Opening Remarks at the Opening Ceremony of MAS Beijing Representative Office on 28 May 2013'. The Westin Beijing Financial Street. Beijing, China. http://www.mas.gov.sg/news-and-publications/speeches-and-monetary-policy-statements/speeches/2013/opening-remarks-by-mr-tharman-shanmugaratnam-at-the-opening-ceremony-of-mas-beijing-office.aspx, accessed 1 June 2017.

Šoštarić, M. 2015. 'Singapore, the Impact Investing Hub of Asia? A Comparison with Hong Kong'. Lien Centre for Social Innovation. Singapore: Singapore Management University.

Sub-Committee on Banking and Financial Services. 1985. Report of the Sub-Committee on Banking and Financial Services. Singapore: The Sub-Committee.

Suhana, M., H. J. Haliza, A. Z. A. Rabiatul, and A. A. Melati. 2012. 'Benchmarking Islamic REITs: Malaysia and Singapore'. Proceedings of World Islamic Banking, Finance and Investment Conference. 17–18 December. Kuala Lumpur, Malaysia. http://www.wbiconpro.com/321-Suhana.pdf, accessed 30 May 2017.

Tan, C. H. 2005. Financial Markets & Institutions in Singapore, 11th edition. Singapore: Singapore University Press.

Tan, C. H. 2011. Financial Services and Wealth Management in Singapore. Singapore: Ridge Books.

Tan, L. 2002. 'DBS Investment Sales Soar Past $300m'. *The Straits Times*, 7 February.

Today. 2014. 'Direct Trading Between Yuan, S'pore Dollar Starts Today'. 28 October. http://www.todayonline.com/business/direct-trading-between-yuan-spore-dollar-starts-today, accessed 1 June 2017.

Venardos, A. 2012. Islamic Banking & Finance in Southeast Asia, 3rd edition. Singapore: World Scientific Books.

Wang, Xiaotian. 2013. 'Singapore Looking to Widen its Yuan Role'. People's Daily Online, 29 May. http://en.people.cn/90778/8261796.html, accessed 1 June 2017.

WealthInsight. 2013. 'The Centre Cannot Hold: Singapore to Overtake Switzerland as Leading Offshore Hub by 2020'. April. London. http://www.privatebankerinternational.com/Uploads/NewsArticle/829644/1a82a8ed-7130-4dae-a951-f8b214e6efd8.pdf, accessed 22 May 2017.

Woo, J. J. 2016. Singapore as an International Financial Centre: History, Policy and Politics. London: Palgrave Macmillan.

Yeung, H. 1999. 'Regulating Investment Abroad: The Political Economy of the Regionalisation of Singaporean Firms'. *Antipode* 31 (3): 245–73.

Z/Yen. 2017. Z/Yen Global Financial Centre Index 21. March. http://www.zyen.com.

9

Tokyo

Still Below its Potential as a Global Financial Centre

Sayuri Shirai

9.1 Introduction

The Japanese government has endeavoured to develop its capital Tokyo as one of the major global financial centres for many decades. Japan's advantages are the sheer size of the Japanese economy (the third largest in terms of gross domestic product (GDP) after the United States and the People's Republic of China) and the status of the Japanese yen as the third international currency after the US dollar and the euro. In addition, Japan Exchange Group (JPX), which includes the Tokyo Stock Exchange, has the largest stock exchange in Japan and the third largest in the world in terms of market capitalization following the NYSE Group and NASDAQ. Japan also has large financial markets—the amount of total financial assets held by financial intermediaries (covering depository corporations, pension funds, insurance firms, and other financial institutions) amounted to about ¥3,303 trillion (about US$30 trillion) in September 2016. This is the fourth largest in the world, following the United States (US$86 trillion) in September 2016, the Eurozone (about US$80 trillion) in June 2016, and the People's Republic of China (about US$35 trillion) in September 2016. Moreover, Japan's financial and capital markets are large with abundant capital.

Thus, Tokyo has the potential to become a regional financial centre that transfers excess capital to emerging Asia given its geographic proximity. So far, this vision has not materialized to the extent that had been expected. This chapter takes an overview of Japan's financial and capital market developments.

Section 9.2 focuses on the Japanese government's initiatives to develop Tokyo as a global financial centre and measures adopted. Section 9.3 focuses on Japan's cross-border financial investment activities. Section 9.4 sheds light on certain features of the banking sector, which is dominant in Japan's financial markets. Debt securities markets are analysed in Section 9.5, and Section 9.6 highlights the equity market and developments of investment trusts. Section 9.7 concludes.

9.2 Government's Vision to Develop a Global Financial Centre and the Current Assessment

The Japanese government has endeavoured to foster Tokyo as a global financial centre for many decades. Since the early 1980s, the government has attempted to realize this vision through internationalizing the yen or increasing usage of the yen in international trade and financial transactions. Moreover, in 1996–2001, comprehensive financial and capital market reforms—the so-called 'Japanese Financial Big Bang'—were implemented with a clear vision for developing Japan's financial and capital markets centre in Tokyo to become comparable to the financial centres in New York and London. Various deregulations took place including liberalizing investment trusts and transactions of securities derivatives; permitting banks, securities companies, and insurance companies to enter each other's business fields; and, introducing new capital markets for start-up firms and electronic trading systems. This section looks at the recent government initiatives with an assessment of their progress and also points out developments related to fintech.

9.2.1 *The Government's Vision to Make Tokyo a Top Global Financial Centre in Asia*

In Japan, the view that Japan could play a major role in transferring abundant capital to emerging economies and developing countries in Asia is widely held. Japan could utilize excess capital to promote financial development and finance long-term investment and infrastructure projects needed to sustain economic growth in the region. This would be achieved also by fostering competitive financial and capital markets and improving the business environment in Japan.

To realize this vision, the Japanese government has taken various measures to attract foreign firms and make Japan's capital markets more attractive. First, the effective corporate tax was lowered from around 38 per cent to around 35 per cent in fiscal year 2014, then further to around 32 per cent in fiscal year 2015, and to 29.97 per cent in fiscal year 2016. Second, the government reformed the basic portfolio of public pension reserve assets (about ¥145 trillion) managed by the Government Pension Investment Fund (GPIF) in October 2014. The target allocation of domestic bonds (mainly comprising Japanese Government Bonds (JGBs)) dropped from 60 per cent to 35 per cent. Instead, the target allocations for the following assets were increased: for domestic equity from 12 per cent to 25 per cent, for external equity from 12 per cent to 25 per cent, for external bonds from 11 per cent to 15 per cent; and the target allocation for short-term assets was eliminated (it was 5 per cent prior to the reform). Third, the government has attempted to induce individuals to take greater risk to accumulate assets and diversify their financial assets by introducing the Nippon Individual Savings Account (NISA) in 2014—modelled on the Individual Savings Account (ISA) adopted in the United Kingdom. Under the NISA, all dividends and capital gains are tax-free, and individuals aged 20 years or over are currently able to invest up to ¥1.2 million per year. In 2016, the Junior NISA was introduced for individuals under 20 years old by allowing their parents and guardians to open an account and contribute up to ¥800,000 annually on behalf of the child.

In 2015, moreover, the government announced that it would provide about US$110 billion over five years to support infrastructure projects in Asia. This would be achieved through increasing yen-denominated official development assistance, strengthening financial support for the Asian Development Bank, and promoting Japanese commercial banks and firms to participate in the investment and financing projects operated by the Asian Development Bank and the Japanese government.

The vision of internationalizing the yen was brought under the spotlight again in May 2017 at the Finance Ministers and Central Bank Governors' Meeting between the Association of Southeast Asian Nations (ASEAN) and Japan, held in Japan for the first time in four years. The statement indicated 'it is important to promote the use of local currencies in cross-border transactions in the region [ASEAN] over the medium term' in order to enhance financial integration and increase activities of Japanese firms in the region. By emphasizing that facilitating the funding of the yen in the ASEAN would contribute to further regional financial stability, the Japanese government proposed to make it possible to withdraw the yen under the existing Bilateral Swap Arrangements (BSAs), which used to be the US dollar basis, as well as to establish a new type of BSA with the size of up to US$40 billion (about ¥4 trillion) to address the short-term liquidity problem. In line with this, Japan concluded a BSA with Thailand, and reached a basic agreement with Malaysia to conclude a BSA.

As a leading local-government authority, the Tokyo Metropolitan Government has taken its own initiatives to promote Tokyo as an attractive and reliable city at the centre of international finance by establishing a task force in 2014. This move was inspired by the decision in September 2013 of the International Olympic Committee to select Tokyo as the host city of the 2020 Olympic Games. The Tokyo Metropolitan Government found that it would be a good opportunity to promote Tokyo as a global financial centre given that a lot of attention would be paid to Tokyo over this period. The vision is to circulate domestic capital and capital from abroad, including New York and London and Asia, and invite foreign financial institutions and firms to establish businesses in Tokyo. This vision has been under the spotlight since Ms Yuriko Koike, who became the first female governor of Tokyo in 2016, brought it to the fore. In December 2016, the local government announced immediate measures to attract more than forty foreign financial firms over the next four years, including establishment of one-stop support centres that would provide various information with simplified procedures for licence acquisition and acceptance of documents in English. A comprehensive report was released in 2017 listing possible policies ranging from a reduction of various corporate tax burdens to improving the living environment for foreign professionals. In September 2017, the local government also announced plans to cut regional corporate taxes for foreign financial firms.

9.2.2 Assessment of the Progress of the Internationalization of the Yen

Despite all these government efforts, the yen has not become internationalized as much as the Japanese government had wished. The progress can be assessed based on the following four measures: (1) currency composition and location of sales desks with regard to various kinds of foreign exchange trade, (2) currency composition and location of active transactions with regard to OTC interest rate derivatives, (3) invoice currency used for Japan's exports and imports, (4) currency composition with regard to foreign reserves held by monetary authorities.

First, the *Triennial Central Bank Survey* compiled by the Bank for International Settlements (BIS 2016) indicates the share of the US dollar in total global foreign exchange trade strengthened moderately from 86 per cent in 2007 to 88 per cent in 2016, maintaining its status as a dominant vehicle currency. The share of the yen also rose moderately from 17 per cent in 2007 to 22 per cent in 2016, while that of the euro dropped from 37 per cent to 31 per cent. In terms of the locations where foreign exchange trade takes place, the United Kingdom was in the lead, with 37 per cent of foreign exchange trading intermediated there in April 2016, followed by the United States (20 per cent), Singapore (8 per cent), Hong Kong (7 per cent), and Japan (6 per cent). The locational advantage of the United Kingdom is maintained with its market share rising from 32 per cent in 2001 to 37 per cent in 2016. The share of the United States also rose, from 16 per cent to 20 per cent over the same period. By contrast, Japan's share dropped from 9 per cent to 6 per cent. In addition, the Japanese yen is transacted more actively in the United Kingdom than in Japan.

Second, with regard to OTC interest rate derivatives trade in April 2016, the yen's presence is less strong than in foreign exchange trade. The most actively traded OTC interest rate derivatives were US dollar-denominated instruments, which accounted for about half of all interest rate derivative turnover, followed by euro-denominated instruments. Yen-denominated instruments were ranked only fifth after British pound sterling- and Australian dollar-denominated instruments, and remained below pre-crisis levels. In terms of geographical distribution, OTC interest rate derivatives were traded most actively in the US, followed by the United Kingdom, France, Hong Kong, Singapore, Australia, and Japan.

Third, the invoice currency used for Japan's international trade remained centred on the US dollar, according to data released by the Ministry of Finance. In terms of Japan's exports, the US dollar accounted for half, followed by the yen (37 per cent). The relatively high share of the yen mainly reflects intra-firm trade transactions between Japanese manufacturers and their subsidiaries and/or contractors operating in Asia. Japan's exports to the US have been dominated by the US dollar, which accounted for 86 per cent, followed by the yen (14 per cent). The US dollar also continues to be a dominant invoice currency for Japan's imports from the world, accounting for about 70 per cent of total imports. This mainly reflects Japan's heavy reliance on commodity imports. This pattern of invoice currency composition has not changed much since 2000, and was similar before and after the Global Financial Crisis.

Fourth, currency composition of official foreign exchange reserves compiled by the International Monetary Fund (IMF) indicates that the US dollar continues to be a dominant reserve currency, although its share of reserves dropped from 72 per cent in 2000 to 64 per cent in 2016. The euro remained the second reserve currency over the same period. The yen was the third reserve currency in 2000, accounting for 6 per cent of reserves, but was then overtaken by the British pound sterling, with its share of reserves declining to 3 per cent in 2007 and rising moderately to 4 per cent in 2016. The British pound sterling's share rose from 3 per cent in 2007 to 5 per cent in 2007 and maintained this share in 2016.

9.2.3 *Tokyo Ranked Fifth Financial Centre since 2007*

Tokyo has been ranked the fifth most important financial centre according to the Global Financial Centre Index (GFCI) published by Z/Yen from its first release in 2007 until its most recent release in September 2017. While the gaps are narrowing, Tokyo remains far behind London and New York, which stand out as the only truly global financial centres. Tokyo also remains constantly behind Singapore and Hong Kong. GFCI ranking is assessed based on five categories (business environment, human capital, infrastructure, financial sector development, and reputation). Tokyo is ranked fifth in terms of reputation, sixth in terms of business environment and financial sector development, seventh in terms of infrastructure, and ninth in terms of human capital. One should note that the GFCI category ranking can change abruptly due to the changes in the instrumental factors and/or subjective perception of respondents used to construct the index. For instance, in the GFCI released in March 2017, Tokyo was ranked fifth in terms of human capital and seventh in terms of reputation (as opposed to the ninth and fifth in the September 2017 release).

The relatively low ranking on business environment could be attributable to high corporate taxes, moderate economic growth, and some labour-market rigidity, despite a favourable score for political stability without strong anti-government, anti-globalization, or populist movements. The corporate tax rate was cut starting in fiscal year 2014, as pointed out in Section 9.2.1. The rate is currently comparable to that of Germany (30.18 per cent) and lower than that of the United States (38.9 per cent), but still higher than that of the United Kingdom (19 per cent), Singapore (17 per cent), Republic of Korea (24 per cent), and Australia (25 per cent). The labour market still requires reforms that clarify layoff conditions, enable workers to achieve a better balance between work and life by reducing long working hours, eliminate income tax and social security incentives that promote female labour-market participation on a part-time basis, and reduce differences in wages and social security benefits between regular and non-regular workers. Moreover, the relatively low ranking on financial sector development could be related to lack of diversity in the financial and capital markets as well as declining market liquidity partially caused by massive monetary easing, as explained in Sections 9.4–9.6. It may be also associated with industry clusters lacking depth, particularly in the financial services and related sectors including financial advisory, consulting, accounting, legal advice, and financial technology.

9.2.4 *New Initiatives to Foster the Fintech Industry*

In line with the boom in the global fintech industry, the Japanese government has begun to recognize that the fintech industry should be promoted as a part of its growth strategy since fintech could be utilized to improve productivity of Japanese firms and improve users' convenience. So far, the development of the fintech industry is moderate and the public continues to use physical money rather than digital currencies (e.g. notes in circulation account for about 18 per cent of GDP as compared with about 10 per cent in the Eurozone and 1 per cent in Sweden). Several measures were taken (Kodama 2016). First, the Banking Law of Japan was partially revised in 2016 with regard to banks' ownership of non-finance firms. Previously, the law set a 5 per cent (15 per cent) cap on the ratio of banks' (bank holding companies') ownership of total voting rights in a non-finance firm. Given that fintech venture companies are often categorized as non-finance firms, this law made it difficult for banks to expand fintech-related businesses. The revision was made so that both banks and bank holding companies are now permitted to purchase shares of up to 100 per cent in fintech companies that provide innovative technologies to advance banks' operations or benefit bank customers—with the approval of the Financial Services Agency (FSA).

Second, the government introduced a new virtual currency regulation in 2016, which has been in effect since April 2017—the first initiative in the world aiming at promoting usage of virtual currencies (such as bitcoin) and blockchain development as well as improving transparency and protecting consumers. The regulation defines virtual currencies that have the function of payment and can be exchanged for the yen, the US dollar, or any other legal tenders and that can be recorded electronically (virtual currencies are not legal tenders). The operators of virtual currency exchanges must: (1) be registered with the FSA, which has the authority to conduct on-site investigations and issue administrative orders; (2) provide proper information (such as the features, risks, and fees) to users; (3) verify the identities of those opening accounts, maintain and store transaction records, and report suspicious transactions to the FSA under Japan's anti-money-laundering law; and (4) manage their own assets separately from those of users. In addition, operators must meet a minimum capital reserve requirement of ¥10 million. Operators or exchanges must submit annual financial reports to the FSA. The operators or exchanges are responsible for using computer systems to protect users' personal information. As of July 2017, no operators had registered with the FSA.

In 2016, the JPX announced the creation of a consortium of Japanese financial institutions to conduct proof of concept (PoC) testing for blockchain/distributed ledger technology. The consortium was set up in March 2017 with a total of twenty-six financial institutions to launch a community website for registered participants. So far, the number of fintech enterprises is small (only about 130, according to Kodama 2016) and the fintech industry is not as active as in other advanced economies, while there is growing interest in investing in fintech companies that provide new financial products and services using artificial intelligence (AI), PCs, smartphones, big data analysis, cloud computing, blockchain, etc. Large banks and other financial institutions are also attempting to collaborate with fintech firms and financing fintech start-ups.

9.3 Japan's Cross-Border Financial Investment and Financial Integration with the World

The Japanese government's long-standing vision of fostering a global financial centre, especially one for Asia, is aimed at promoting greater private-sector cross-border financial activities between Japan and Asia. This section, therefore, focuses on Japan's cross-border capital flows by examining changes in external financial assets and liabilities.

9.3.1 *Japan's Financial Assets Concentrated towards Advanced Economies*

Developing Tokyo as a regional financial centre in Asia could be a challenging task given that Japan's cross-border outbound and inbound transactions remain predominantly with advanced economies such as the United States and Europe.

Table 9.1 shows that Japan's total external assets accumulated from foreign direct investment (FDI), portfolio investment, foreign reserves, and others (including loans and deposits) rose sharply from ¥341 trillion yen in 2000 to ¥998 trillion in 2016. Net external assets—the difference between external assets and liabilities—also rose, from ¥133 trillion in 2000 to ¥349 trillion in 2016. This indicates that Japan remains a net international creditor nation.

Among various external assets, assets related to portfolio (securities) investment accounted for the largest component. According to the portfolio investment destination by region (using data available from the Ministry of Finance for 2014–16), it largely comprised debt securities from the United States, which include treasury securities, agency bonds (bonds issued by government-sponsored enterprises (GSEs)), agency mortgage-backed securities (MBSs issued by the GSEs), etc. Holdings of debt securities issued by the United States accounted for 36 per cent of external assets related to portfolio investment in 2014, and they rose to 41 per cent in 2016. The second-largest debt security assets are those issued in Europe—they accounted for 33 per cent of total external assets related to portfolio investment in 2014, but dropped to 30 per cent in 2015 and further to 28 per cent in 2016. Together with foreign reserves held by the Japanese government, holdings of US securities are quite large.

The preference for relatively safer external debt securities over external equity reflects that Japan's investors are largely risk-averse. This may be attributable to the lack of diversity with regard to the investor base—composed largely of commercial banks, insurance firms, and pension funds. Commercial banks and institutional investors have increased investment in external debt securities since the introduction of massive monetary easing called

Table 9.1. Japan's external assets and liabilities

Year				External Assets				
				Portfolio Investment			Foreign	
		Total	FDI	Total	Equity	Debt Securities	Reserves	Others
2000	¥ Billion	341,520	32,307	150,115	30,133	119,982	41,478	117,620
	% of Total		9	44	9	35	12	34
2007	¥ Billion	611,050	62,416	287,687	65,376	222,311	110,279	150,668
	% of Total		10	47	11	36	18	25
2016	¥ Billion	997,771	159,194	452,917	162,879	290,037	142,560	243,100
	% of Total		16	45	16	29	14	24

Year				External Liabilities			
				Portfolio Investment			
		Total	FDI	Total	Equity	Debt Securities	Others
2000	¥ Billion	208,473	6,096	101,609	63,222	38,387	100,768
	% of Total		3	49	30	18	48
2007	¥ Billion	360,828	15,703	221,487	142,031	79,456	123,638
	% of Total		4	61	39	22	34
2016	¥ Billion	648,658	27,840	324,469	181,530	142,938	296,349
	% of Total		4	50	28	22	46

Year				Net External Assets			
				Portfolio Investment			
		Total	FDI	Total	Equity	Debt Securities	Others
2000	¥ Billion	133,047	26,211	48,506	−33,089	81,595	16,852
2007	¥ Billion	250,222	46,713	66,200	−76,655	142,855	27,030
2016	¥ Billion	349,113	131,354	128,448	−18,651	147,099	−53,249

Note: FDI = foreign direct investment.

Source: Author, based on data from the Bank of Japan.

'Quantitative and Qualitative Monetary Easing' (QQE) in April 2013, which has resulted in substantially low returns in Japan. They tend to prefer debt securities due to financial regulations and their asset–liability management for pension funds and insurers. It is noteworthy that the share of external equity holdings rose gradually from 9 per cent of external assets on portfolio investment in 2000 to 16 per cent in 2016. This is partly attributable to the reform of the basic portfolio of public pension reserve assets managed by the GPIF as mentioned in Section 9.2.1. Despite a diversification of outbound portfolio investment, Japan's preference for external debt securities remains largely unchanged.

Regarding loans extended abroad, large Japanese banks have increased overseas lending activities including trade finance, particularly in Asia from 2009, by replacing a decline in the presence of European banks in the region.

9.3.2 Foreign Investors' Preference for Japan's Equity over Debt Securities

Japan's total liability accumulated from FDI, portfolio investment, and other activities rose from ¥208 trillion in 2000 to ¥645 trillion in 2016. Most portfolio investment in Japan originates from the United States and Europe. Unlike Japan's portfolio investment abroad, however, portfolio investment from US and Eurozone companies in Japan has concentrated on Japan's equity rather than Japan's debt securities since 2000. This trend continued after the adoption of QQE.

From December 2012, moreover, foreign investors began to increase equity investment in response to a rise in stock prices driven by the launch of 'Abenomics' and the subsequent QQE. Stock prices rose sharply, as shown by major stock price measures including the Nikkei 225, the Tokyo Stock Price Index (TOPIX), and the JPX Nikkei 400 (see Figure 9.1). The Nikkei 225 exceeded the highest level recorded prior to the Global Financial Crisis. Nevertheless, Japan's stock prices have never recovered to the historically

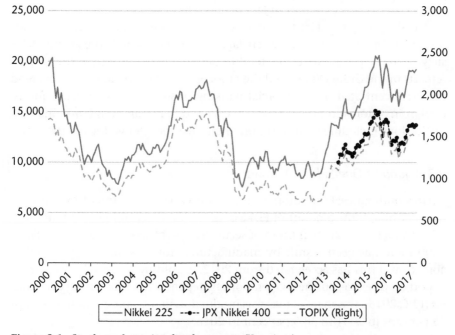

Figure 9.1. Stock market price developments (¥, points)

Note: Units of JPX Nikkei 400 and TOPIX are points, and the unit of Nikkei 225 is yen (¥).

Source: Author, based on data published by the CEIC.

highest level achieved in December 1989 (¥38,947 in the case of the Nikkei 225 and 2,884 points in the case of TOPIX). The bubbles in the late 1980s were generated due to the government's increase in public investment projects and the BOJ's cut in the interest rate to cope with the recession driven by the 1985 Plaza Accord and the associated sharp appreciation of the yen. Market prices recovered to about half of the maximum price levels on two occasions: once in early 2000 and again after the launch of QQE (in 2015 and from late 2016 to the present after Donald Trump's victory in the US presidential election in November 2016). However, prices have been quite volatile.

Returns on debt securities were low before QQE and became lower under QQE, so bonds are too expensive for foreign investors unless they are able to obtain the yen cheaply through the cross-currency basis swap against the US dollar. Since the cost of obtaining the yen for these investors is much cheaper than negative returns from holding treasury discount bills (TBs), non-residents accounted for 51 per cent of the outstanding TBs issued in December 2016. Until September 2016 the BOJ was the largest holder of TBs, but it reduced its holdings, perhaps due to an increase in their prices. Foreign investors accounted for only 5.5 per cent of the outstanding JGBs. In terms of outstanding JGBs and TBs combined, foreign investors held 10.5 per cent. This suggests that non-residents' holding of TBs reflects low funding cost rather than intrinsic interest in Japanese bonds.

Overall, equity is riskier than debt securities. Thus, the differences in portfolio investment patterns between Japanese investors and foreign investors suggest that Japanese investors tend to be more risk-averse than their counterparts in the United States and the Eurozone. While Japanese investors tend to be concentrated in commercial banking, insurance, and pension funds, foreign investors tend to be more diverse and many are non-bank financial institutions including short-term-oriented investors and various funds.

9.3.3 Japan's One-Sided FDI Flows

Japan's outbound FDI is another important type of investment by Japanese firms, although the amount of FDI assets (accumulated amount of outbound FDI) is much smaller than those of securities and others (see Table 9.1). Since 2000 there has been a shift by manufacturers towards locating production abroad, and this has accelerated from 2012. According to the FY 2016 Survey Report on Overseas Business Operations by Japanese Manufacturing Companies (JBIC 2016), the share of overseas production in total production rose from 25 per cent in 2001 to 38.5 per cent in 2016.

Regional decomposition is available for 2014–16. Asia accounts for about 30 per cent of Japan's outbound FDI assets throughout the period, suggesting the region is an important destination of capital for Japanese firms. Indeed, the presence of Japanese manufacturers including automobile producers is large and noticeable in many Asian economies. The amounts of assets related to outbound FDI to the United States and Europe is equally large, accounting for about 35 per cent and about 25 per cent of total outward FDI respectively. Again, advanced economies are important destinations of Japan's FDI capital.

With regard to external liability related to FDI (accumulated amount of inbound FDI), the amount is relatively small compared with external assets related to FDI and accounts for only 17 per cent of external assets related to FDI. Despite a cut in the corporate tax rate, as mentioned in Section 9.2.1, the FDI inflow remains limited. Among source regions, Europe is the most active FDI investor in Japan, accounting for about 50 per cent of external liability related to FDI.

9.4 Japan's Banking Sector Coping with Abundant Bank Deposits

Japan's financial assets held by financial intermediaries are dominated by depository corporations. Depository corporations include domestically licensed banks, foreign banks in Japan, and financial institutions for small businesses. This section focuses on Japan's banking sector, whose deposits from households and firms have been large and growing.

9.4.1 *Banking Sector with the Low Loan–Deposit Ratio*

Japan's banking sector has abundant deposits, but demand for credit has been limited for a long time. This is a structural phenomenon, as evidenced by the persistently low and declining bank loans-to-deposit ratios. The ratio dropped from 66 per cent in 2000 to 53 per cent in 2016 (see Figure 9.2). This means that the increase in bank deposits has been faster than the increase in bank loans. The gap between loans and deposits is mainly filled by JGB holdings. This suggests that abundant capital has not been utilized efficiently for productive purposes in the private sector.

9.4.2 *Long-Standing Limited Credit Demand*

Long-standing limited demand for credit reflects not only the current rapidly ageing and declining population, but also the shrinking markets for goods and services. Since 2013, 'Abenomics' and QQE have enabled stagnant loan growth to turn positive. This is a welcome trend, but the current year-on-year loan growth of 2–3 per cent remains too moderate to offset a decline in the interest rate margins (the difference between lending and deposit rates).

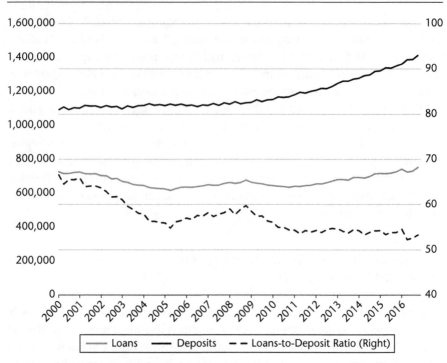

Figure 9.2. Loans, deposits, and loans–deposit ratio of depository corporations (¥ billion, %)

Source: Author, based on data in the Flow of Funds, published by the Bank of Japan.

The interest rate margin fell below 1 per cent in 2012 due to monetary easing by the BOJ adopted in 2010 until the introduction of QQE. The margin continued to drop under QQE and further after the announcement of a negative interest rate policy in January 2016. Deposit growth, rather than slowing down, accelerated in relation to bank loans, especially after the negative interest rate policy; thus, the already low loan-to-deposit ratio dropped even further (see Figure 9.2).

The main objective of QQE is to achieve the 2 per cent price stability target by promoting portfolio rebalancing of financial institutions from safe assets (i.e. JGBs) to risk assets (such as bank loans, FDI, and other domestic and foreign securities investment). Figure 9.3 indicates that the ratio of loans to total financial assets has declined over the past four years. The decline in the ratio of holdings of debt securities (largely comprising JGBs)—mainly as a result of selling JGBs to the BOJ—was replaced by an increase in deposits (largely comprising the current account balances at the BOJ).

The ratio of foreign investment to total financial assets did not show a rising trend over the same period. The presence of the Japanese banking sector remained relatively large globally until the first half of the 1990s, with the number of overseas branches reaching a peak of 380 in 1996. Since then,

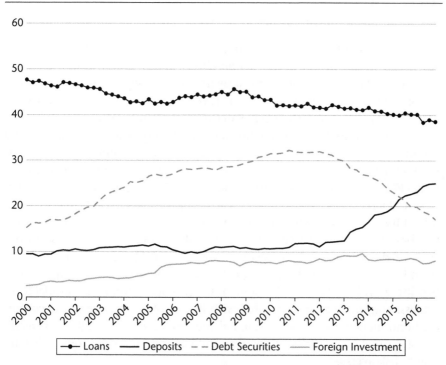

Figure 9.3. Asset composition of depository corporations (% of total financial assets)
Source: Author, based on data in the Flow of Funds, published by the Bank of Japan.

domestic non-performing loans have risen rapidly, and the growing banking-sector problems led to mergers and acquisitions within the sector and a decline in the number of overseas branches in the late 1990s and the 2000s (to 92 by 2011). In 2012, the number of foreign branches began to rise moderately, reaching 102 as of September 2016, reflecting the soundness of the banking sector and the need to develop new business opportunities in other countries in the face of substantially low interest rates and limited credit demand domestically. One noticeable positive change is the move of the Mitsubishi UFJ Financial Group, one of the three largest groups in Japan, which has become keen on expanding foreign businesses by increasing the number of subsidiaries and branches, and is now present in more than forty economies globally. In 2008, the Bank of Tokyo-Mitsubishi UFJ (BTMU) group formed a global strategic alliance with Morgan Stanley and, as part of the alliance, made an equity investment in Morgan Stanley. In 2008, moreover, BTMU completed the acquisition of all of the shares of common stock of Union-BanCal Corporation in the United States, which then became a wholly-owned indirect subsidiary of MUFG. In 2013, BTMU acquired approximately 72 per cent of the total outstanding shares of Bank of Ayudhya in Thailand, which then became a consolidated subsidiary of BTMU.

9.4.3 *Household's Excessive Reliance on Bank Deposits*

Japanese households traditionally prefer banks deposits. Deposits and currency accounted for around 50 per cent of households' total financial assets from 2000 to 2016 (see Figure 9.4). Such large-scale holdings of deposits are quite remarkable given that the deposit interest rate is very low—it was so even before QQE and has been close to zero per cent since the adoption of QQE.

QQE contributed to raising households' equity and investment fund holdings as a share of total financial assets from around 9–10 per cent in 2008–12 to 12 per cent in 2016. However, the ratio did not exceed the peak (17 per cent) reached in 2007 and the 15–16 per cent before the Global Financial Crisis. The moderate increase during 2013–16 reflects mainly stock price hikes, because households have remained a net seller of equities over the past four years. By contrast, households' holdings of debt securities accounted for only 1–2 per cent of total financial assets over the same period. Their equity holdings are greater than debt securities holdings, partly because a wide range of JGBs and other corporate bonds are available to professional investors as compared with households. The size of the corporate bond market also remains small as mentioned in Section 9.5.2. Overall, the sheer size of holdings of deposits and currency indicate households are highly risk-averse.

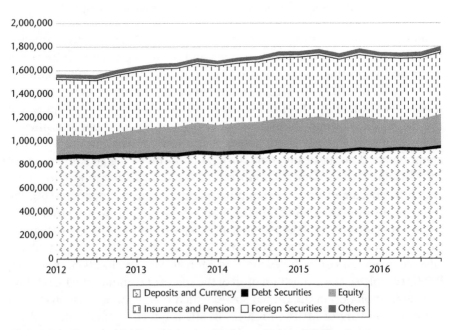

Figure 9.4. Households' financial assets by type of assets (¥ billion)

Source: Author, based on data in the Flow of Funds, published by the Bank of Japan.

9.4.4 Cautious Corporate Sector with Ample Deposits and Cash

Like households, Japanese firms are known to be highly risk-averse, as demonstrated by their large holdings of deposits and currency. The amount of deposits and currency held by firms began to rise from 2011 and rose at an accelerated pace from 2013 owing to an increase in corporate profits. In 2016, the amount of deposits and currency exceeded ¥240 trillion—about one-quarter of firms' financial assets and about 45 per cent of GDP in 2016 (see Figure 9.5). Corporate profits rose rapidly in 2013 and companies maintained high profit levels in 2014–16. This high profitability was attributable to various factors: (1) the substantial depreciation of the yen, (2) low borrowing cost, (3) a series of cuts in the corporate tax rate, (4) a sharp decline in commodity prices and imported materials in 2014–16, and (5) an increase in foreign demand since 2015. This reflects the choice of firms to accumulate profits in the form of retained earnings rather than allocating them to expanding business in terms of fixed investment, mergers and acquisitions, research and development, foreign portfolio investment, and FDI.

Since 2013, firms have increased their non-residential fixed investment. However, the amount of the increase has been moderate and has remained well below cash flows or changes in deposits and currency. Since 2013, firms have been expanding outbound FDI, with assets growing from ¥72 trillion in

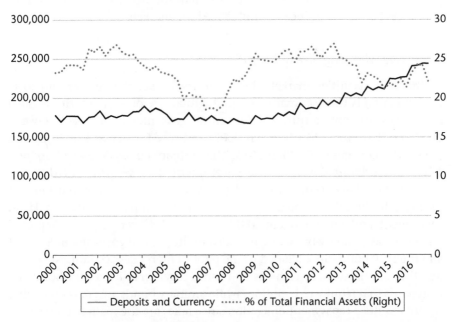

Figure 9.5. Firms' holdings of deposits and currency (¥ billion, % of total financial assets)
Source: Author, based on data in the Flow of Funds, published by the Bank of Japan.

2013 to ¥123 trillion in 2016. The increase has been moderate and foreign assets related to FDI accounted for only half of deposits and currency in 2016. Meanwhile, firms in the US also increased their holdings of deposits to about US$1 trillion in December 2016 due to an increase in profits. However, the outstanding amount of deposits is relatively small compared with Japan, accounting for only 5 per cent of total financial assets and 5 per cent of GDP. In addition, US firms actively engaged in outbound FDI so that the amount of foreign assets related to FDI measured US$5 trillion, about five times the amount of deposits. Firms' non-residential fixed investment exceeded cash flows or changes in deposits.

9.5 Debt Securities Markets with Growing Issuance by the Public Sector

The capital markets comprise the debt securities market and the equity market. The total size of the debt securities market reached about ¥1,263 trillion in December 2016 and accounted for 235 per cent of GDP. This size is greater than that of the equity market (equity market capitalization accounted for about 100 per cent of GDP), which is a reflection of the sheer size of the government's mounting debt. This section focuses on public- and private-sector debt securities markets as well as the BOJ's asset purchase programmes that have significantly influenced the markets.

9.5.1 *Overwhelming Size of the JGB Market*

In the debt securities market, the government (i.e. the central and local governments) is the dominant issuer. The total size of debt securities issued by the government (mostly by the central government) doubled between 2000 and 2007 to ¥720 trillion in 2007, and rose further to ¥1,046 trillion (about 195 per cent of GDP) in 2016. The ordinary bonds (¥854 trillion) and TBs (¥117 trillion) dominate the government debt securities market and accounted for 93 per cent of the total government debt securities outstanding in 2016. It should be noted that JGBs include ordinary bonds and Fiscal Investment and Loan Program (FILP) bonds. However, they are reported separately, as ordinary bonds are included in the general government account and the FILP bonds are included in the public enterprises account. Nevertheless, they are classified collectively and issued together as JGBs. FILP bonds are loan funds that require redemption, while ordinary bonds are grant funds that do not require a repayment obligation since taxes are the main fiscal sources. In 2016, the FILP bonds measured about ¥104 trillion (or about 20 per cent of GDP) so that the amount of JGBs outstanding issued came to ¥958 trillion.

9.5.2 Small and Stagnant Private-Sector Debt Securities Market

The second-largest issuers of debt securities are private non-financial corporations. Their securities cover mainly corporate bonds and commercial papers. Their amount outstanding issued remained small and largely stable after the Global Financial Crisis and was equivalent to 13 per cent of GDP in 2016 (see Figure 9.6). Since 2013, the amount outstanding has risen moderately by about ¥6 trillion. Some large firms issued super-long corporate bonds (with remaining maturity of over ten years) due to a substantial decline in JGB yields with all maturities, especially after the adoption of the negative interest rate policy. However, this increase in super-long corporate bonds contributed to expanding the corporate bonds market only moderately. The relatively small size of the corporate bond market reflects the fact that credit demand by firms has been limited. Firms can borrow funds cheaply from commercial banks and many firms maintain retained earnings in the form of deposits and currency, as mentioned in Section 9.4.4.

The third-largest issuers are domestically licensed banks, and their debt securities are mainly bank debentures and commercial papers. The amount outstanding remained largely constant after the Global Financial Crisis, accounting for only 8 per cent of GDP in 2016. From 2013 to 2016, the amount outstanding rose by about ¥6 trillion as commercial banks issued longer-term bonds like non-financial corporations. As banks have ample

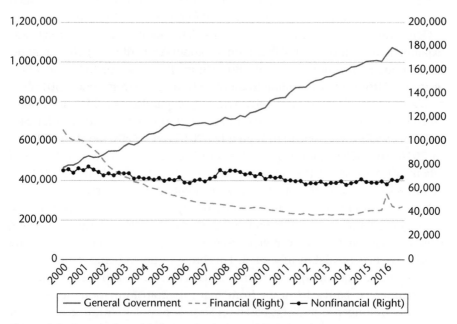

Figure 9.6. Outstanding debt securities by issuers (¥ billion)

Source: Author, based on data in the Flow of Funds, published by the Bank of Japan.

deposits and thus limited need to find alternative funding sources, the bank debenture market remained stagnant.

9.5.3 *Growing Amount of JGB Holdings by the BOJ*

The huge and growing JGB market reflects an accumulation of the central government fiscal deficit. The Bank of Japan Law prohibits the BOJ from monetizing its fiscal deficit or financing the government directly. Under QQE, therefore, the BOJ has purchased JGBs from financial institutions that hold current account balances with the BOJ. The purchase of JGBs is a major monetary easing tool aimed at raising aggregate demand in order to achieve the 2 per cent price stability target—rather than financing the government deficit. Therefore, the BOJ stresses that the practice should not be viewed as monetization. The BOJ's large-scale purchases of JGBs raised JGBs' prices and reduced yields substantially, generating a very accommodative monetary environment.

In April 2013, the BOJ adopted monetary base control by abandoning the policy rate target and initially set an annual pace of increase in the monetary base of about ¥60–70 trillion. To meet this monetary base target, JGB purchases of about ¥50 trillion (about 10 per cent of GDP) with maturity up to a maximum 40 years were essential (for details, see Shirai 2017a). JGBs are the only assets that enable the BOJ to continue such large-scale purchases (see Figure 9.7). Other assets purchased include two risk assets—exchange traded funds (ETFs) (about ¥1 trillion annually) and REITs (about ¥30 billion annually).

QQE was expanded in October 2014. The monetary base target was expanded from about ¥60–70 trillion to about ¥80 trillion; JGB purchases from about ¥50 trillion to about ¥80 trillion. Purchases of ETFs and REITs were raised from about ¥1 trillion to about ¥3 trillion and from about ¥30 billion to about ¥90 billion, respectively. The BOJ expanded the ETFs to around ¥6 trillion in July 2016. A negative interest rate policy was added in January 2016 and yield curve control in September 2016 (for details, see Shirai 2017b). In 2016, the BOJ's holdings of JGBs and TBs reached about ¥371 trillion (about 40 per cent of the outstanding JGBs issued) and about ¥50 trillion (about 43 per cent of the outstanding TBs issued), respectively.

Especially after a negative interest rate policy, JGB yields declined substantially and all the yields with remaining maturities up to 10 years became negative. The lowest 10-year yield reached around –0.3 per cent and the yield curve became flat in July 2016. This brought down banks' lending rates and the interest rate margin further. The flat yield curve also made it difficult for commercial banks to profit from maturity transformation (lending or investing in longer-term assets based on shorter-term liabilities) as well as for insurance firms to gain reasonable returns from savings-type products. With the subsequent yield curve control, the ten-year yield was raised and stabilized

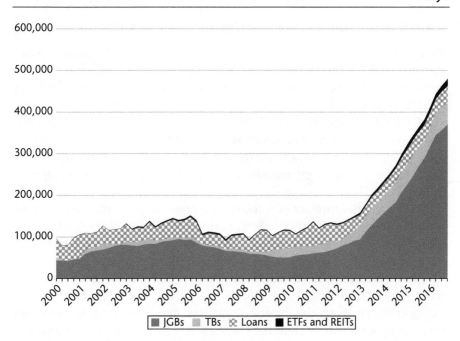

Figure 9.7. Assets held by the Bank of Japan (¥ billion)

Notes: JGB = JPN Government Bonds; TBs = Treasury Bills; ETFs = Exchange Traded Funds; REITs = Real Estate Investment Trusts.

Source: Author based on data in the Flow of Funds, published by the Bank of Japan.

at around zero per cent. The yield curve steepened moderately for the yields with remaining maturity above ten years. This new action was de facto tightening, but it helped to stabilize the yields and to expand the interest rate differentials against the United States. Particularly after Donald Trump's victory in the November 2016 US Presidential election, the US yields rose rapidly and led to a depreciation of the yen against the US dollar and many other currencies due to wider interest differentials (and an appreciation of the US dollar against the yen and many other currencies). The depreciation of the yen helped to raise Japan's equity prices.

9.6 Development of Equity Markets and Investment Trusts

The equity market performance deteriorated after the Global Financial Crisis, but was revived somewhat from late 2012, as was evident from a stock price hike. The net assets of investment trusts including the ETFs and REITs have also expanded rapidly and achieved their highest levels as of March 2017. This section focuses on the features of Japan's equity markets and investment trusts.

9.6.1 *Listed Companies Dominated by Domestic Companies*

There are currently four stock exchanges in Japan (Tokyo, Nagoya, Sapporo, and Fukuoka). Among them, the JPX is the biggest. The JPX was established in January 2013 by combining the two largest securities exchanges: the Tokyo Stock Exchange and Osaka Securities Exchange. The Tokyo Stock Exchange and Osaka Exchange are currently the JPX's subsidiaries. The spot markets of the Tokyo and Osaka stock exchanges were merged in July 2013 and the number of listed enterprises together amounted to 3,423 companies. After that, the number of companies increased by 132 firms to 3,557 companies in May 2017.

By contrast, the number of foreign companies dropped from eleven companies in July 2013 to only five firms currently. The number of foreign listed companies has a been on a declining trend since 1992 after the collapse of the stock market bubble in 1990. The maximum number of foreign listed firms on the Tokyo Stock Exchange was 127 companies in 1991. The declining trend reflects Japan's weakened macroeconomic performance, language barriers, listing costs, Japan-specific business practices, and other factors. As a result, listed companies mainly from the United States and Europe have withdrawn from the Tokyo Stock Exchange to reduce costs arising from double listing. The Tokyo Stock Exchange made efforts to improve the situation in 2010, for example by exempting foreign companies listed on major overseas stock exchanges from listing examination procedures and by allowing disclosure of financial documents in English. Despite such efforts, the Tokyo Stock Exchange has not been successful in raising the number of foreign listed companies. Indeed, the domestic orientation of Japan's stock exchanges has increased. The limited presence of foreign companies could be one of the factors working against Tokyo in terms of its ambition to be recognized as a global financial centre.

Market capitalization of all the markets belonging to the JPX reached ¥586 trillion and accounted for about 110 per cent of GDP in March 2017. The 1st Section has the biggest market capitalization, accounting for about 96 per cent of the total.

9.6.2 *Essential Role Played by Foreign Investors in the Equity Market*

While there are only a few foreign listed companies, foreign investors have found it increasingly attractive to invest in Japanese stocks. They have become major market players in the equity market, as already pointed out in Section 9.3. Foreign investors' holdings of shares listed on the four stock exchanges on a market-value basis rose from 19 per cent in fiscal year 2000 to about 30 per cent in fiscal year 2015. Foreign investors have been the largest group of investors since 2010. This rising trend is remarkable given that their market share was a mere 4 per cent in the 1980s and 1990s.

Financial institutions (including commercial banks and insurers) are the second-largest group of investors, but their market share has gradually fallen since the early 2000s. They used to hold large ownership stakes in listed companies as a way of maintaining long-term business relationships with them. In line with changing practices of corporate governance, financial institutions have begun to sell their stakes. The move was started by commercial banks and later followed by insurers. In terms of market value, their total market share dropped from 39 per cent in fiscal year 2000 to 28 per cent in fiscal year 2015.

As for individual investors, their market share fluctuated—rising from 19 per cent in fiscal year 2000 to 20 per cent in fiscal year 2012 and then dropping to 17 per cent in fiscal years 2014–15. Many individual investors took advantage of a stock price hike from late 2012 as an opportunity to sell shares they had held onto for a long time while stock prices were sluggish, as mentioned in Section 9.4.3. Although they profited from capital gains, this did not lead to accelerating equity investment. The subsequent volatile movements of stock prices may have discouraged individual investors from increasing investment in risk assets. Their position as a net seller from fiscal year 2009 was maintained until fiscal year 2016.

9.6.3 *Performance of Investment Trusts: ETFs and REITs*

Japan's total net assets of investment trusts amounted to US$1.4 trillion in December 2016—the eighth largest in the world according to data released by the Investment Trusts Association. The total net assets of investment trusts in the United States (US$18.8 trillion) overwhelmed those in other countries. Out of Japan's net assets in investment trusts, about 60 per cent are allocated to publicly offered investment trusts and the rest to privately placed investment trusts. The net assets of publicly offered investment trusts have grown rapidly since 2013 and reached about ¥100 trillion in March 2017—the highest level registered since 1998, when data started becoming available—¥86 trillion of which were stock investment trusts (including ETFs worth about ¥23 trillion), accounting for about 90 per cent of the net assets of publicly offered investment trusts. The net assets of publicly offered stock investments are largely denominated in yen. The market share of yen-denominated assets rose from 43 per cent in 2009 to 67 per cent in March 2017 (of which net assets excluding ETFs rose from 40 per cent to 54 per cent over the same period). This was a result of a rapid increase in investment in Japanese equities since 2013. The expansion of the ETF market is associated with the BOJ's ETF purchases. Japan's ETFs are largely stock ETFs. The net assets of

ETFs were small before the Global Financial Crisis, reaching a maximum of about ¥4 trillion in 2006, followed by a decline in 2007–9. From 2013 they rose rapidly, from ¥4.2 trillion in 2012 to ¥23 trillion in March 2017.

With regard to listed REITs, the market has faced a similar rising trend to that of the ETFs since 2013. Several factors contributed to this trend: the BOJ's purchases of REITs, a low-interest-rate environment, and the speculation on higher real estate prices driven by the 2020 Tokyo Olympic Games, etc. The net assets of listed REITs reached about ¥4 trillion in 2009 and remained at that level until 2011. The net assets then rose rapidly from ¥4.6 trillion in 2012 to ¥8.5 trillion in February 2017 (the market value of REITs rose from ¥4 trillion to ¥12 trillion over the same period). The number of REITs subsequently rose from thirty-seven in 2012 to fifty-eight in February 2017. However, the TOSHO REIT index (the index of the REITs listed on the Tokyo Stock Exchange) saw an end to its rising trend in early 2015 and has since fluctuated between 1,700 and 1,900 points.

9.7 Conclusions

While the Japanese government has attempted to develop its capital Tokyo as one of the major global financial centres with various measures, this vision has not materialized so far—as Tokyo has been ranked the fifth-largest financial centre ever since the Global Financial Centres Index was launched in 2007. While Tokyo has the potential to become a regional financial centre that would transfer excess capital to emerging Asia for productive purposes given its geographic proximity, the major destination of financial investment continues to be biased toward the United States and Europe. Japan's investment in Asia is largely FDI and its size remains limited relative to Japan's total external assets. Moreover, Japan's FDI performance can be characterized as a one-way (namely, outbound) flow. A wider gap between FDI-related external assets and FDI-related external liabilities is indicative of the limited entry of foreign firms and the limited success of foreign firms operating in Japan. This is different from the United States and Europe, where both inbound and outbound FDI with the rest of the world are fairly balanced. Japan's one-way flow of capital is more evident with regard to FDI as compared with portfolio and other types of investment.

Japan's banking sector has been struggling with its long-standing problem of how to utilize abundant deposits given the limited demand for credit. An increase in corporate profits since 2013 has further increased corporate holdings of deposits and currency. Households continue to prefer bank deposits and cash as major financial assets. Japan's debt securities markets lack diversity. The JGBs stand out and private-sector debt securities (issued by financial institutions and non-financial enterprises) amounted to only ¥114 trillion and accounted for just 21 per cent of GDP, which is well below the size of the equity market. For firms, ample deposits and currency holdings reduce their need to issue corporate bonds. For financial institutions, ample bank deposits reduce their need to issue bank debentures. This could be one of the factors making it more challenging for Tokyo to be recognized as a global financial centre, since other cities like New York enjoy a wider range of debt securities. In addition, investors and market players perceive the BOJ's growing presence in the JGB markets as an indication of the declining function of the markets.

On the ETF (and equity) and REIT markets, the BOJ's purchases have helped develop them. However, concerns are also raised about the functioning of the equity market due to the growing presence of the BOJ—with regard to reducing the downside risk related to stock prices (as the BOJ's purchases are expected to take place when stock prices fall) as well as on potentially undermining corporate governance (as a result of its growing presence as a tacit large investor not exercising voting rights). Some equity market participants are concerned that a further increase in the BOJ's ETF purchases may lead to a situation where market prices of individual companies do not necessarily reflect firms' specific information and fundamentals. While foreign investors have been actively investing in Japan's stocks as market players, the number of foreign listed firms has been declining steadily to only five currently—confirming that Japan's equity market remains domestically-oriented.

Meanwhile, some investors in the REIT (and real estate) markets hold the view that these markets are likely to remain active and favourable at least until the 2020 Olympic Games due to an expected increase in construction activities (such as for sport facilities, hotels, and restaurants)—even if the BOJ reduces the amount of REIT purchases. An important issue in the future, therefore, will be how the markets will respond to any change in the BOJ's policy, which is likely to move towards normalization or a more sustainable framework in the foreseeable future.

References

Bank of Japan. 2016. 'Flows of Funds—Overview of Japan, the United States, and the Euro Area: the Third Quarter of 2016'. 22 December.

BIS (Bank for International Settlements). 2016. 'Triennial Central Bank Survey of Foreign Exchange and OTC Derivatives Market in 2016'. Geneva: BIS.

JBIC (Japan Bank for International Cooperation). 2016. 'The FY 2016 Survey Report on Overseas Business Operations by Japanese Manufacturing Companies'. December.

Kodama, Toru. 2016. 'Japan's Initiative for Fintech Innovation'. Swedish Agency for Growth Policy Analysis.

Shirai, S. 2017a. Mission Incomplete: Reflating Japan's Economy. Tokyo: Asian Development Bank Institute.

Shirai, S. 2017b. 'The BOJ's Risky Yield Curve Control Experiment'. *Central Banking Journal*, 9 May.

10

Conclusions

A Global Overview from a Geographical Perspective

Dariusz Wójcik and Theodor F. Cojoianu

10.1 Summarizing Trends

The main objective of this book is to review the development of international financial centres since the Global Financial Crisis. The first chapter by Youssef Cassis has introduced the topic and previewed our findings from a historical perspective by focusing on the long-term trajectories of financial centres. In this chapter we shall summarize observations made in the volume thus far and complement them from a more geographical perspective, putting developments in the eight countries and eleven financial centres covered in the book in a global context.

Perhaps the main conclusion of our book is that international financial centres have fared surprisingly well in the last decade. As the preceding chapters demonstrate, New York and London have recovered from the crisis relatively quickly and remain the leading global financial centres, even if the level of employment in financial services in New York has slightly declined. Paris and Frankfurt were affected by both the US subprime crisis and the Eurozone crisis, but they too have proved rather resilient. At the same time, chapters on China and Singapore document that their financial centres have grown quite spectacularly. Even the chapter on Tokyo points to a recent growth in its international financial activity, although in international finance Tokyo is definitely punching below Japan's economic weight. The chapter on Switzerland probably paints the most pessimistic picture of all, proclaiming the end of a golden era for Zurich and Geneva, but on closer reading even there one can find more evidence on stagnation than decline.

The major reason for this relative stability in the landscape of international financial centres lies arguably in the management of the crisis. The concerted action of governments and central banks, largely orchestrated by the US government and its central bank, as described by Richard Sylla in Chapter 2, prevented a global financial meltdown. With very few exceptions, big banks have been saved from failing, and a big part of the toxic debts they have produced has been taken over by governments. In other words, we might say that financial centres themselves have been saved from failure, which was a distinct possibility during the heat of the crisis in 2008. In this light, we should be careful when we use the term resilience to describe the post-crisis performance of financial centres. It is open to debate to what extent financial centres exhibited robustness that allowed them to recover relatively quickly, and to what degree they were saved by external intervention.

The role of the state–finance nexus in the development of financial centres has certainly increased. The size and power of central banks and regulatory agencies have increased, particularly in North America and Europe. As these institutions are typically headquartered in leading financial centres, this trend has generated additional employment, cushioning job losses in the private financial sector. New financial regulation led by Dodd–Frank Wall Street Reform Act, higher capital adequacy requirements of Basel III, and new EU directives, have restricted some financial activities such as proprietary trading by banks, forced deleveraging, and stimulated a degree of bank downsizing. On the other hand, however, the new regulatory environment of finance has stimulated the creation of thousands of jobs in risk management and compliance, thus boosting employment in financial and related business services. It should be noted that these new employment opportunities were created mainly in leading financial centres, which host the headquarters of financial institutions and national and supranational regulatory agencies, not in regional and local financial centres.

A major force underlying the evolution of international financial centres is the ongoing shift of the world's economic centre of gravity towards Asia. The global landscape of financial centres has always been part and parcel of the global distribution of economic and political power: geo-economics and geo-politics. One of the patterns in the history of international financial centres is that the power of a centre is built on the economic and political power of the underlying economy, and can last for a long time after the economic and political power fades away (Cassis 2006; Spufford 2006). In other words, changes in geo-finance, understood as the global distribution of financial power, and reflected in the geography of international financial centres, typically lag behind changes in geo-economics and geo-politics. China may already have the largest GDP in the world in PPP terms, but its nominal GDP, which matters more in international finance, is still much smaller than that of the United States. China is asserting its power through increasing influence in international financial institutions like the IMF and the World Bank, and by establishing its own institutions such as the Asian Infrastructure Investment Bank headquartered in Beijing and the New Development Bank, formerly referred to as the 'BRICS bank', based in Shanghai. It may take much longer, however, before mainland Chinese financial centres challenge or join New York and London at the apex of the global hierarchy of financial centres. Key ingredients of this process will undoubtedly include the internationalization of the Chinese currency, and changes in China's rule of law, discussed by David Meyer in Chapter 7 and Karen Lai in Chapter 8. While the former process may seem inevitable, the latter is far from guaranteed.

At a lower level, within the financial industry, we have seen an important process of restructuring, with a relative decline of banks, and investment banks in particular, and the rise of the asset management industry. Based on data from Dealogic, fees from core investment banking activities in 2015 were down by 40 per cent from their 2007 level. Meanwhile, according to Willis Towers Watson, total assets managed by the world's 500 largest asset managers increased by 10 per cent in the same period. BlackRock, the world's largest asset management company, is now considered among the most influential private financial companies in the world, with its CEO Larry Fink attracting the kind of attention that used to be the domain of investment bank executives. Some reasons behind this rebalancing between investment banking as the sell-side of the securities industry and asset management as the buy-side are clear. The asset management industry was not involved in the Global Financial Crisis as directly as investment banks. While banks have suffered from a reputational crisis and much of the new regulation has been targeted at them, asset managers have come out from the crisis relatively unscathed. This restructuring has put a lot of pressure on centres that relied to a large extent on the pre-crisis expansion of investment banking, including Zurich, as discussed by Tobias Straumann in Chapter 6.

There are many other trends in international financial centre development discussed in the volume, which we shall touch upon in the remainder of this chapter. We shall combine observations based on preceding chapters with new data that will help us compare developments across the eleven financial centres and beyond them, taking into consideration financial centres that our book did not focus on. We shall start by looking at the elite of the financial sector, comparing the world's top centres of investment banking and asset management. Next, we shall broaden our focus by reviewing trends and patterns of employment in the financial and business services sector as a whole. In Section 10.4, we shall get a glimpse of offshore finance and its development since the crisis. Section 10.5 will provide an overview and comparison of developments in fintech and its potential impacts on the global map of financial centres. The concluding section will consider new geographical ways of conceptualizing relationships among financial centres, financial and business services, and offshore finance, and will make suggestions for future research.

10.2 Ranking Elite Financial Centres

Table 10.1 presents the top ten centres of investment banking and asset management. Data used to construct it uncovers only part of these high-value-added activities. For investment banking, it captures fees from core investment banking deals in primary capital markets, assigned to the subsidiary or headquarters of each service provider. For asset management, it is based

Table 10.1. Top ten centres in investment banking and asset management and their share in global activity

Investment banking 2015		Investment banking 2007	
New York	36.6%	New York	45.9%
London	11.0%	London	9.1%
Tokyo	9.4%	Zurich	6.8%
Toronto	6.3%	Tokyo	4.3%
Paris	4.4%	Frankfurt	3.9%
Charlotte	3.5%	San Francisco	3.5%
Frankfurt	3.3%	Toronto	3.2%
Zurich	2.5%	Paris	2.9%
Beijing	1.9%	Charlotte	1.7%
Hong Kong	1.7%	Amsterdam	1.7%
Top 10	80.5%	Top 10	83.0%

Asset management 2015		Asset management 2007	
New York	21.8%	New York	14.3%
Boston	7.6%	London	10.0%
Paris	7.3%	Paris	7.9%
London	7.0%	Boston	7.2%
Philadelphia	6.0%	Tokyo	4.7%
Tokyo	4.0%	Zurich	4.1%
Toronto	3.3%	Frankfurt	3.6%
Zurich	3.1%	Munich	3.3%
San Francisco	3.0%	Philadelphia	2.9%
Los Angeles	3.0%	Los Angeles	2.8%
Top 10	66.2%	Top 10	60.7%

Notes: Investment banking activity is measured as the value of fees from core investment banking deals: equity and debt issuance underwriting, syndicated lending, and advice on mergers and acquisitions. Fees are allocated to the subsidiaries of investment banking service providers that conducted each deal. For details of the estimation methodology, see Wójcik et al. 2018.

Asset management activity is measured as the value of assets under management allocated to the operational headquarters of asset management companies.

Source: Authors' calculations based on data from Dealogic and Willis Tower Watson and estimations by Vladimír Pažitka.

on assets under management managed by the world's largest asset management companies, and allocated to their global headquarters. Despite these limitations, the data offers a useful indication of what has happened to the geography of the securities industry, the elite of the financial sector.

New York dominates due to the sheer size of its domestic capital market. Over 80 per cent of fees from investment banking activities conducted by New York-based banks was paid by US customers. The share of New York in global investment banking activity has declined since 2007, but it was still nearly 37 per cent. In asset management, the share of New York-headquartered asset management firms has increased significantly. In a step that decisively helped its meteoric rise in size and power, in 2009 New York-based BlackRock took over London-headquartered Barclays Global Investors. But New York's position in asset management is broad-based, as the city was home to over fifty of the 500 largest asset managers in the world as of late 2015.

London maintained its second position, and even increased its share in investment banking, but its share and rank in asset management has declined. It should be noted, however, that allocation of assets under management according to global headquarters of asset management firms underestimates the significance of London in this industry, as London is home to the European headquarters of many foreign asset management firms, including BlackRock.

The table reminds us that there are many large financial centres in the United States beyond New York. In investment banking San Francisco and Charlotte featured as top-ten industry centres in 2007. San Francisco had dropped out of top ten by 2015, but Charlotte had reinforced its position. This was due mainly to the merger of Bank of America and Merrill Lynch in 2008, and Wells Fargo Securities (the securities arm of Wells Fargo) moving headquarters from San Francisco to Charlotte in 2009. In asset management, as many as five US cities were the top ten in 2015: Boston, Philadelphia, San Francisco, and Los Angeles, besides New York.

Both sides of the securities industry have witnessed the rise of Toronto. In investment banking, Toronto nearly doubled its market share and rose to the fourth position. In asset management, it entered top ten. With a relatively buoyant economy and robust financial regulation, Canadian banks maintained much stronger balance sheets and reputations for quality, allowing them to expand internationally, with RBC in the lead (Bordo et al. 2015).

Our table puts Tokyo far ahead of any other financial centre in Asia. This is determined to a large extent by the fact that our data does not capture the full activity of foreign investment banks and any activity of foreign asset managers in financial centres. As these are particularly important in Hong Kong and Singapore, their positions are underestimated. In investment banking Hong Kong was behind Beijing and Shanghai was not in the top ten. Beijing typically hosts headquarters of Chinese and foreign institutions operating in mainland China, even if much of their financial activity is conducted out of Shanghai. It is nevertheless a reminder that Beijing should be taken seriously as an international financial centre.

Data issues notwithstanding, Tokyo's position is impressive. While investment banking globally has significantly declined, Japanese banks have expanded their activity. Following the crises experienced in the 1990s, Japanese banks entered the 2000s with more capital, less leverage, and less risk appetite than their European and American counterparts. When the crisis erupted in 2008, the Japanese economy was not affected directly, and Japanese banks stood ready to take advantage of their competitors' weaknesses. Nomura took over Lehman Brothers' operations in Europe and Asia, while Mitsubishi UFJ bought a major equity stake in Morgan Stanley and created successful investment banking joint ventures with the US bank. In addition, Japanese banks took advantage of the rise in the foreign activity of Japanese companies. Abenomics has played a part, as some economic reforms, including a change in corporate governance to make companies more shareholder value-oriented, a revitalization of capital markets, and a push towards a more diversified investment strategy of the Government Pension Investment Fund, directly or indirectly generate demand for investment banking services.

Among continental European centres, Paris appears more resilient than Frankfurt or Zurich. Paris-based banks, with BNP Paribas, Société Générale, and Crédit Agricole in the lead, have reduced their investment banking activity since 2007, but less than banks in Frankfurt. The latter also dropped out of the top ten in asset management, taking eleventh position with a 2.6 per cent global market share, on a par with Munich. Zurich-headquartered investment banks, with UBS and Credit Suisse in the lead, suffered large losses, even if much of their pre-crisis business had been conducted out of London and New York. Geneva does not make it to the top ten in any of the above rankings. Its share in global investment banking was less than 0.1 per cent, while its share in asset management fell from 1 per cent in 2007 to 0.6 per cent in 2015. This lends additional support for the findings of Tobias Straumann in Chapter 6 concerning the end of the golden age of Swiss financial centres. It should be added, though, that from these tables alone, Frankfurt does not look as resilient as Eike Schamp suggested in Chapter 5. This may be because the rise in regulatory functions in Frankfurt offset losses in the private financial industry in the city.

Two final notes are in order when interpreting Table 10.1. First, both investment banking and asset management are highly concentrated activities, with top-ten centres accounting for over 80 per cent and 66 per cent of global activity in 2015. This level of concentration and dominance of leading centres cannot really be captured in indices focusing on competitiveness, such as the

GFCI series. In the latest (22nd) edition of GFCI, London leads with a rating of 780, New York follows with 756, with Toronto in seventh place with 710, and Montreal twelfth with 697. This makes the financial centre hierarchy look flatter than it is, as if lower-ranked financial centres had the potential to challenge those at the very top, with Montreal for example as a potential challenger to Toronto. This approach underestimates the significance of localization and agglomeration economies present in large financial centres. Financial firms are attracted to other financial firms and big cities, which makes it difficult for challenger centres to dislodge incumbents.

The localization and agglomeration economies also help to explain why the centres of investment banking overlap so much with those of asset management. Both groups of companies benefit from global knowledge about rates, prices, and market trends. Both thrive in places with a large number of professionals with financial industry expertise and from infrastructure for clearing and settlement of trades. In fact, investment banking and asset management are often conducted by the same companies. JPMorgan, BNP Paribas, HSBC, and many other banks are also some of the leading asset managers in the world. Of course, there is some room for specialization. Boston, Philadelphia, and Munich, for example, appear among the top asset management centres, without being leading centres of investment banking.

10.3 Thinking Broadly about Financial and Business Services

Investment banking and asset management are part of the securities industry, which occupies a privileged position in the financial sector, with fees, salaries, and bonuses typically higher than those in the rest of the financial sector. Literature in geography, however, has for a long time made a case for thinking about financial centres in much broader terms, as centres of financial and business services, including law, accountancy, marketing, public relations, business consulting, human resources, and others (Sassen 2001; Taylor 2004; Cassis 2006). Consider big financial transactions with companies raising capital or buying other companies. Such transactions always involve lawyers, accountants, and business consultants in addition to financiers. On the retail side, consider real estate and mortgage deals, which involve a nexus of financial and other firms. Thinking in terms of localization and agglomeration economies, jobs in the financial services sector create jobs in other business services and vice versa. The presence of the headquarters of Linklaters and EY reflects and contributes to the status of London as a global financial centre, just as the presence of McKinsey, S&P, or Moody's does to the status of New York.

Table 10.2. Financial and business services sector (FABS) in selected cities

City	Employment at the end of 2015 (thousands)	Share in total employment	Growth in employment since 2007	Share of FABS in GVA 2015	Growth in FABS GVA since 2007
New York	2,253	24%	4%	46%	8%
London	2,616	30%	20%	42%	16%
Paris	1,774	27%	5%	38%	8%
Frankfurt	426	27%	6%	37%	2%
Zurich	333	26%	20%	32%	11%
Geneva	107	28%	18%	25%	9%
Beijing	2,286	29%	53%	35%	91%
Hong Kong	744	20%	23%	31%	26%
Shanghai	1,505	21%	92%	27%	89%
Singapore	741	21%	58%	29%	46%
Tokyo	2,699	14%	14%	31%	1%

Notes: Financial and business services sector includes: financial and insurance activities, real estate activities, professional, scientific & technical activities, and administrative & support service sectors.

GVA—gross value added; GVA growth is measured in real terms, after accounting for inflation in the respective country.

Cities are defined as metropolitan areas.

Source: Authors, based on Oxford Economics and authors' calculations.

To capture this broad approach to financial centres, Table 10.2 presents the size and dynamics of the whole financial and business services (FABS) sector in the eleven cities covered in the book. To start with, FABS is a very large sector. In 2015 there were fourteen metropolitan areas in the world that employed more than a million people in FABS. These included six financial centres covered in this book plus São Paulo, Moscow, Los Angeles, Chicago, Mumbai, Jakarta, Mexico City, and Seoul. In our sample of eleven centres, FABS constituted between 14 per cent of total employment in Tokyo and 30 per cent in London. The share of FABS in gross value added (GVA) was even bigger, exceeding 40 per cent in New York and London. The financial sector itself was typically responsible for a quarter of FABS jobs and a third of GVA.

In all eleven cities we focus on in the book, FABS employment has grown and so did FABS GVA. Growth was recorded even in cities for which preceding chapters indicated a slight decline (New York) or stagnation in financial sector employment (Frankfurt, Zurich, and Geneva). Several reasons, already hinted at earlier in the book, can help explain this apparent paradox. To cut costs, many financial firms outsourced some jobs to business services firms. In addition, new regulation created a lot of new jobs in risk management and compliance, both inside financial institutions and in business services. The shift to new markets, including Asia, has also created demand for business services, including consulting, accounting, and law. Even Brexit creates a lot of demand (at least short-term) for legal and consulting services to help financial firms with contingency plans and to establish and extend operations on the European continent. In general, economic globalization may have slowed down since the crisis, but it has not stopped, and companies around the world seem to continue to outsource their central coordinating functions including financial functions to specialist firms that create financial centres by their very presence in these cities. Technological development, which definitely has not slowed down since the crisis, only enhances these outsourcing opportunities.

Not surprisingly, growth in FABS employment and GVA has been very uneven. While employment in New York, Paris, and Frankfurt has grown by single-digit figures since 2007, in Hong Kong it has grown by 23 per cent, in Singapore by 58 per cent, in Beijing by 53 per cent, and in Shanghai it nearly doubled. To be sure, Shanghai is not an exception. According to Oxford Economics, there were dozens of metropolitan areas in the world where FABS employment grew even faster than in Shanghai. These include Casablanca in Morocco, Bengaluru and Delhi in India, Hangzhou in China, as well as Istanbul, Abu Dhabi, and Doha in the Middle East. In Europe, cities with FABS employment growing at a rate exceeding 50 per cent since 2007 include Wrocław, Poznań, and Kraków, Polish cities with populations between 0.5 and 1 million that became major destinations of business process outsourcing by foreign companies. In Africa, besides Casablanca, cities with the fastest growth in the sector were Lagos, Nairobi, Cape Town, and Johannesburg.

Overall, this data reminds us how much cities, and not only megacities, depend on FABS. By consequence, understanding FABS, with financial services at their core, is crucial for understanding the world economy in the twenty-first century. While the growth of the financial sector might have stalled in some places, the broader FABS complex, to which finance is central, is forging ahead, contributing to the picture of resilience in leading international financial centres.

10.4 Locating Offshore Finance

While all chapters have talked about cross-border activities of leading financial centres, offshore financial centres have not been the focus of this book. In general, there has been a lot of confusion and controversy regarding the definition of offshore finance and offshore financial centres. The IMF has defined an offshore financial centre as 'a country or jurisdiction that provides financial services to non-residents on a scale that is incommensurate with the size and the financing of its domestic economy' (Zoromé 2007, p. 7). This, however, equates offshore with cross-border finance, and neglects offshore financial activities conducted in large economies and leading financial centres. To deal with these issues, a new definition has recently been proposed

215

by geographers, defining offshore finance as 'the activity of booking and/or registering financial claims in a jurisdiction to avoid policy constraints in other jurisdictions' (Clark et al. 2015).

Measuring offshore finance is very difficult by the very nature of the phenomenon. In Table 10.3 we have gathered data from the Bank for International Settlements on the outstanding cross-border claims booked in banks located in various jurisdictions. This is by no means a ranking of offshore financial centres, not least because the data is available only for countries, not cities. More importantly, only some of the claims that figure in the table would count as offshore finance in the light of the above definition. In addition, there are offshore financial activities beyond the banking sector, not covered in the table. Nevertheless, if we relate figures in the table to what we know about the size of the domestic banking sector and the physical presence of foreign banks in these jurisdictions, the data might serve as a useful starting point for locating offshore financial centres.

Table 10.3. Outstanding cross-border claims by banks located in a given country/jurisdiction ($ million)

Rank	Country/jurisdiction	31/03/2017	31/03/2007
1	United Kingdom	4,484,002	5,697,471
2	Japan	3,500,056	1,959,468
3	United States	2,764,479	2,644,738
4	France	2,191,124	2,475,131
5	Germany	2,096,111	2,948,364
6	Hong Kong SAR	1,383,295	619,670
7	Netherlands	1,078,140	1,052,772
8	Cayman Islands	1,038,396	1,743,400
9	China	931,206	n/a
10	Switzerland	761,970	1,347,259
11	Singapore	732,788	556,829
12	Canada	581,726	248,132
13	Luxembourg	576,704	925,393
14	Belgium	548,356	922,144
15	Sweden	527,199	293,846
16	Italy	469,569	478,969
17	Spain	425,612	508,832
18	Australia	409,381	164,387
19	Chinese Taipei	380,764	149,642
20	Ireland	284,195	868,242
	Selected jurisdictions outside of top 20		
25	Bahamas	182,210	347,223
27	Jersey	146,162	464,142
28	Guernsey	143,046	213,331
29	Bahrain	130,204	162,493
30	Macao SAR	110,388	22,569
	World total	27,710,832	28,076,226

Source: Authors, based on locational banking statistics from the Bank for International Settlements.

First of all, it is notable that the total value of cross-border claims has declined slightly in absolute terms, but not in a way that could be described as financial de-globalization. Major declines in cross-border claims of banks located in the Cayman Islands, Switzerland, Luxembourg, Ireland, the Bahamas, Jersey, and Guernsey suggest a decline of these jurisdictions as offshore financial centres. In Switzerland, this is a development related to the erosion of banking secrecy, as discussed by Tobias Straumann in Chapter 6. In Switzerland and elsewhere it may be related to new measures aimed at increasing transparency in international finance led by G20 and the OECD, much of it motivated by the increasing determination of crisis-stricken governments to limit tax evasion and tax avoidance. On the other hand, we see spectacular increases in claims registered in Hong Kong, Singapore, Chinese Taipei, and Macao, which are consistent with research demonstrating the increasing role of Chinese capital in offshore finance (Haberly and Wójcik 2015). Put simply, the centre of offshore finance is moving slowly to Asia. Major increases in cross-border claims in Japan and Canada add further evidence on the strengthening positions of Tokyo and Toronto, highlighted in Table 10.1. Consistent with findings of Table 10.1 is also the fact that France's position in cross-border bank claims decreased less than that of Germany.

As already mentioned, offshore finance exists in international insurance, asset management, and other parts of the financial sector in addition to banking. In fact, there are signs that with post-crisis financial regulation targeting banking, offshore financial activity has moved to and flourished in the non-bank financial sector. According to the data collected by the Financial Stability Board, the share of banks in total assets booked in the Cayman Islands has declined from 45 per cent in 2007 to 15 per cent in 2015, with the share of other financial intermediaries rising from 55 per cent to 85 per cent (FSB 2017, p. 17). At the end of 2015, other financial intermediaries located in Ireland held assets of approximately $1.4 trillion, several times larger than total bank assets. According to data collected by McKinsey, the total foreign assets and liabilities booked in Luxembourg, the Netherlands, Ireland, Hong Kong, Switzerland, Singapore, and Mauritius exceeded 1,000 per cent of their GDPs, and in the case of Luxembourg 36,000 per cent (2017). Overall, offshore finance remains an important building block of international financial centre activity.

10.5 Mapping Fintech

Fintech can be defined as 'a dynamic segment at the intersection of the financial services and technology sectors where technology-focused start-ups and new market entrants innovate the products and services currently provided by the traditional financial services industry' (PWC 2016, p. 3). Ever since clay tablets were used in Mesopotamia around 2500 BC to record claims, technology has been key to the development of financial services (Ingham 2004). Key moments in the history of modern financial innovation included the installation of the transatlantic cable connecting North America and Europe in 1866 and the introduction of ATMs in 1967 by Barclays. According to Arner et al. (2015), 1967 marked the end of the analogue era of financial technology (or fintech 1.0) and the beginning of an era focused on the applications of digital technology, including electronic payments systems, electronic securities trading, and online banking (fintech 2.0). In their view, the global financial crisis of 2007–8 marks the beginning of a new stage in the relationship between financial services and technology. Whereas before the crisis established financial firms dominated the introduction of new technology to financial services, since then new start-ups and established technology firms have started to deliver financial products and services to companies and retail customers directly. Who drives financial innovation is thus the distinctive feature of what Arner et al. describe as fintech 3.0, and what we refer to simply as fintech. Another distinctive feature of the last decade is the speed of innovation. For example, a new fully online money market fund launched by Alibaba, a Chinese technology firm, became the fourth-largest fund of this type in the world within merely nine months (Arner et al. 2015).

The crisis created conditions for the rise of fintech as it made the established financial sector more vulnerable to competition from technology firms and new start-ups. The crises damaged the reputation of financial firms, particularly banks. Some of their pre-crisis financial innovations, including those related to securitization of subprime mortgages, were considered self-serving and dangerous. Banks have embarked on a long process of cleaning up their balance sheets, reducing costs, and complying with a myriad of post-crisis regulations. Many banks trimmed their branch networks and reduced their lending activities, leaving much of the market, particularly SMEs and retail customers, underserved. At the same time, the technology sector has enjoyed a good reputation among investors and the public, and little regulation. Armed with smartphones (the iPhone was launched in 2007), Internet infrastructure, and data science, the technology sector was ready to enter the market for financial services, not only in the mature economies of North America, Europe, and Japan, but also in emerging and developing economies, where hundreds of millions of adults do not have a bank account, and where physical banking infrastructure never or hardly existed. The Internet- and technology-savvy millennial generation seems to be ready to access and use financial services in ways radically different from those of their parents and grandparents. As Richard Sylla stresses in Chapter 2, 'for more than a century in the United States the financial sector has charged about $2 for every $100 of assets it intermediates'. The challenge for fintech is to change this long-established pattern.

In the last decade, fintech has permeated the whole range of financial products and services, from mobile payments, digital wallets, and cryptocurrencies, through peer-to-peer lending and insurance, to blockchain, crowdfunding, and robo-advisors. Fintech is changing the way financial companies relate to their customers, to each other, and how they operate internally, with fintech applications in risk management and compliance in addition to product design.

Even though fintech is defined by the prominence of start-ups, established financial services firms as incumbents and established technology firms as challengers are crucial for understanding the dynamics of the industry. Financial firms serve as both producers and consumers of fintech. It was estimated that in 2016 alone the financial sector globally spent nearly $500 billion on information technology (IDC 2016). So far financial firms have reacted to fintech in three ways: by developing fintech solutions in-house, by acquiring fintech firms, and by investing in and partnering with fintech firms. In the United States, in 2016 only, JPMorgan has spent more than $9.5 billion on revamping its IT infrastructure, out of which $600 million was spent on developing fintech solutions, either in-house or through partnerships (McDowell 2017). Goldman Sachs invested heavily in payments technologies and real-estate fintech, while Citi invested and partnered with many data analytics and financial services infrastructure software companies. In Europe, Banco Santander engages with fintech mainly through its corporate venture capital arm, Santander InnoVentures (CBInsights 2017; Crunchbase 2017). Ping An Insurance Group has emerged as a key fintech player in Asia through its investment in Lufax, the world's most valuable private fintech company. It has also invested in R3, a blockchain consortium funded by major banks across the United States and Europe (Cryptocoins News 2017; Reuters 2016).

Established technology firms engage in fintech by developing their own fintech solutions, spinning off specialized fintech firms, as well as investing in and partnering with them. AmazonLoans extends short-term credit to small and micro businesses selling on Amazon marketplace. Google offers payment services through Google Wallet. Alibaba, China's largest e-commerce company, developed Alipay, which in 2013 became the largest mobile payment company in the world, overtaking PayPal (Business Insider 2014). While technology firms including industry giants eagerly develop fintech solutions and feed the fintech industry with capital and talent, one of the factors that make them reluctant to a wholesale commitment to fintech is the fear of falling subject to financial regulation. In other words, while established technology firms do not want to become financial firms, established financial firms lack the core competencies and culture to become technology firms. Thus, fintech represents a convergence between the financial services and information-technology sectors, but one that expresses itself, at least so far, in the proliferation of specialized fintech firms.

Governments and the public sector are also key players in fintech. One reason is the close relationship between fintech and infrastructure. Fintech solutions rely on existing infrastructure, such as the Internet, and develop new financial infrastructures, e.g. for payment services, vital for economic development (PWC 2016). Governments need to understand fintech and its implications for financial development and financial stability. A debate is ongoing as to what aspects of fintech should be regulated and how (Arner et al. 2015). Fintech offers new tools for governments to monitor financial markets and institutions. A whole branch of fintech, referred to as regulatory technology (regtech), helps financial firms streamline and automate risk management and compliance with financial regulation, but it also helps governments improve the efficacy of regulatory activity, e.g. through real-time compliance and fraud detection. Last but not least, governments see fintech as a promising innovative sector generating high-quality jobs and tax revenues. As a result, it is not surprising to see governments investing in fintech firms and nurturing the development of fintech through industry incubators and accelerators. Previous chapters have given plenty of examples of such initiatives in different financial centres. It should also be mentioned that government intervention protects the proliferation of specialized start-ups in fintech by preventing large financial firms and technology firms from monopolizing fintech. In 2016, for example, Lloyds, Barclays, HSBC, and RBS were forced by the UK government to divest their joint stake in VocaLink, the company providing the UK's payments infrastructure (Accenture 2016).

While previous chapters have presented recent fintech developments in individual centres, here we shall focus on a comparative geographical perspective, from world regions, through countries, to cities. This will help us identify some broad geographical patterns of the industry.

According to Autonomous Research (2017) new fintech investment rose from $2.5 billion in 2012 to $17.3 billion in 2016. While in 2012, North America accounted for 80 per cent of new investment, in 2016 the amount of new investment in China (at $7.7 billion) surpassed that in the USA ($6.2 billion). Total new investment in Europe was $2.2 billion, with the UK in the lead ($0.8 billion). China's rise in fintech was driven by investments made by the giants of the Chinese Internet industry as well as the state-controlled investment funds. Alibaba's affiliate company Ant Financial alone raised over $4 billion from investors such as China Investment Corporation and China Development Bank Capital (TechCrunch 2016).

To analyse fintech investments by city, we have built our own dataset based on data on equity and debt funds raised by all fintech start-ups founded between the start of 2007 and the end of the second quarter of 2017, using Crunchbase and data from the CBInsights Fintech 250 List.[1] The coverage of the whole decade allows us to paint a big picture rather than focus on fluctuations in year-to-year investment flows. It also allows us to capture fintech as a sector of financial centre activity during the decade since the outbreak of the subprime crisis in the United States. The total number of start-ups captured in our dataset is 5,381, but data on funding was available for only half of them. Hence our results should be treated with caution and only as indicative. However incomplete, they are broadly compatible with the results of other surveys and present a useful insight into the spatial structure of the fintech industry.

Table 10.4, presenting the top twenty countries according to fintech start-up funding, confirms the dominance of US firms, accounting for 60 per cent of total funding. China comes second, but with a relatively small number of deals and start-ups. Funding per deal in China is larger than in any other country, a reflection of the involvement of giant Chinese Internet firms and the state-controlled investment funds. In Hong Kong SAR the average deal size is also relatively large. In Europe, the UK seems to have a firm lead in fintech, and hosts the second-largest number of fintech start-ups after the United States. Germany holds the second position in Europe, followed by Sweden, France, Russia, Ireland, Spain, and the Netherlands. Switzerland occupies only the twenty-second position. Canada appears as a prominent location of fintech, with the fifth-largest value of investments in the world. Other countries in the top ten are India, Israel, Singapore, and Brazil. Japan is not in the top ten.

Table 10.5 presents the top twenty-five cities in the world based on total funding raised by fintech start-ups between 2007 and Q2 2017. San Francisco metropolitan statistical area represents by far the largest centre of fintech in

---

[1] To create our universe of fintech start-ups, we conducted two searches. First, we found all firms with any of the following keywords in the description of their activity: Fintech, Bitcoin, Cryptocurrency, InsurTech, Mobile Payments, Funding Platform, Crowdfunding, Trading Platform. In addition, we found all firms whose activity description included a combination of at least one of the keywords Financial Services, Finance, Banking, Insurance, Payments, Personal Finance, Wealth Management, Stock Exchanges, Credit Cards, Lending, Auto Insurance, Transaction Processing, Compliance, Health Insurance, Micro, Lending, Debt Collections, Debit Cards, Prediction Markets, Life Insurance, Commercial Insurance, Property Insurance, Consumer Lending, with at least one of the keywords Software Information Technology, Enterprise Software, SaaS, Big Data, Cloud Computing, Internet of Things, Artificial Intelligence, Machine Learning, Predictive Analytics, Cloud Infrastructure, Software Engineering, Data Mining, PaaS, Natural Language Processing, IaaS. The list of companies obtained thus is merged with the CBInsights Fintech 250 List. This led to a sample of 5,381 companies with complete headquarter address details, including 2,547 companies (47%) for which data on funding was available.

Table 10.4. Top twenty countries based on total fintech funding between 2007 and Q2 2017

Rank	Country	Funding (US$m)	No. of start-ups
1	United States	31,636	2,625
2	China	8,981	104
3	United Kingdom	4,008	596
4	Germany	1,440	133
5	Canada	872	195
6	Hong Kong SAR	639	55
7	India	612	180
8	Sweden	444	38
9	Israel	367	80
10	Singapore	365	107
11	Brazil	342	72
12	Australia	328	95
13	South Korea	320	27
14	Japan	249	21
15	France	233	100
16	New Zealand	143	12
17	Russian Federation	129	39
18	Ireland	126	55
19	Spain	113	109
20	The Netherlands	94	58
	World total	52,367	5,381

Source: Authors, based on data from Crunchbase data and the CBInsights Fintech 250.

the world, and if we combine it with San Jose MSA, they account for more than a quarter of global investment. The San Francisco Bay area, including Silicon Valley, is home to the largest technology firms like Alphabet (Google) and Apple, which invest in fintech, and home to nine out of the twenty-six fintech 'unicorns' (start-ups with a valuation in excess of $1billion) in the world as of the end of Q2 2017: Stripe, SoFi, Credit Karma, Zenefits, Prosper, Robinhood, Clover Health, Gusto, and Symphony. As Jamie Dimon, JPMorgan's CEO, remarked in his 2014 annual letter to shareholders, 'Silicon Valley is coming' (JPMorgan 2015). As San Francisco is also a major financial centre in the United States, including the headquarters of one of the world's largest banks (Wells Fargo), fintech has the potential to elevate San Francisco to a position of much higher importance in the network of international financial centres than it has hitherto occupied.

New York takes the second spot in our table. It is home to such start-ups as CommonBond, which offers loans to students to fund their study; Betterment, an automated investment advisory service; Oscar Health, applying fintech solutions to healthcare insurance; and Bond Street, providing an online platform for small business loans. New York City and State promote fintech development through such initiatives as the Fintech Innovation Lab and a new fintech centre on Roosevelt Island. As Richard Sylla notes in Chapter 2, New York has had a large high-technology industry for a long

Table 10.5. Leading centres of fintech based on total funding between 2007 and Q2 2017

Rank	City/metropolitan area	Funding (US$m)	No. of start-ups
1	San Francisco	11,881	439
2	New York	5,812	490
3	Shanghai	3,646	23
4	London	3,585	481
5	Beijing	3,417	48
6	Chicago	2,322	99
7	Boston	1,676	106
8	San Jose	1,448	166
9	Los Angeles	1,281	138
10	Atlanta	1,256	52
11	Austin	776	53
12	Shenzhen	726	15
13	Hong Kong	636	48
14	Hamburg	619	10
15	Toronto	598	77
16	Washington	558	51
17	Seattle	551	79
18	Berlin	512	57
19	Stockholm	441	27
20	Hangzhou	420	5
21	San Diego	388	27
22	Singapore	365	107
23	Dongguan	351	1
24	Phoenix	340	19
25	Minneapolis	336	11

Selected cities outside of top 25

30	Tokyo	243	19
33	Paris	219	68
73	Zurich	46	20
96	Frankfurt	28	10
203	Geneva	3	5
	World total	52,367	5,381

Source: Authors, based on data from Crunchbase and the CBInsights Fintech 250.

time, recently associated with the metonym Silicon Alley, located in Midtown and Lower Manhattan. There are as many as ten other US metropolitan areas in the top twenty-five. This shows how widespread the fintech activity is in the United States. Most of these cities can be easily identified as major technology centres such as Austin, San Diego, or Seattle, major financial centres such as Chicago, or centres of both such as Boston.

London features as the leading fintech centre in Europe by a large margin. The city has been branded as an 'all-rounder' in fintech, as it offers the 'Fin of New York, the tech of the West coast and the policymakers of Washington' all in one place (Deloitte 2017). Level 39 in Canary Wharf has become one of the biggest fintech hubs in the world, hosting over 100 start-ups and acting as a model for other financial centres trying to emulate London's success. The UK government is heavily involved in the promotion of fintech. The recently published Green Paper for the New British Industrial Strategy mentions fintech as one of the key sectors (HM Government 2017). Uncertainty over Brexit, however, has had a negative influence on London's fintech community. One of the largest London-based fintech firms, Transferwise, has announced that it is considering moving its headquarters to mainland Europe (Reuters 2017).

Shanghai and Beijing appear as the leading centres of Chinese fintech, with Shenzhen, Hong Kong, Hangzhou, and Dongguan also in the top twenty-five. As already noted, Chinese fintech investments are typically smaller in number but large in value. Six out of the twenty-six fintech unicorns globally are located in China. The largest of them, Lufax, is headquartered in Lujiazui, Shanghai's financial district, and specializes in P2P lending and online investment. Zhong An is China's first fully online insurance company, based in Shanghai and created by the Chinese insurance company Ping An in collaboration with Internet giants Alibaba and Tencent. Beijing is home to Lakala and Rong360, specializing in online payments and lending respectively. Hangzhou is the home of Alibaba and the fintech unicorn 51XinYongka/u51.com, which helps customers manage credit-card bills. Shenzhen is home of Tencent and Ping An, and the major technology centre of China alongside Beijing, Shanghai, and Hangzhou. In China, we thus see a pattern similar to that in the United States, with fintech following the location of financial and technology centres.

As mentioned by Eike Schamp in Chapter 5, Frankfurt is not the leading fintech centre in Germany. In our table, both Hamburg and Berlin are far ahead of Frankfurt, which was in ninety-sixth place globally with $28 million of investments and ten start-ups. Berlin has been a more vibrant centre of the technology industry than Frankfurt for a long time. The position of Hamburg in the table is influenced by a large fundraising deal by Kreditech Holding, a lender using artificial intelligence to calculate credit scores. In fact, according to our data, in fintech Frankfurt was trailing not only Hamburg and Berlin but also Düsseldorf and Munich. This is another example of the relatively decentralized structure of the German economy and its financial system, and specialization among its economic and financial centres (Wójcik and MacDonald-Korth 2015).

Apart from Frankfurt, four other financial centres covered in this volume do not feature in the table of the top twenty-five fintech centres. Tokyo is in 30th place, Paris in 33rd, Zurich in 73rd, and Geneva in 203rd with a negligible level of fintech investment. Our data is only indicative, but consistent with other studies on fintech showing the paucity of this activity in Japan, France, and Switzerland. It seems that initiatives to promote fintech in these countries, as described in previous chapters, have not yet yielded major results.

In summary, fintech activity measured in terms of investments is spread very unevenly. The map of fintech is very spiky. Fintech is concentrated in cities with pre-existing technology or financial services industries, and thrives particularly in cities where it can build on the strength of both industries. While fintech may help economies leapfrog whole stages of financial development, and help them overcome the lack of some types of physical financial infrastructure, such as branch networks, no major fintech centres seem to have emerged without a pre-existing base in technology or finance industry. There are no obvious fintech centres outside of big cities and metropolitan areas. Fintech does not arise out of cyberspace. It is rooted in established centres of technological innovation and finance, with their infrastructure and deep labour markets. As Karen Lai stated in Chapter 8, 'Taking a financial geography perspective, financial markets and actors are understood as being firmly rooted in IFCs as the physical locations where the production and exchange of financial services take place. Markets are not just abstractions that exist "out there" and operated by "invisible hands"; they are spatially embedded and socially constructed.' This statement seems to apply as much to fintech centres as it did to financial centres before the rise of fintech.

Our observations here go against predictions that fintech will make financial centres redundant. They do not, however, imply that fintech does not have potential to change financial centres and their global landscape. Our data already suggests a degree of convergence between technology and financial centres. As fintech progresses, technology centres are likely to become more important in global financial networks, while financial centres without fintech may lose in competition with those that have it. This may increase the concentration in the financial services sector rather than reduce it. Fintech is also likely to reduce employment in financial services, particularly those serving retail customers, and change its distribution. Fintech facilitates the extension and fragmentation of financial services value chains, with parts of the chain becoming outsourced and offshored, and with some employment migrating from financial centres like London and New York to cities in India or Poland. Any radical predictions on fintech decimating employment in financial centres should, however, be tempered by considering the latter as centres of FABS. Impacts of fintech on employment in accounting, law, and consulting services may be much weaker than those in the financial sector. Remember that in Table 10.2 we have seen the business services employment growing consistently since 2007, even in advanced economies.

Fintech may affect the very structure of financial centres. While in the 1980s–2000s new financial districts were emerging as the financial sector was expanding into new locations within financial centres (think of Canary Wharf, IFSC Dublin, Midtown Manhattan, or Kowloon), in the last five years financial districts are diversifying into technology and new fintech locations are emerging, including Canary Wharf with its Level39 and 'Silicon Round-about' in London, 'Crypto Valley' in Zug, near Zurich, or Roosevelt Island next to Manhattan. Considering that women face barriers to science, technology, and engineering careers, fintech may maintain or even increase gender inequality in the financial sector, as it increases demand for such skills. It should also be noted that the fintech mania has also prevented a much-expected decrease in the level of salaries and bonuses in the financial sector in the wake of the crisis, as financial firms compete to attract fintech talent, and technology firms compete for finance professionals with expertise applicable to fintech (Wójcik and Cojoianu 2018).

10.6 Looking Ahead

Looking ahead, this book makes us think of a number of challenges and opportunities for the study of international financial centres. These challenges and opportunities concern theoretical, methodological, and empirical issues.

On the theoretical front, geographical research on financial centres has undergone major change in recent decades (Wójcik 2013). First, with globalization attention has moved from national financial systems and centres to international ones. Second, the focus has shifted from competition to collaboration among financial centres, and various ways in which they complement each other as nodes in an international network of financial centres. Third, much research on financial centres now emphasizes relationships between financial and other business services such as accounting and law. An example of all three trends is the World City Network (WCN) project, with broad empirical focus, covering office networks of financial and producer services firms in hundreds of cities (Beaverstock et al. 2000; Taylor 2004). To be sure, while new themes have emerged, some important topics have been neglected. For example, after a small but significant body of work on offshore finance in the late 1990s and early 2000s, focusing on the importance of small, often island, economies in the international financial system, there was curiously little attention to offshore finance in geography until recently, with most studies focusing on leading international financial centres (Clark, Lai, and Wójcik 2015).

How could we conceptualize financial centres in the twenty-first century in ways that take into account networks, offshore finance, and financial and business services at the same time? One idea that attempts to deal with these questions is the concept of global financial networks (GFNs).

GFNs can be defined networks of FABS, financial centres, and offshore jurisdictions (Wójcik 2018). FABS are the key agents and master weavers in these networks. Their command-and-control functions concentrate in financial centres, as nodes in GFNs, which offer large and deep labour markets, infrastructure, and access to customers, whether these are big corporations, wealthy households, or governments. In short, financial centres offer economies of localization and agglomeration. Financial centres are also places where the trading of and control over financial assets is concentrated. Financial assets, however, are often booked or registered in offshore jurisdictions, away from the places where these assets originate, are controlled, managed, or traded. They are booked or registered in offshore jurisdictions for reasons related to tax, regulation, and secrecy. These jurisdictions are not necessarily states or countries. They can be colonies, dependent territories, or subnational jurisdictions, like the US states. Fintech can be integrated within the GFN concept by considering it a new component of the FABS complex.

GFNs play a key part in the global economy. FABS as intermediaries influence relationships among governments, among businesses, and among households, but also those between governments, businesses, and households. Fintech in particular, affects the very way in which financial services are consumed. FABS also influence the way we look at the map of the world economy and measure economic performance. Concepts such as emerging markets, value at risk, or BRICs have been devised and popularized by FABS, with securities industry firms in the lead. We might even call these firms the cartographers of modern capitalism. When businesses or wealthy individuals are interested in offshore financial services, they do not shop around visiting various offshore jurisdictions; they go to a FABS firm in a financial centre to obtain a menu of such services. As such, the GFNs represent networks of transactions but also of power. The concept builds on an intellectual tradition in geography, urban studies, and network theory. Its recent applications show, for example, the role played by GFNs in the expansion of Chinese companies, which raise capital from global financial markets using the services of western FABS firms, through financial centres with Hong Kong in the lead, and an intricate network of financial vehicles registered in offshore jurisdictions, mainly the British Virgin Islands and Cayman Islands (Wójcik and Camilleri 2015).

In terms of methodology, despite recent progress mentioned in the introductory chapter by Youssef Cassis, research on financial centres continues to struggle with the paucity of financial data at the urban level. Most publicly available financial data is collected for countries, with no breakdown at subnational level. One way around this is to collect data at firm level and aggregate it by cities. Then, however, we quickly encounter the problem of allocating all activity of a firm to the location of its legal or operational headquarters, as the data on the internal geography of financial firms concerned is rarely available. One solution is to acquire access to proprietary datasets, such as Dealogic (used in Table 10.1), which offer insight into the geographical location of financial transactions.

Another methodological issue is the need for a clearer and rigorous distinction between different geographical descriptions of financial activity: domestic, international, and offshore. Many studies compare international financial centres using data on the market capitalization or trading volumes of stock exchanges they host, even though most of the companies listed are domestic and much of the trading is among domestic traders, and so strictly speaking does not represent the international activity of a financial centre. One way to distinguish between domestic and international activity would be to consider the nationality and location of the service provider in relation to those of the customer.

Considering problems with quantitative data on financial centres, case studies, particularly comparative case studies, remain an important avenue for studying financial centres. In a sense, this volume had been a contribution to this mode of research, offering case studies of leading financial centres in eight countries. One of the questions that future case studies could focus on is the relationship between financial firms, technology firms, and fintech start-ups. Such research could help tease out the competitive and collaborative aspects of such relationships in product, services, and labour markets, as well as factors in the environment of the fintech industry that affect its development. One possible scenario that could be explored here is whether fintech increases the significance of city-regions as nodes in financial networks. We already see centres of financial data and computing in places such as Basildon near London or the part of New Jersey adjacent to Manhattan. May the San Francisco Bay Area in the United States or the Pearl River Delta in China emerge as the world's financial city-regions, with different parts of the city-region specializing in different FABS including fintech?

On the empirical front, as this book goes to press, attention is focused on Brexit. Our contributors have been cautious when predicting its impacts on the global landscape of financial centres. Brexit is recognized as a major threat to London's future, but one that would make London's dominance as Europe's leading financial centre diminish rather than vanish. Frankfurt and Paris, as well as Dublin and Luxembourg, are mentioned as the centres most likely to benefit from opportunities created by Brexit, as is New York. On the other hand, the potential impact of Brexit on Asian financial centres appears to our contributors as almost negligible.

Another exciting empirical question is the future of Asian financial centres. While the time-zones of the Americas and Europe–Middle East–Africa are dominated by one global financial centre each, in the Asian time-zone the landscape seems far from settled, and if anything, the field is becoming more crowded, with Hong Kong and Singapore being joined by Shanghai, Beijing, and perhaps Shenzhen, and possibly rejoined by Tokyo. Will the future lead to increasing concentration or more specialization among these centres? What lessons can be drawn from the history of US financial centres for the future of Chinese financial centres, from one continental-sized economy to another? Are these lessons relevant in times of fintech?

Studying financial centres is fascinating in its own right. But 'capitals of capital' are also capitals of capitalism, and as such research on financial centres is a great and important lens through which to study the world economy. In this sense, the resilience of leading international financial centres documented in this volume may be interpreted by some as the resilience of neoliberalism and financial capitalism, a reflection that the 2007–9 crisis has been by and large, in the words of Eric Helleiner, 'a status quo crisis' (Helleiner 2014). Recent political backlash against globalization that manifested itself in the UK's EU referendum, the US presidential election of 2016, and less acutely in the French election may be read as a vote against islands of prosperity and opportunity, including financial centres, in an archipelago economy, to borrow the term of the French social scientist Pierre Veltz (2000). Thus, the future research agenda must address the impacts of financial centre formation, structure, and networks on economic growth, but also inequality, economic stability, and sustainability. To meet this challenge, we need more dialogue between financial historians and geographers, but also among them and other social and economic scientists.

Acknowledgements

Our work on this chapter has been supported with funding from the European Research Council (ERC) under the European Union's Horizon 2020 research and innovation programme (grant agreement number 681337). The article reflects only our views and the ERC is not responsible for any use that may be made of the information it contains.

References

Accenture. 2016. 'Fintech and the Evolving Landscape: Landing points for the industry'. London.

Arner, D.W., J. Barberis, and B. P. Buckley. 2015. 'The Evolution of Fintech: A New Post-Crisis Paradigm?' Univ. Hong Kong Fac. Law Res. Pap. 2015/047, 1689–99. doi: 10.1017/CBO9781107415324.004

Autonomous Research. 2017. 'Breakdown of Global Fintech Investment by Region'. https://next.autonomous.com/insights/breakdown-of-global-fintech-investment-by-region, accessed 1 November 2017.

Beaverstock, J. V., R. G. Smith, and P. J. Taylor. 2000. 'World-City Network: A New Metageography?'. *Annals of the Association of American Geographers* 90 (1): 123–34.

Bordo, M. D., A. Redish, and H. Rockoff. 2015. 'Why Didn't Canada Have a Banking Crisis in 2008 (or in 1930, or 1907, or ...)?'. *Economic History Review* 68 (1): 218–43. doi:10.1111/1468-0289.665.

Business Insider. 2014. 'Alipay Overtakes PayPal as the Largest Mobile Payments Platform In The World'. http://uk.businessinsider.com/alipay-overtakes-paypal-as-the-largest-mobile-payments-platform-in-the-world-2014-2?r=US&IR=T, accessed 20 September 2017.

Cassis, Y. 2006. Capitals of Capital. The History of International Financial Centres, 1780–2005. Cambridge: Cambridge University Press.

CBInsights. 2017. 'Where Top European Banks Are Investing in Fintech in One Graphic'. https://www.cbinsights.com/research/europe-bank-fintech-startup-invest ments/, accessed 5 November 2017.

Clark, G. L., K. P. Y. Lai, and D. Wójcik. 2015. 'Editorial Introduction to the Special Section: Deconstructing Offshore Finance'. *Economic Geography* 91 (3): 237–49. doi:10.1111/ecge.12098.

Crunchbase. 2017. Santander InnoVentures Profile https://www.crunchbase.com/organization/santander-innoventures#/entity, accessed 5 November 2017.

Cryptocoins News. 2017. 'Asian Fintech Startups See a Record $5.4 Billion VC Funding in 2016, Driven by China'. https://www.cryptocoinsnews.com/asian-fintech-startups-see-record-5-4-billion-vc-funding-2016-driven-china/, accessed 3 November 2017.

Deloitte. 2017. 'A Tale of 44 Cities—Connecting Global FinTech: Interim Hub Review 2017'. London: Deloitte.

FSB. 2017. 'Global Shadow Banking Monitoring Report 2016'.

Haberly, D. and D. Wójcik. 2015. 'Tax Havens and the Production of Offshore FDI: An Empirical Analysis'. *Journal of Economic Geography* 15 (1): 75–101. doi:10.1093/jeg/lbu003.

Helleiner, E. 2014. The Status Quo Crisis. Oxford: Oxford University Press.

HM Government. 2017. 'Building our Industrial Strategy—Green Paper'. London.

IDC. 2016. 'Financial Services IT Spending to Reach $480 Billion Worldwide in 2016'. https://www.idc.com/getdoc.jsp?containerId=prUS41216616, accessed 5 November 2017.

Ingham, G. K. 2004. The Nature of Money. Cambridge: Polity.

JPMorgan. 2015. JPMorgan Chase & Co. Annual Report 2014. New York.

McDowell, H. 2017. 'JP Morgan Spent $9.5 Billion on Tech Revamp Last Year'. The Trade. https://www.thetradenews.com/Sell-side/JP-Morgan-spent-$9-5-billion-on-tech-revamp-last-year/, accessed 15 January 2018.

PWC. 2016. 'Blurred Lines: How FinTech is Shaping Financial Services'. Global FinTech Report, March.

Reuters. 2016. 'Ping An Becomes First Chinese Member of R3 Blockchain Consortium'. http://uk.reuters.com/article/us-insurance-blockchain-china/ping-an-becomes-first-chinese-member-of-r3-blockchain-consortium-idUKKCN0YF0R5, accessed 25 September 2017.

Reuters. 2017. 'Brexit Prompts Transferwise to Move Europe Headquarter from UK to Continent'. https://uk.reuters.com/article/uk-fintech-transferwise-brexit/brexit-prompts-transferwise-to-move-europe-headquarter-from-uk-to-continent-idUKKBN17E1KC, accessed 3 November 2017.

Sassen, S. 2001. The Global City: London, New York, Tokyo, revised edition. Princeton: Princeton University Press.

Spufford, P. 2006. 'From Antwerp and Amsterdam to London: The Decline of Financial Centres in Europe'. *Economist* (Leiden). 154: 143–75. doi:10.1007/s10645-006-9000-7

Taylor, P. J. 2004. World City Network: A Global Urban Analysis. London: Routledge.

TechCrunch. 2016. 'Ant Financial, the Alibaba Affiliate that Operates Alipay, Raises $4.5B at a $60B Valuation'. https://techcrunch.com/2016/04/25/ant-financial-the-alibaba-affiliate-that-operates-alipay-raises-4-5b-at-a-60b-valuation/, accessed 2 November 2017.

Veltz, P. 2000. 'European Cities in the World Economy'. In Cities in Contemporary Europe, edited by A. Bagnasco and P. Le Galés. Cambridge: Cambridge University Press, pp. 33–47.

Wójcik, D. 2013. 'The Dark Side of NY-LON: Financial Centres and the Global Financial Crisis'. *Urban Studies* 50 (13): 2736–52. doi:10.1177/0042098012474513.

Wójcik, D. 2018. 'Global financial networks' in Clark, G.L., Gertler, M.S., Feldman, M. (eds), The New Oxford Handbook on Economic Geography. Oxford: Oxford University Press, pp. 557–574.

Wójcik, D. and J. Camilleri. 2015. '"Capitalist Tools in Socialist Hands?" China Mobile in Global Financial Networks'. *Transactions of the Institute of British Geographers* 40 (4): 464–78. doi:10.1111/tran.12089.

Wójcik, D. and T. F. Cojoianu. 2018. 'Resilience of the US securities industry to the global financial crisis'. *Geoforum* 91: 182–194.

Wójcik, D., E. Knight, P. O'Neill, and V. Pažitka. 2017. 'Economic Geography of Investment Banking since 2008: Geography of Shrinkage and Shift'. Financial Geography Working Paper Series—ISSN 2515–0111.

Wójcik, D. and D. MacDonald-Korth. 2015. 'The British and the German Financial Sectors in the Wake of the Crisis: Size, Structure and Spatial Concentration'. *Journal of Economic Geography* 15 (5): 1033–54. doi:10.1093/jeg/lbu056.

Zoromé, A. 2007. 'Concept of Offshore Financial Centers: In Search of an Operational Definition'. IMF Working Papers 7, 1. doi:10.5089/9781451866513.001.

Index

Tables and figures are indicated by an italic *t*, or *f*, following the page number.